The
Last Years
Of
The Big Four

Atlantic

AN ORIGINAL WORK BY:

PROFESSOR ALAN EARNSHAW
&
DAVID JENKINSON B.ED

PUBLISHED BY:

ATLANTIC PUBLISHERS

TREVITHICK HOUSE • WEST END
PENRYN • CORNWALL
TR10 8HE

RESEARCH ASSISTANT
ALISTAIR AYNSCOUGH

DESIGN:
KEVIN BRADLEY
BURWAIN STUDIOS • PENRITH • CUMBRIA

REPRODUCTION:
BARNABUS DESIGN & REPRO
THREEMILESTONE • TRURO • CORNWALL

PRINTED BY:
AMADEUS PRESS LIMITED • HUDDERSFIELD • WEST YORKSHIRE

Text © Alan Earnshaw & David Jenkinson 1997
Photographs: all from joint author's collections unless otherwise stated

ISBN 0-906899-79-6

British Cataloguing in Publication Data
A catalogue record for this book is available from the British Library.

CONTENTS

Introduction

The hands of Big Ben swept inexorably towards midnight, and as they had chimed twelve on so many New Year's Eves before, so they did at the end of 1947. For the revellers gathered around London's various public squares, or those who were at home listening to the chimes being broadcast on the BBC that Tuesday night, it was a time for celebration. Glasses would be raised, Auld Lang Syne would be sung, and 'first footers' would be calling at the doors. This was just the third peace-time New Year since the ending of the Second World War. It heralded a new dawn, but it was also the end of an era.

Months before the sound of Big Ben heralded the arrival of 1948, decisions had been taken in the cloistered halls of the Palace of Westminster below which would change the face of British transport, when that particular midnight hour arrived. With it came a new national transport policy, and with it four great railway companies were consigned to the pages of history. Four railway companies which had been born as a result of one major period of conflict, were now to be abolished as the consequences of another World War. On the morrow a new railway would be born, for the politicians had decreed that as part of social change and reform a nationally-owned railway would be created. Gone would be the 'Big Four', in would come British Railways.

Almost five decades later another Government would have begun the process of reversing that policy, but in the meantime successive political parties would have decimated the nationalised rail system, either by design or by default. Having become nationalised the railways then became a political football and as such they could have no chance of real development. Never would they be as great as they had been in the 'Last Years of the Big Four'!

This book takes a reflective look back at these last years of Britain's independently owned railway system and primarily reviews the period from 1st January 1938 to 31st December 1947, in other words the last decade of these four great companies. Although, to set the scene we must first travel back to the start of World War I, for in its wake national conditions actually gave birth to the Big Four. From there on we chart the development of the companies as they moved through the difficult post-war years, the General Strike and the Depression as well as through the great achievements of the record-breaking 'thirties. In his contribution of five chapters in the book, my fellow author David Jenkinson also charts the locomotive and rolling stock developments of the big four companies between 1938 and 1948.

In our view of the period concerned, we must appreciate that the fortunes of Britain's railways were inexorably linked with socio-economic developments in the country, and to a lesser extent the same factors in the world scene. It is essential that the book delves into secular history from time to time, as railway history can not be taken in isolation from world or national events. Therefore, we will be taking a look at topics as diverse as the Great Depression, the fall of the BEF and its retreat from Dunkirk, to the D-Day landings, and then through to the formation of a Socialist programme of reform in post-war Britain. The development of the political scene is especially important in this book because, from the outset, we must appreciate that during this period the railways were under a form of direct state control which lasted from September 1939 until well after the end of the Second World War in the summer of 1945.

It is not surprising, therefore, that much of this period of history is also inextricably linked with that terrible period of conflict which saw Britain poised on the very brink of annihilation. Indeed, it is no false claim to set forth the proposition, that had it not been for the sterling efforts of Britain's railway companies and the people employed thereon, then the course of the war might have gone very differently. For much of this last decade, we see a period of time when the railways were facing almost insurmountable odds, with shortages in every field but particularly material, manpower and money.

From the outset of state control in September 1939, the Big Four faced the same sort of conditions as those which had decimated the private railway companies during World War I, and therefore led to the Railway Grouping of 1923. Extreme pressures of under-funding, deferred maintenance and extremely high traffic levels were to do, in this second period of conflict, exactly what had transpired on the railways in the Great War of 1914-18. Like the period leading up to the Grouping in 1923, so it was in the period from the summer of 1945 to the end of 1947.

The railways were worn out and reeling from the over-use and abuse that they had faced during the preceding six years. Sadly these were not matters which could be cured overnight, and it bestowed upon the newly formed British Railways a legacy of worn-out track, ageing locomotives and a work-force stretched to (and often beyond) capacity. It is, for this reason, that the last days of the Big Four were plagued with one mishap after another, and many of these mishaps led to disaster. Compounding the miseries was the pervading problem of coal, as supplies of steam-coal not only deteriorated in quality but almost completely disappeared in post-war Britain as exporting became of primary importance.

Yet, despite this, it was not all doom and gloom, and the Big Four railway companies fought a splendid rear-guard action in a final attempt to maintain their independence. They also strove to re-establish many of the prestigious services which had been abolished at the outbreak of war, and on the face of it normality was quickly resumed. Yet, the days of the Big Four were numbered, and it is evident that post-war political-thinking saw the railways as being ripe for nationalisation. The under-funding and over use of the past six years had made them into a very soft target indeed.

The story of this last decade is one of fascinating contrasts, with our account featuring, achievement, heroism, dedication and adversity in a time of national need, and continues to the ultimate betrayal by a nation and its politicians who very quickly forgot what had been achieved in **The Last Years of the Big Four.**

CHAPTER ONE
Prologue

Following the Railways Act of 1921, all the major railway companies in Great Britain (and most of the minor ones) were Grouped into just four principal undertakings. The Southern Railway, as its name implied, covered almost all of the southern part of Britain, stretching from the English Channel ports down into the West Country. It was an intensified system in parts of Kent, Surrey and Sussex, into which counties commuter lines radiated from London. Also running west of London was the Great Western, which went as far down into Cornwall as Penzance. It also ran in to West and South Wales, Birmingham and the Midlands, and as far north as Birkenhead. The rest of the country, and Scotland, was basically divided into two halves. The western side of the realm was predominantly served by the London, Midland & Scottish Railway. The eastern part of Britain was generally the domain of the London & North Eastern Railway, but this was a widely varying territory which imposed is own special problems that often resulted in financial difficulties for the new group.

These were the Big Four, but there could easily have been a case for arguing that six companies, not four, should have been created as an answer to the transport problems of post-World War I Britain. Scotland was a prime case for a separate operating company, but strange to relate in these days of devolution proposals, it was the Scots themselves who were against separation. Accordingly, it was left to the LMS and LNER to absorb the Scottish pre-Group companies. The other case for another company was evident in the Midlands, where it would have made considerable logic to create a single operating system by the merger of companies like the Midland and Great Central, which in turn could have absorbed part of the LNWR and GWR systems. However, with the benefit of hindsight, no-one could ever say that the Railways Act of 1921 was logical, or even a half-way solution to the problems which faced the railway at the end of World War I.

In many ways the Grouping was a best-effort attempt of a Government which had to absorb the real truth of the costs involved in waging total war for four years. The phenomenal pressure this period of conflict had placed on the Exchequer is still hard to appreciate, but it was such that it became impossible for the nation to honour many of the promises it had made when it enlisted the support of commerce and industry when their services were most needed. Undoubtedly, the greatest civilian organisations to contribute to the 'national effort' during the 'Great War' were the railway companies. It had always been seen that the railways would have a role to play in times of war, and in such times it was essential that petty squabbles and territory disputes be put aside for the national good. Naturally this meant that some form of Governmental control would be necessary, yet this was both an intractable and thorny problem which the railway companies and Government would have to resolve.

Above:
A typical Southern Railway motive power scene between the two wars.

Opposite Left:
The creation of the Big Four led to a new era of locomotive development, more powerful engines were developed to meet the growing demands placed upon the railways as post - World War I recovery began. In the field of heavy goods traffic the Robinson 2-8-0 had shown the way forward, both at home and abroad, when it was chosen as the ROD standard. Its mantle in the 1939-45 conflict would fall on the Stanier 2-8-0s such as No.8703 pictured here at Derby.
Photo: LMS Official

Below:
It was not all mainline passenger and heavy freight traffic however, on the Big Four in the mid 1930s as this idyllic picture of the Vale of Rheidol Railway shows.
Photo: J.I.C.Boyd.

Above:
There was always a very close connection between the railways and the military, as will be evident from the very large number of engines that were given the names of army regiments, famous naval ships, or (much later) aircraft. Quite why this was so could be put down to a number of reasons, but the most likely one is found in the flexibility that rail offered to the military. In Germany mobilisation of the armed forces in times of war was planned at a very early stage in railway history, and the American Civil War had shown the effectiveness of railways to the advantage of the differing factions at various times. A good example of the growing bond between railway and military was witnessed in Britain when the LMS renamed several of its Royal Scot class 4-6-0s with nameplates that had a military connection. Names like Jenny Lind *became* Rifle Brigade, Vulcan *the* Green Howards, Goliath *the* Border Regiment, *whilst* Condor *which is seen here at a renaming ceremony at Halifax station in 1935 became* The Duke of Wellington's Regiment (West Riding). *Then allocated to Camden Shed, the engine had come to the LMS/LNER joint station as this was the home town of this famous army regiment.*

There was, of course, already existing legislation by which the Government could assume control of any civil or public undertaking in the form of the National Defence Act 1888. But at the same time, there was considerable resistance on the part of the railway companies to allow the Government to take absolute control of the network, as it argued that the Civil Service or War Office were not the best suited organisations to run a national transport system. The operators favoured the older Regulation of the Forces Act 1871, through which the State could operate the network under military law. But, coupled with this they also advocated two other important measures, which would ensure the continuity of railway management.

In turn these 'terms' were to result in the creation of a permanent body of railway managers to operate the railways whilst they were under state control, and the creation of a consultative group comprising railway managers, military officers and civil servants which could be brought together to ensure smooth running of the system for mutual benefits. As a consequence, the Railway Executive Committee was formed at the Board of Trade on 5th November 1912. Its first members comprised senior officials from the following companies: CR, GCR, GNR, GWR LNWR, LSWR, LYR, MR, and NER, under the chairmanship of Frank Ree (LNWR). Later on representatives from the South Eastern & Chatham and the BoT were appointed.

As the war in Europe turned from a great adventure into a period of attrition on the 'home front', the demand on Britain's railways increased five-fold. Firstly, more and more railway employees were called up for military service, with callow youths or female workers being brought in to replace them, yet (worse still) many were not replaced at all. Next came the demands on the railways to carry more and more military traffic, both freight and personnel, all of which was run to specific priorities. Thirdly, locomotives and rolling stock were urgently needed in France, so huge quantities of railway equipment (including whole branch lines) were removed en-mass to the continent. Next came the demand for railway workshops to turn over large parts of their manufacturing capacity for armament production. Finally, shortages of materials, especially steel and timber, imposed the added burden of limited raw materials to work with.

These factors led to critical shortages in one form after another, and as soon as the late summer of 1914 civilian travel restrictions were being recorded as excursion trains and holiday specials were withdrawn. By 1916 it was even worse, and a wholesale programme of station closures and service withdrawals followed. Even where trains were well-used by munitions factory workers, such as the Brampton branch of the NER in Cumberland, services were slashed without any excuse. Yet, even so, the Railway Operating Department was demanding the War Office to send a minimum of 370 more freight engines to France. The near-sighted approach to locomotive manufacture and maintenance almost cost the country dearly, for in addition to the demands for engines overseas, nearly 500 locomotives were 'stopped' in Britain awaiting major repairs at the end of 1916. Every last inch was being squeezed out of the railways, and it was not only the locomotive departments that were feeling the pinch.

Coach and wagon building, except for military purposes, had almost ground to a complete halt, whilst track renewal and repair had reached an all-time low. On top of this aerial bombing attacks by Zeppelins, and a spate of tragic accidents (particularly evident in 1915) were seriously affecting an already exhausted railway system. The influx of Commonwealth (and later American) servicemen that were flooding into Britain with their equipment also had to be catered for, as did the ever-increasing flow of ambulance trains that were repatriating the wounded from the battlefields of Europe. Even when the war finally came to its end, the railways' work was not finished, and the flow of servicemen returning to demobilisation centres had to be handled as expeditiously as possible. The main period of demobilisation commenced on 9th December 1918, but it ran on well into the summer of 1919. Even then, the levels of traffic being carried by the railways, were still far in advance of the pre-war figures on which compensation was to be paid.

By aggregating the compensation on the sum of pre-war traffic, the Government had squeezed so much life-blood out of the railway companies, that they could not possibly survive in their present form for much longer. Already it was evident that the arrears of maintenance and the deferred capital expenditure was so great, that it would bankrupt most of the companies to get back to their 1914 position. Something more radical was needed, and as the Government could not afford to pay the true levels of compensation, the only real solution was nationalisation. Indeed, one may wonder whether, having had a taste of strong control over the railways, the State had not enjoyed what it had nibbled at and thus decided to take a bigger bite! Winston Churchill was a strong advocate of nationalisation in that post-war era, and it was felt that his views were shared by many other influential people. Rationalisation was obviously needed, as was funding to provide at least some redress for the losses that the railways had endured, but just how far were Government prepared to go?

Actually, the House of Commons had appointed a Select Committee on Railways in August 1918, and it reported three months later, just after the Armistice had been signed. It concluded that a return to pre-war status would be wrong, but it held back from coming out in favour of any single course of action. It merely presented a number of options:

1. Further amalgamation of the various companies as a step towards unification.
2. Unification achieved by private ownership with commercial management.
3. Unification by means of nationalisation.

If the latter course was to be adopted, a further three stages would need to be considered:

1. Establishment of a Government department to manage railways (and the appointment of a Minister thereof).
2. Formation of a Board of Management, but which had no representation in Parliament.
3. Nationalising the system, and then leasing it to one or more operating companies.

Whilst no outward signals were indicated at this time, it is significant that the Government formed the Ministry of Transport in 1919 and appointed Sir Eric Campbell Geddes, (a former Deputy General Manager of the NER) as its first Minister. His rise to fame had been meteoric, having commenced in a minor position in the NER's Claims Office, to rise to the post of Director General of Military Railways in 1916 and finally First Lord of the Admiralty in May 1917. Geddes soon stamped his mark on the new Ministry, and the organisation which ensued bore all the hallmarks of a railway company headquarters' staff.

A study of the methodology proposed for the new Ministry indicates, at least to me, that Geddes' thinking was solely centred around the formation of a nationalised railway. Yet, at the same time, it seems that the rest of Government-thinking was hardening against the idea of a completely unified railway system, and heading more towards the Select Committee's first alternative. Whether or not complete nationalisation was just too big a bite to take at that time remains a matter of conjecture, but the proposals of 1920 which led to the 1921 Act were probably the most politically expedient, most readily achievable, and therefore probably the next best thing as far as the State was concerned.

Once established, each of the four new companies would have had an almost exclusive segment of the country, and yet there would still be considerable scope for competition. Indeed, it seemed that competition was something which the Government wished to

Below:
The first demand on the Railway Executive at the outbreak of war was that of Mobilisation. Following a carefully pre-ordained timetable this swung into action, taking troops from army barracks, territorial reserve depots and so on, to their designated ports. Mobilisation saw the first British Expeditionary Forces arriving in Southampton on 9th August 1914, and the process was completed when the last of the BEF reinforcements were embarked on 31st August. In the meantime some 670 trains had been run. Next came a process of collaboration which had hitherto been unheard of on the railways in Victorian or Edwardian England, when competition rather than co-operation had been the order of the day. Through traffics were handled more swiftly, particularly those connected with military purposes that had to pass over the systems of several railways between points of origination and destination. Long-haul traffic soon became the order of the day, with specific examples being the naval specials; 'Jellicoe Specials' taking coal from South Wales to the far north of Scotland, and leave trains from Ashford to Inverness one of which is pictured here arriving at Inverness. Conveying a number of sailors for Invergordon and Wick they now have a change of trains, (and in view of the need to obtain rest and refreshments) the men were allowed a minimum of two hours 'stand-easy' in Inverness.

Above:
One of the notable facets of pre-war rail travel was the special marketing that the companies applied to holiday services. A particular exponent of this technique was the Southern Railway who published its own holiday guides. The GWR also promoted its Holiday Haunts publication and ran special express services in connection with it as may be seen by the one behind No.6025 King Henry III.
Photo: The late M.W.Earley

Below:
Much use was made of mechanisation after the great Depression, and many firms began to introduce automated handling systems, such as hoists, cranes, conveyors etc. included amongst whom were the firm of Constable, Hart & Co. who erected a Cowans, Sheldon crane at their private delivery siding.

encourage (to an extent), in order to prevent the railways exploiting a near-monopoly over the carriage of middle to long distance passengers and freight. In many ways this view alone explains why the Southern were allowed to retain the 'long withered arm' down into the West Country. Further prevention of monopolies was to be insured by another section of the 1921 Act, which decreed the establishment of the Railway Rates Tribunal that provided a statutory system of rate fixing for the railways.

As a prelude to the Grouping some mergers were already coming into place before 1923, notably those between the LNWR and LYR, and the Welsh railways which came into the new 'western' group. These took place on 1st January 1922, but it is interesting to note the completely different effects that resulted. For example, the Welsh companies that were absorbed by the GWR, namely the Alexandra Docks & Railway, Barry Railway, Cambrian Railways, Cardiff Railway, Rhymney Railway and Taff Vale Railway, were all suffused to such an extent that their original identities became masked by the overall personality of the GWR. Meanwhile, the purely regional Lancashire & Yorkshire Railway in the north was to put up a great fight for its identity; and although absorbed into the LNWR, it was 'Lanky' people and policies which began to shine through. Indeed, it was so much so, that it was Horwich-trained men that took over most of the prominent positions in the LMS after its formation; undoubtedly much to the chagrin of Derby and Crewe.

The formation of the Southern did not lead (at first) to too great a change as the company initially operated the lines of its pre-Grouped constituents as separate divisions, each with its own management team and sets of policies. Both of the two main companies that were absorbed into the Southern, the London Brighton & South Coast Railway and the London & South Western Railway, had also already commenced experiments into electric traction. On the intensified commuter services out of London, electrification would prove to be a great advantage and the contribution that both the companies had made prior to 1923 set the basis for the Southern's later success. Sadly, the two systems were at complete variance with one another and this was to provide quite a few 'sparks' before the company adopted the LSWR 600v DC third-rail system in preference to the Brighton designed 6,600v AC overhead electric's.

The LNER, destined to be the poorest of the Big Four, made an astute choice in its first chairman, William Whitelaw. He had previously been chairman of the small Highland Railway, where he had demonstrated the courtesy and consideration which was essential in getting to know many of his staff personally. This was easily achieved in a small company, but not so readily attainable on a railway the size of the LNER. There were also conflicts of opinion with management who resented a Chairman who liked to have a 'hands on' approach (and Whitelaw loved riding on the footplate), so it is not surprising that the relationship with his Chief General Manager did not get off to the best possible start. Yet, as the years progressed, under people like Whitelaw and Gresley the LNER were to rise to a prominence which was not even hinted at in 1923.

Yet, once Grouping had been achieved, the problems for the railways were far from being over. First of all large volumes of 'war traffic' still had to be handled, and it is remarkable that the files held in the Public Record Office at Kew, show that military freight continued at high levels until well into the mid-1920s. Coupled with this came the fact that considerable retraining was required to bring the workforce back up to scratch, and also to replace the many experienced railwaymen who had lost their lives in and amongst the 16 millions who had been slaughtered in this awful period of world conflict. Coupled with this, the Spanish Influenza epidemic that swept the country claimed the lives of many more railway servants. Included in the casualties was Sir Guy Calthrop the General Manager of the LNWR who, but for his untimely death, would probably have played a major role in the development of the LMS. In the wake of war and adversity, it has long been evident that social reform or change follows in one guise or another. Expectations of social change were particularly evident in the lower social classes, especially from men who had 'given their all for King and Country'. No longer could railwaymen be expected to work in subservient conditions, where long hours and poor conditions were their daily lot.

A national strike on the railways had already been held in 1911, and at this the railway management caved in to the strikers' demands. A more bitter post-war strike occurred in 1919, bringing Britain into a period of insurmountable turmoil and possibly, as at least one historian recounts, almost to the brink of civil war. The men struck for better conditions, pay and improved safety, but the police and armed forces were employed to break up the protests. Even so, many of the military commanders recognised that there was a ground-swell of support for the railwaymen amongst the army, and the Government were duly advised to concede to some of the demands. So was born the 8-hour working day, and with it the number of railway accidents (especially personal injury incidents) were dramatically reduced. Yet, this had a severe knock-on effect for railway management who were already facing increased costs in post-war Britain. Indeed, many costs could simply not be absorbed and the 8-hour day led to many pieces of rationalisation. One such was the demise of the NBR's Port Carlisle branch which finally succumbed, because it just was not profitable to sustain the employment of two separate locomotive crews and station staffs.

The 8-hour day took no account of the very many railway services which operated for just 9 or 10 hours a day, and it was a pity that the companies had not given in to the demands much earlier, as systems of flexible rostering might have been adopted more readily if attitudes had not become so hardened after the 1919 strike. Another week and a half long strike, by the Associated Society of Locomotive Engineers and Firemen hit the companies hard at the start of 1925, because an award by the National Wages Board had said that mileage payments over and above the basic rate for an 8-hour day should be paid after 150 miles of running, rather than the 120 miles which had previously been the agreed rate. All of this was to have its affect on the Grouped railways, although in many ways its end results were submerged for many years to come.

Some of these issues reared their ugly head in the General Strike of 1926 when, once again, industrial unrest affected the national transport scene between 3rd and 12th May. In 1927 just under 9% of the insured workforce were unemployed, with around one million out of work. But despite this, by the end of the 1920s, the traffic on all the railways had begun to rise again, arrears of maintenance were being finally overcome and a capital expenditure programme was clearly in evidence. Yet all of this was to change again on a black day in October 1929, with an event across the Atlantic Ocean which had its repercussions in every major city of the world and even on every little branch line in Britain. This was, of course, the Wall Street Crash which led to the Great Depression. By 1933 almost a quarter of the British workforce, around three million people, were unemployed and the cost of living index fell to an all time low. By 1934 about a third of this figure had returned to gainful work, and the following year it was somewhat better still. Yet, much of this re-employment was only due to rearmament policies as Britain geared itself up for another and an increasingly more inevitable war with Germany.

The railways faced the Great Depression phlegmatically, even though increasing competition was evident in the form of better long distance and local bus services, improved road haulage, and greater numbers of private motor cars. The railways were, however, cushioned from the effects of this competition because Government, as governments will, found new forms of taxation to rake in its share from the growing interest in road transport. Driving tests, petrol taxation etc. all combining to make motoring an expensive exercise and thus deter the masses from making a switch on to a winding, inadequate road system which was still little better than it had been in the days of horse and cart. What is more, many of the loads that had been the traditional preserve of the railways, (coal, iron and steel) could not be accommodated on the roads in any great volume. Yet, even in these staple industries the railways were suffering because of reduced output as a consequence of the Depression.

By 1937 coal was peaking at about 240 million tons, but this was still substantially down on pre-1929 levels. Likewise iron and steel output, which increased by 80% between 1933 and 1937, was still way below what had been produced before the Wall Street Crash. Passenger traffic was relatively unaffected at least as far as middle-long distance journeys were concerned, though a number of rural and workers' train services did decline dramatically. Overall the drop in passenger numbers carried was a mere 10% in the four years following the Wall Street Crash, and by 1937 the figures were around 20% higher than 1929.

This remarkable recovery was, in no small way, due to the excellent efforts that the railway companies had made to improve services and make them more attractive. This they did by improving the two cornerstones of any good railway service, comfort and speed. Best of all were the LMS and LNER in this regard, as the race for the Anglo-Scottish and northern England traffic led to intense competition and rivalry. From this resulted crack express services such as the Coronation, Coronation Scot, Silver Jubilee, and the West Riding Limited.

Above:
One of the saddest events of this period, as far as the railways are concerned, was the deliberate derailment of the Flying Scotsman at Cramlington in May 1926. Although no-one was badly hurt, passengers emerging from the wrecked coaches behind Merrie Hampton *were jeered and booed by onlookers who saw them as part of the upper classes with whom they were in dispute. Sad and tragic days indeed. The pages of a railway history dealing with the Last Years of the Big Four are not the place to discuss the economic situation of the 1920s, but it has to be appreciated how great were the effects of the General Strike and the Depression, for in their own way these also played a significant part in the build-up to nationalisation.*

Below:
A fairly representative view of traffic on the LMS between 1923 and 1947 is captured in this picture of 0-6-0 No. 17668 on a coal empties at Uddington just before nationalisation.

Above:
This undated view is representative of East Coast mainline practice in the latter half of the LNER era. As A3 class 4-6-2 No. 51 Blink Bonny heads north with a mid-summer express one of the crew takes a backwards glance to see what the photographer was doing. To the right of the tender will be seen Copenhagen Tunnel Signal Box.
Photo: LNER Official / Wethersett

Below:
More mundane than the above train, but nevertheless of equal importance, were cross country services such as this stopping train from Gloucester to Bristol, which is pictured just prior to the start of its journey behind LMS No.935 from Bristol shed.

There were similar developments in the south and west, and whilst not as significant as the Anglo-Scottish improvements, no-one could dismiss the speeding up of the GWR service to Cheltenham. Furthermore the Southern's superb electrification scheme was, by now, paying remarkable dividends, although few of their passengers might have realised that the 'new' electric sets were little more than old steam stock coaches mounted on new underframes. Even so, no other company achieved the same levels of passenger increase as the Southern. Actually the LMS came nearest to recapturing its pre-1929 levels, although the GWR and LNER both showed an overall loss in passenger revenue when 1937 is compared with pre-1929 numbers.

An interesting form of support for the railways at last came from the Government during the 1930s, as three distinct pieces of action by the state finally led to the much needed improvements and capital expenditure. The first of these was the Royal Commission on Transport's report into the state of the railways, which had looked at the worsening situation following World War I. As early as 1928 the Commission was urging Westminster to make finances available for the railways, and it seems likely that their influence was behind the Development (Loan Guarantees and Grants) Act of 1929, but more of that later. To understand the thinking in the Commission we need to look at their third report which was published in February 1931, and made nine major recommendations for the railways.

1. Railway services should be speeded up.
2. Revision and lowering of fares would assist the recovery of traffic.
3. Statutory obligations upon the railways to provide a seat for each passenger on a main line train at its starting point.
4. Joint or overlapping lines to be merged into one or other of the groups.
5. All competitive traffic to be pooled.
6. All suburban services to be electrified at all major cities, not just London.
7. Great encouragement should be extended for the use of larger wagons; specifically making reference to the GWR 20-ton wagons as an example for others to follow.
8. Development of containerisation to facilitate ease of load, road/rail transfer etc.
9. Financial and statistical returns should be reviewed in order to see if they could be reduced or simplified.

All of these recommendations were, of course completely logical and highly desirable, but in a time when the railways were fighting to regain the ground lost in the war years, let alone absorb the affects of the Depression, such aims could clearly not be funded from revenue. This therefore brings us neatly back to the 1929 Act by which the Government were offering guarantees, in one form or another, to facilitate investment in large-scale railway improvement programmes. All of the four companies availed themselves of these facilities, and the Southern did particularly well with its electrification and docks programmes, followed by the GWR who expended £13.3 million on capital projects between 1929 and 1939. The LMS and LNER all made significant developments, aided by a programme which I feel sure had an alternative motive. Ostensibly, it would seem that the Government were only putting back what the nation had taken out of the railways in the Great War, but several historians feel more than satisfied that this investment was more likely an attempt to help the railways gear up for the second European war that was inevitably going to follow the first.

It is clear, from a study of the approved programmes (compared with those that were rejected), that only those which had a strategic value (in one form or another) were going to succeed in gaining the go-ahead. For example, engine sheds, marshalling yards, warehouses, coaling arrangements, electrification programmes and emergency/breakdown trains were warmly accepted, whilst station developments, rolling-stock improvements etc. were generally only funded out of revenue-based profits as opposed to grants. Whilst this is a very generalistic idea, it is fairly safe to hold the view that only those items that would aid the smooth running of the railways in the time of war, were the ones which were likely to receive grants or guarantees. As an example we might consider the construction of the 261 new stations that were built between 1923 and 1938, and see how little Government funding was received towards these projects; then we must compare the high levels of grant-aid which went into the 19 new goods depots built in the same period. This was even more identifiable when it came to the provision of new locomotive depots and facilities. Now, if this altruistic approach to railway finance can be detected by summary of the 1929 Act, it stands out as a glaringly obvious fact in the funding that followed.

These grant regimes came about as a result of the London Passenger Transport (Agreement) Act of 1935, that was used to provide a role model upon which funding could be provided for the Big Four. Under the resulting Railways (Agreement) Act, a Railway Finance Corporation was formed by HM Treasury. From this Corporation, the Big Four companies could borrow the capital it required for 'approved' schemes at very advantageous rates of interest. It would be quite a lengthy task to present the reasons why we say that these 'approved schemes' were allowed primarily for their potential 'war contributions', but a detailed look at all those that were given authorisation clearly reveals that they were nearly all of considerable benefit to both the railways and the state during the period 1939-45. Certainly, very few of these schemes could have been justified by revenue-based profits, at least not in the short to medium term, no matter how desirable they may have been from an operating point of view.

Government commitment was even more clearly demonstrated in the formation of the Railway Technical Committee, under whose auspices much preparatory work would be undertaken to provide railway facilities for a second war with Germany, which by then seemed almost inevitable. The third piece of Government involvement in railways came about as a result of the 1931 Weir Report, which dealt with the electrification of the railways. In turn this led to a Ministry of Transport Order in 1932 which mapped out the future for electrification and stipulated that all future projects would use either 1,500 volts dc overhead current or 750 volts dc on a third-rail system. Following continental practice, the desire to increase electrification on the railways was certainly foremost in the minds of all concerned despite the high capital outlay required for its introduction.

It has to be remembered that the continuing effects of the Depression, coupled with the long overdue maintenance problems left very little from revenue for capital expenditure. Certainly, such profit could never have permitted major expenditure on modernisation, had there not been some considerable degree of Government support. Yet, as may be clearly perceived from a study of British history, Government rarely supports anything unless it has an ulterior motive. It can be stated that war was foreseen from the mid-1930s onwards, and the threat was being acknowledged as early as 1937. Accordingly, the various General Managers of Britain's railway companies were in touch with the Government about the eventuality of war and the ways in which the railways might be required to serve a national need. Not least in this were the concerns on what the railways would have to carry, and what their workshops would have to manufacture on the Government's behalf.

As early as 1936 the railways were asking for radio telephone equipment to provide an alternative resource to fixed telegraph systems, but as such equipment was in short supply the request was denied until well after the war had begun. A reliance was therefore put on strengthening existing land-line circuits, but despite two years of continuous development, at the outbreak of war in 1939, the railways still found themselves to be short of 21,000 miles of telephone and telegraph wire. Yet the organisation for bomb damage was thoroughly developed, and elsewhere we relate the ARP and anti-gas measures, so for the moment we will just concentrate on repair work preparations.

Above:
An undoubted casualty of the Depression, and the critical times of the 1920s and 30s', was the little narrow gauge Lynton & Barnstaple section of the Southern Railway. Although conceived to meet both a tourist and local need, by the 1930s it was badly affected by the growing operation of motor coaches, even though these had the added difficulty of climbing the tortuous hills around Porlock and Lynton. The line itself closed on 30th September 1935. Seen above is the American-built 2-4-2T, No.762 Lyn.

Below:
Whilst some lines closed others had to be modernised if they were effectively to meet the challenges of the 1930s revival. One such station was Temple Meads at Bristol which needed to be enlarged to meet the demands being put upon it. When the work was finally completed the station would cover an area twice its previous size and see the longest platform increased from 307 yards to just over 410 yards in length.
Photo: GWR Official / Soole

In 1937 a decision was taken to upgrade the railways' breakdown and heavy lifting facilities, and early in the following year it was determined that each district should have its own emergency depot. This resulted in the concentration of stores of materials, rails, sleepers, bricks, baulks of timber, ply-wood sheeting, bridge beams, girders, corrugated-iron, plexi-glass and so on. In fact, anything which could be used to effect a speedy repair to railway lines and their infrastructure.

As an example of the reserves set aside, we might look at the LMS who, over ten centres, distributed sufficient material to replace 22 miles of track, 130 points, 1,330 crossings and 25 bridges. The same company even began experimenting with high explosives on derelict buildings in 1938, to try and learn what the effects of air raid damage were likely to be. To assist with the heavy lifting that would result from bomb damage, a complete review of breakdown crane policy was undertaken, and new cranes were ordered for areas where the existing ones were to be found wanting. Mobile workshops were formed and equipped with welding gear, lathes, drilling machines etc., and 73 of the breakdown and repair trains were also provided with gas decontamination apparatus.

As times worsened around the time of the Munich Pact on 29th September 1938, the railways and the Ministry of Transport formulated the means by which the Railway Executive would take control of the public undertakings when war was declared. Sir Ralph Wedgwood of the LNER was appointed as its chairman. From this stage on, we can see even more evidence of Government funding flowing into the railways, in one form or another, thus enabling them to undertake even more vitally necessary work. Nevertheless, the railways were not idle at resolving their own problems, and as far as revenue activities were concerned they were making very positive steps to redress the critical times in which they were operating. For example, a good many of the companies' losses were being overcome by more efficient working and greater co-operation, standardisation and exchange of traffic.

Joint publicity arrangements were entered into, and many railway pictures of the era show GWR or SR posters appearing on the notice boards of LNER or LMS stations. Other posters, advertising holiday destinations in the South-west carried both sets of initials, SR and GWR. The LMS and LNER applied for, and received, Ministerial approval for pooling traffic between certain points, permitting a greater degree of flexibility to the travelling public (and in turn this seems to have stimulated a growth in demand). International promotion was undertaken at various events, notably the 'World Fair' in New York, where British railways were represented as a whole.

Above:

The book Timetable To Victory *by Evan John, commented about the late 1930s in the following way: 'They [passengers] did not know, as the August of 1938 sped them in their thousands to the sea, what the railways were doing in unpublicised places. It was naturally a secret that, for more than a year now, railway workshops had been turning aside from the building of engines and rolling-stock to the fashioning of tanks and aeroplanes.' The terrible devastation wreaked on communication lines by dive-bombers in the Spanish Civil War had set a precedent for what might happen elsewhere in Europe, and the powers that be were alive to the threat that it posed to British railways. However, despite all of this the Fall of France was both swift and largely unanticipated. Even as the Panzers encircled Dunkirk supplies of equipment were being needlessly sent to France. Fortunately a large order that was due to be shipped from the Birmingham Railway & Carriage Works was not sent and the equipment pictured here was later used in other theatres of war. On May 23rd 1940 a variety of wagons, coaches, and gun limbers are seen in the yard in company with an LPTB tube carriage.*

Right:

Preparations for the war were widely evidenced on British railways, but more noticeably so on Northern Irish lines as it was evident that railways like the LMS's Northern Counties Committee would have to be improved to carry the substantial traffic that war would bring.

By the summer of 1939 roughly two decades had elapsed since the end of World War I, and in that time the railways had achieved remarkable ends against overwhelming odds.

In the face of social change, economic hardship and world-wide Depression, they had become a unified operation. Collectively they operated 60,000 miles of track, 95 miles of dock-side quays, and 130 steamships. They also employed 650,000 men and women, had a quarter of a million railway freight vehicles and owned sufficient coaching stock to carry 2,500,000 passengers at a time.

The Big Four had spent the first five years of their existence overcoming the difficulties of four years of total war, and then restoring services to their pre-war levels.

From the time the Grouping took effect, and for the next ten years Britain's railways were to witness a period of consolidation and, to an extent, rationalisation. This came in the midst of a time of major economic and social unrest, and it would not have been unreasonable for little progress to have been made in view of these problems. We only have to look at the examples of some other countries to prove what could have happened, and we might purposefully cite post-revolution Russia as a prime example. The fact that our railways did progress, albeit slowly at first, says much for their management rather than any official assistance.

In the 1930s the railways turned the corner, and there came all the major advances with the great acceleration in speed, specifically on the Anglo-Scottish routes. Much of this acceleration was born out of the continuing spirit of competition, but as the decade drew to its end, the railways were coming closer together than might be readily imagined. True, many of the areas of co-operation were in fields where a unified approach by railway operators was designed to fend off competition from outside operators, but it was a general meeting of minds. Indeed, it could be concluded that in their own way the railways, whilst maintaining their own identities, were moving ever closer to the goals that the Parliamentary Select Committee had proposed. In many ways, had the companies been allowed to go their own way, then a greater form of unification might have been achieved than resulted from the nationalisation of 1948, but for now we can only speculate on what might have been as we look at the four railways individually.

Above:
During the difficult years of the war routine maintenance of locomotives was bound to suffer, so the Railway Executive Committee instructed the railway companies to simplify all areas of non essential work. One such area was in the painting and lining out of locomotives and simplified liveries were thus introduced. Nowhere was this more evident than on the LNER, where the decision was taken to simplify the company abbreviation to NE and this was duly painted on locomotive tenders etc. Undoubtedly this was seen by many enthusiasts as an allusion to the old North Eastern Railway, and it did not go down too well as a result. An example of this livery is seen on class D17/2 a 4-4-0 of 1897 vintage. Pictured in its 50th year at Brough, No. 1902 awaits departure with the 1:23 PM to Hull.
Photo: LNER Official / Wethersett

Left:
A successful locomotive design concept that was employed throughout the world was the Beyer-Garratt engine. A number were acquired by the LMS for working heavy coal trains, but they were not the success they could have been had the manufacturers been allowed freedom of movement in their construction, here No.4994 is seen at Cricklewood in 1935.
Photo: R.J.Essery Collection

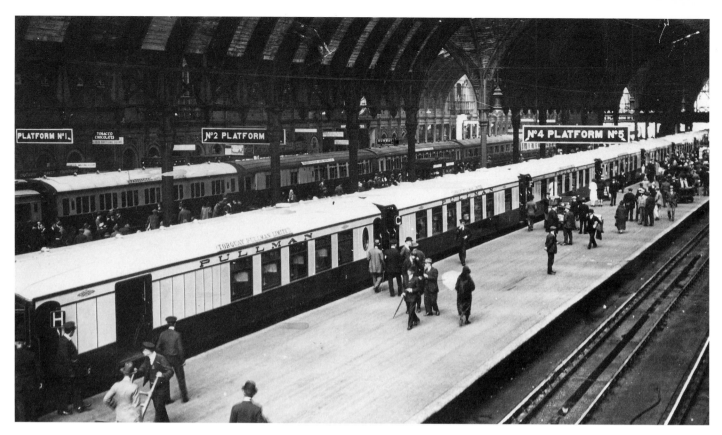

Above:

In 1929 the GWR's Torbay Limited service was joined by another luxury train using Pullman stock - naturally this became known as the Torbay Pullman Limited. The service actually began on 8th July 1929 and it was the first regular use of Pullman coaches on the GWR. The service was inaugurated from Paddington by James Milne (the new General Manager) and C.B.Collett. The train engine was none other than No.6000 King George V with its famous brass bell, and this was rung by Collett just before the train departed.

Below:

The Abermule disaster claimed 17 lives after confusion between incompetent station staff allowing two trains on to a single track line. The two trains met head on and both were completely wrecked as the picture below graphically shows.

CHAPTER TWO
The GWR Pre-war

The GWR, whatever your personal view, has to be considered as one of the most successful and charismatic railway companies that ever operated. The whole operation was built on a series of solid foundations, and whilst prudently frugal in some avenues of operation (a few Welsh branch lines spring readily to mind for instance), it could also provide quite lavish accommodation for those customers who could afford to travel first class.

It was initially conceived to link Bristol and London, a circumstance that owed much to the prominence of the west country city's maritime industry and its then important position of being the nation's 'Second City'. The flamboyance of the GWR's engineer Isambard Kingdom Brunel was matched only by his spectacular achievements which included many notable feats of civil and mechanical engineering; amongst which the single arch span of the bridge across the Thames at Maidenhead most confounded his critics. Brunel's legacy and influence remained with the GWR in the years that followed, and in no small measure did this contribute to the stability which so greatly benefited the enlarged Great Western after the Grouping of 1923.

It was the old GWR's predominant position in the country's railway network that enabled it to claim the right to being the nucleus of the new Western Group that was formed after 1923 and it was therefore only right and just that the name should continue as well. Equally, many of the railways that were amalgamated into the new group were just about destitute, or at best financially impoverished by the circumstances of the all-out national effort during World War I. An example that readily springs to mind is the Cambrian Railway, which served central and western Wales. Hardly the most populous region, the Cambrian could enjoy only slim pickings from many of the stations it served en-route, and most of its route mileage was just single track. Yet the terrible state of the Cambrian is perhaps demonstrated in that most classic and infamous of railway disasters, Abermule, which occurred on 26th January 1921.

The official report into the disaster which resulted from the head-on collision of two passenger trains on a single track line, illustrates to what a low pitch efficiency had slipped at the small Welsh station. The staff there were critically censured for their failings, but their malaise was not (it seems) unique and was probably indicative of the underlying trends on not just the Cambrian, but many of the small railways which the GWR were about to absorb. It was, therefore the duty of the new regime to bring these railways firmly into the 20th century, and that is something they certainly did, as throughout the period covered by this book - right down to the bitter end in December 1947 - the GWR promoted a policy of standardisation that was aimed at eliminating inefficiency and waste.

Train Services and Developments

We begin this section with a general introduction to the trains of the GWR in the difficult years of the early-1930s. Fortunately there was something of a buffer against these problems as the old GWR's policies of locomotive standardisation, overall economies, and train safety were largely unaffected by the Grouping. Therefore, as the dominant partner in the new company of the same name, the enlarged GWR did not undergo the many sea changes experienced in the other large pre-Grouped companies. Swindon ruled, at least in mechanical terms, and that was only for the good of all concerned. None of the other works in the new GWR had the size, ability or personalities to influence the way forward like Swindon.

It was, of course a much more different story on the LMS, where men from Crewe, Horwich, Derby and so on, all vied for position of top dog. Consequently the GWR had the advantage, and it showed. As David Jenkinson will later explain by the end of the 1920s the GWR had already set its standards for its main locomotive classes. We also have to take into consideration the introduction of steam locomotive classes and, of course, the desire for standardising diesel railcars which set the practical alternative to electrification of suburban services and also made substantial economies to branch line operations. Not only were these railcars useful in this regard, but they were also to be gainfully employed on cross-country express workings as was shown by their introduction on the Cardiff - Birmingham service, where passengers willingly paid a supplement of 2s 6d (12.5p). Moving on to the stock side, the vehicles introduced for the Cornish Riviera Limited in 1935 were masterpieces of corporate design that included high-specification passenger features and considerable technical advances. It was similar with the stock introduced for the 'Ocean Liner' trains, introduced in the early 1930s, which embodied all the luxury features of the Pullman cars that had preceded them.

Freight developments were nowhere near as exciting, and the GWR seemed happy to contend with a high percentage of un-braked freights which ambled along at average speeds of less than 10 mph. In a more positive vein the GWR had developed the 20-ton all-steel coal wagon, authorising a batch of 5,000 in 1933 thanks to Government finance from the 1929 Act. Variants on the 20-ton capacity vehicles came in the form of the 'Mink-G' van and the steel grain hopper known as the 'Grano'. Another general traffic development was the use of containers and demountable tankers, especially those used in the carriage of milk. Containerisation, it will be recalled, was a recommendation of the Royal Commission on Transport's third report, and it is an area where the GWR took a notable early lead over its contemporaries.

Many authors have commented on the inadequacies of the standard 10 feet wheel-base of the basic British railway wagon, and pointed at the reluctance to upgrade from this to larger capacity wagons as being one of the major reasons in the demise of rail freight in the 1950s and 60s. Yet, as experience with road/rail freight transfer clearly showed in the Suez crisis of 1956, commercial customers highly regarded the flexibility of small containers, as these could be delivered to the customer's factory or warehouse, loaded by the sender's own staff, and sent on to a distant destination by a convenient means of integrated road, rail and even sea transportation without the need for re-packing, transhipment or warehouse storage.

Left:
It is believed that but for World War II, the GWR would have introduced an extensive programme of container development which would have included the vacuum braking of the wagons employed in this traffic. The containers had a great advantage, as they were equally at home on the back of a 10 feet wheel-base railway wagon, a motor lorry, or even a mechanical horse. The containers were used for a variety of things such as furniture, electrical goods, cycles, motor-cycles, fruit and vegetables. This latter traffic was also being catered for by conventional 12-ton vans, some of which were fitted with cooling equipment operated by the ICI's patent 'Dricold' carbon-dioxide refrigerant agent.
Photo: GWR Official

The summer of 1934 also saw a new form of railway vehicle development, though on this occasion the vehicles concerned were to have a very low mileage indeed as most of their time was spent on disused sidings. I refer, of course, to the concept of Camping Coaches which were embraced by the railways as a means of encouraging travel and providing low-cost family holidays. At selected sites all over England and Wales, the GWR camping coaches began to appear, initially using old clerestory vehicles which had been modified to provide sleeping, eating and living accommodation. Most of those who booked camping coach holidays, such as this one in Wales, would probably expect to take out Holiday Season Tickets, the fore-runner of 'rail rover' passes, so that they could explore the area around their given holiday destination by rail. It was yet another piece of shrewd marketing, for it provided a 'holiday to remember' for all who partook of them.

Below:

Interestingly, the 1930s' increase in fruit, flower and vegetable traffic, especially from the West Country, the Scilly Isles (via Penzance) and the Channel Isles (via Weymouth) came at a time when traditional animal traffic was showing a marked decline. Consequently a number of surplus cattle vans were modified for perishable traffic, although it was something of a standing joke amongst railwaymen at Marazion in Cornwall, that 'their broccoli was so fresh they sent it in vans that used to have manure on the floor'. It is this traffic that is being unloaded at Paddington goods station in the Spring of 1942; note the number of female porters.

Photos: Both GWR Official.

One of the most interesting facets of pre-war travel on the GWR were 'Railcar Excursions' which the company began to organise as a means of demonstrating the advantages of its new diesel railcars. With quite slick marketing flair, the GWR laid on a number of outings for various chambers of commerce. One such was put on for the Birmingham Chamber of Commerce, and ran from England's second city to Weston-super-Mare by way of Swindon Works. With just one intermediate stop, the railcar reached Swindon in 2 hours, not bad for a journey of 100 miles. After providing a guided tour of the works the railcar was on its way once again, this time with stewards serving lunch on the 80 minute leg to Weston. Speeds of up to 70 mph were reached on this part of the trip, but slow passages through Bath and Bristol considerably reduced the overall timings. This of course was just one of the specially promoted GWR railcar excursions, others had included South Wales, Birkenhead and even Aberystwyth, but all served to demonstrate the advantages of this new-fangled form of rail travel to an appreciative and influential audience. Elsewhere, the GWR continued its improvements to branch and suburban services with a great many benefiting from significant cuts in the running schedules, but as we will discuss later they never took the courageous step of suburban electrification like the other three companies.

Yet, as far as the travelling public were concerned, the yard-stick by which a railway could be measured were its crack expresses. We shall mention the GWR's most interesting, the Cheltenham Spa Express, a little later on, but for now we might mention some of the other GWR improvements in the pre-war years. One of the stages came in the adoption of the American process of streamlining trains, and the GWR were no slouches at following modern trends. The concept is more readily associated with the streamlined railcars of the GWR and the developments on the LNER, but the GWR introduced their streamlined services in the same month as their East Coast counterparts, namely September 1935. The Bristolian, when it was introduced led to a significant improvement on the route west, and as much as 23 minutes was slashed from some journey times.

Track developments, also discussed later, led to substantial improvements in the schedules. For example, the Cornish Riviera was cut to just under 4 hours between Paddington and Plymouth, while the Torbay Express lost five minutes off its timings. New services were also introduced to the west, with the Cornishman also being introduced in 1935. Furthermore, in the same two years of 1934-5, around 1,000 new services were introduced, although we must admit that most were Saturday-only workings. Newspaper trains were also to see general improvements, and one of the South Wales services enjoyed the distinction of being the 'Fastest Newspaper Train In The World'. The summer timetable of 1938 saw a major number of improvements, with Swansea getting a 3 hour 45 minute service from Paddington, whilst the 7.30am from Birmingham to Paddington saw its arrival time being slashed by a whole quarter of an hour.

Of course there were closures as well as improvements, but the GWR fared remarkably better through this period than did the LMS and LNER. One notable closure was the antiquated Cleobury Mortimer & Ditton Priors Light Railway which was a superannuated affair even when it was new. When it was closed in 1938, there must have been mixed feelings about the withdrawal of its elderly 4-wheeled coaches with stepped running boards that were needed to facilitate access to and from the line's low platforms. Another closure of 1938 was the Portreath Branch in Cornwall, which met its demise in its centennial year. The quaint, three mile long line that ran from Carn Brae down to the tiny harbour on the north Cornish coast would, today, have made an attractive tourist railway. However, its closure demonstrated the almost total decline of the Cornish tin-mining industry, and for most of its length it had been little used for many years prior to that.

In the last summer before the war, the GWR became involved in some extraordinary traffic flows to Windsor in connection with the Royal Show which took place in Windsor Great Park. The first of these flows were consignments of 20,600 old sleepers (7,200 of these were supplied by the Southern), which were delivered in June for the purpose of making roadways on the show site. Next came large amounts of equipment that had been kept in store at Cardiff following the 1938 show which had to be moved, and this traffic alone totalled some 1,650 tons. To handle all the additional pre-show traffic, a fleet of 22 Scammell 'mechanical horses' were drafted in, but as the show dates neared, the fleet of cartage units based at Windsor Low Level Goods Yard increased to an extra 135 units, including four wheel tractors, lorries, box vans, horse boxes, and traditional horses and carts.

The Southern Railway had about 85 extra units working from its yard in the town. Livestock was handled at platform four of the GWR passenger station, and an ingenious one-way system led to a speedy unloading (and later reloading) operation. The GWR also handled all the LMS show trains, both passenger and freight. One of the latter was a special train from Lockwood near Huddersfield, which was conveying supplies of the first all-British tractor, the David Brown VAK1 that was making its debut appearance that July.

A number of LNER trains also used the GWR facilities, including through expresses from Scotland, although LNER services from Yorkshire, Lincolnshire and East Anglia were mostly worked to the Southern's Windsor & Eton Riverside station. The show was a great success and, for a short while at least, it took people's minds off the fast approaching war. More importantly the event showed close co-operation between the railways and its agricultural customers, and in the months and years that followed the goodwill engendered at the 1939 Royal Show was to be of significant advantage.

New Ways and Works.

As the 1930s progressed, the GWR made much use of the 1929 Act, and by 1931, 34 schemes had been authorised. The first two to be completed were the doubling of the Scorrier - Redruth and Goonbarrow Junction - Bugle sections in Cornwall. New marshalling yard improvements were authorised for Banbury, Severn Tunnel Junction, and Rogerstone, whilst goods facilities were upgraded at Wolverhampton, Paignton, Hockley, Swansea (High Street), Lye and Birmingham Small Heath. New engine sheds or improved facilities were introduced at Radyr, Treherbert and Pantyffynnon. Duffryn yard received an extensive improvement in coaling facilities, whilst the workshops at Swindon and Cardiff (Cathays) also benefited substantially from the expansion programme. Improvements were also to be noted in station buildings, as for example Paignton which was completely reconstructed at the same time as the goods depot.

Below:
Whether it was replacing viaducts in Cornwall, painting the Saltash bridge or doubling important sections of track, the GWR made much use of its rail cranes as seen here in bridge replacement work.
Photo: GWR Official

Improving The Line

New lines, widening, and quadrupling schemes were a feature of the GWR's pre-war development. For example, on the West of England line the cut-off routes at Westbury and Frome were opened in 1932, as was the quadrupling of the line west of Cogload Junction through Taunton and as far as Norton Fitzwarren. Actually, this much needed expansion was undertaken in a slightly frugal fashion and the earthworks were not widened sufficiently to allow the normal positioning of signals. This caused a few minor problems on the eight mile long section of line down to the junction for the West Somerset and Barnstaple branches, but none so bad as those on a dark night in November 1940; when this non-standard signalling was to become one of the contributory factors leading to the disaster which befell the crew of No. 6028 *King George VI*. Further west a number of stations were to receive the benefit of platform loops, thus allowing facilities for express services to overtake stopping trains. Even the Falmouth branch was to receive attention, and the last of Brunel's timber viaducts in Cornwall was replaced when a new structure opened on 22nd July 1934. Another Cornish viaduct rebuilding project at Trenance was completed in 1938 as part of improvements to the Newquay branch which saw exceptionally busy periods in the summer months.

Below:
More fully covered in the Atlantic book Brunel's Cornish Viaducts, *the subject of viaduct replacement such as this one at Liskeard in 1926, forms a fascinating part in the GWR's modernisation plan.*
Photo: GWR Official

The most notable reconstruction programme, was that of London's Paddington station, which came about following a report entitled 'The Future of Paddington Station'. This far-reaching document called for extensive building works, but the proposals for an overall concrete roof and a 300 feet high clock tower were not implemented. However, in the period 1932-4, the platforms were extended whilst the track-layout was completely remodelled and provided with colour-light signalling and powered points. Four new suburban platforms were constructed on the site of the old Bishop's Road station and a new parcels depot was built nearby. New office buildings were also provided, whilst the carriage sidings at nearby Old Oak Common were enlarged and improved. Bristol's Temple Meads was another principle GWR station to be upgraded, and was enlarged so significantly as to cover twice its original area. Didcot was extensively remodelled as were the Welsh stations of Newport High Street, Swansea High Street, and Cardiff. Yet it was not just large stations which were developed as the little halts at Ninian Park (Cardiff) and The Hawthorns (West Bromwich) were provided to cater for visiting football fans.

Holiday makers to Penzance witnessed work on both the station and the sea defences, whilst a scheme promoted at the end of 1937, saw the complete rebuilding of Porthcawl station in Wales. The new facilities there were to include seven platforms radiating from a large circulating area around which would be built a new booking hall, waiting rooms, cloakrooms and other offices. New carriage sidings (940 to 1,150 feet) were provided, as well as a modern turntable big enough to accommodate the largest engines. In 1938 work was put in hand to improve facilities at Plymouth North Road, but this was still not completed when war broke out and the station was subsequently damaged during the air raids of the early 1940s. Exeter St. David's was another casualty of the war, this time not because of enemy action, but rather a Railway Executive Committee decision to defer the proposed alterations. This is by no means a complete list of works undertaken, but it is representative of a period of expansion

The year 1938 brought electrification very much to the fore, and whilst this might be more commonly associated with the Southern and the LNER, in February came news that the GWR were also looking into the subject. Lord Horne, Chairman of the GWR, announced that they were to investigate the possibility of a section from Taunton to Penzance, engaging consultant engineers Merz & McLellan Ltd. The obvious reasoning behind this proposal was the continuing rise in the price of coal, as every shilling (5p) that was added to the price of a ton was costing the GWR £100,000 per year. This was just one of a number of options that the company were considering, and it is interesting to note that it was looking at a scheme in the West Country rather than the London or Birmingham suburban services which might have been more profitably considered.

How the GWR arrived at the decision for an electrification of the South West lines is something of a mystery, for it made very little logical sense except in the fact that the steep gradients and sharp curves on the route through Devon and Cornwall called for very high engine power. Yet, even with electrification, the schedules west of Taunton would not have been remarkably accelerated. When we consider that it was also proposed to electrify the Kingswear branch, the Par - Newquay line and the Cornish china clay branches, the whole thing seems a nonsense. It could be argued that a study of the traffic figures would reveal these routes as being almost identical to the LNER's Woodhead line, calculated on a basis of engine miles; although a detailed analysis of the same figures would show that a great percentage of this mileage was concentrated in a very short time period, mostly summer Saturdays. What is more, the argument of speeding up the service to the west could not be really taken into account either, because of the time that would be taken for the change-over between steam and electric traction (or vice-versa) which would cause a major bottleneck at Taunton.

A number of historians who have looked at the subject in great depth have, therefore, concluded that the electrification proposals may have been nothing more than a ploy to force down the prices of coal which had risen sharply during the 1930s. This factor was hurting the GWR (and other railways) very badly, but surely not so bad as to partially resolve the problems by a capital expenditure of £4,000,000. In due course the GWR issued a press release which, in part, said: 'The investigations have thus revealed that this section of line is not particularly suited to electrification by reason of its physical characteristics, the nature of the traffic, and the wide variation between summer and winter density, while the high cost of electric locomotives is another adverse factor. In these circumstances we regret that the Great Western Railway board of Directors has decided not to proceed with the project.' Even so the bluff, if bluff it was, had worked and the prices which the collieries were asking the railways for their coal dropped significantly.

On a more practical note, the GWR developed a plan for the economic maintenance of the permanent way, which was obviously an advantageous step forward in view of the many miles of rural secondary track which the company operated. Power equipment was made available to replace some manual operations, such as hole boring in sleepers and rails, whilst electric welding was introduced to build up worn down crossing parts. Steel keys were introduced to replace wooden ones, and automatic weed-killing was introduced in 1932. By 1935 a special weed-killing train had been formed up from a tank wagon and three old locomotive tenders. As part of a determined effort to reduce track maintenance, this new system was capable of treating anything up to 60 miles of track a day.

Remarkable Achievements

Turning now to the subject of Automatic Train Control we can rightly include it in this section as it was one of the most significant technological advances made by the GWR in the 1930s as they continued the system on the main lines as far as Wolverhampton, Plymouth and Swansea. The last main line station to be reached was Penzance, where the installation was completed a few months after the start of World War II. This made the GWR the safest railway in the land, if not the world, as it had almost 3,000 miles of superbly signalled, safe track upon which to run its trains. From my study of railway accidents, I would venture to propose, that had it not been for ATC, then the GWR would probably have suffered as high a percentage of accidents as its contemporaries did in the dark war years that followed.

Unlike the LMS and LNER, the GWR did not go into the business of speed records or highly publicised 'races', it simply settled for what services it had and went on to improve them. Yet, whilst they did not achieve the record-breaking triumphs of *Mallard,* it did have its famous 'Cheltenham Spa Express'. By 1929 it had become the fastest train in the world, achieving an aggregate 66.2 mph between Swindon and Paddington. This world record was taken from the GWR, not by the LNER but the Canadian Pacific Railway which set up a 68.9mph schedule on the principal Toronto - Montreal expresses.

The Cheltenham Flyer, as the service was nicknamed, regained the record in September 1931 when the schedule was set to 69.2 mph. Yet, this was just the beginning and *Launceston Castle* showed that the run to Paddington could be achieved, under favourable conditions, in less than an hour which corresponded to a speed fractionally less than 80 mph. In June 1931 *Tregenna Castle,* did the run in just 56 minutes and 47 seconds, and averaged a speed of 81.7 mph. Thus encouraged, the GWR lifted the schedule to 70 mph and made much play in their advertising and promotional material about their operation of 'The World's Fastest Train'. The timing of its departure was another facet in its popularity for, leaving Cheltenham at 4pm, it made the whole of its journey to London in the daylight hours - even in the winter months. Afternoon teas served on board, especially as the train rolled down the pastoral Thames Valley, undoubtedly added to the appeal.

The 1930s were also something of a time of doubt about the claims that *City of Truro* had achieved the speed of 100 mph back in 1904 and much comment was made about this in the popular railway press. Yet, what ever the case behind that claim, the GWR could rightfully boast in the achievement of *Builth Castle* in 1939 which certainly did attain a speed of 100 mph through the village of Honeybourne.

Above:
In March 1935 Swindon works took in a representative of both the King and Castle classes with a view to experiment with streamlining which was coming into vogue on other railway systems. The two locomotives were No. 5005 Manorbier Castle *and No. 6014* King Henry VII. *As will be seen from the picture above the results were hardly aesthetic, although Swindon did in fact beat the LNER in producing a streamliner by a few months.*

Below:
The 1930s saw improvements to a number of GWR harbour facilities, but few could have been as urgently needed as those for Weymouth jetty seen below.
Photo: GWR Official

Above:
One of the many services provided by the GWR was that of mail trains and whilst the company were not as famous as the LMS for its travelling post offices, they nevertheless ran an effective service on behalf of the Royal Mail. Pictured in a train of very mixed stock one of the TPO's is seen behind No. 6094 Dynevor Castle *prior to the outbreak of war.*

Below:
The involvement of British railways in other forms of transport had long been evident, as for example canals, road haulage, commercial shipping and ferries; so it was not unreasonable to expect them to get involved in developing air services. Pictured here is the Railway Air Services De Havilland DH84 Dragon Rapide which was introduced in 1934.
Photos: Both GWR Official

Ancillary Services

In an overview of any of the Big Four companies' pre-war activities, we are obliged to take a brief look at their non-railway operations. Mind you, that is something of a misnomer, as activities such as docks, road vehicles, hotels etc., were all part and parcel of the all-pervading commercial activities the railways engaged in.

When the GWR was formed, it was the largest dock-owning company in the world. True, many of the ports were small and increasingly inadequate for 20th century shipping, and most were located on the shores of the Bristol Channel, but they were generally successful and highly profitable as a whole. They had boomed in the late-Victorian and Edwardian eras, and been buoyed up due to artificially high traffic levels in the Great War. Yet, with the General Strike, the Depression and the world-wide slump that followed the Wall Street Crash in 1929, the GWR's docks were to find themselves in serious trouble.

The fall off in exports of coal from South Wales was particularly significant and in its 1929 Act, the GWR obtained powers to close the Town Dock at Newport. Since 1923 coal exports had declined by nearly ten million tons from the South Wales ports up to 1930, and in the next five years it dropped again by a similar figure. Clearly the GWR, whose fortunes in South Wales were centred on the carriage of coal from the valley mines to the coastal ports, were facing fairly serious problems.

By 1932 the company were seeking to close the 3,000 feet long Penarth dock, but they were kept open through combined acts of local diplomacy. However, despite the repeated cutbacks, it was not all doom and gloom, and new investment was also in evidence. New works were installed at Newport North Dock and Cardiff, whilst the GWR-owned Mumbles Lighthouse was converted from oil to electricity. Cattle-traffic saw its ups and downs too, as several outbreaks of notifiable diseases in Ireland restricted movement of livestock and thus affected imports. As this compounded the drop in cattle traffic following an outbreak of foot and mouth in Pembrokeshire in 1931, the GWR began importing both meat and livestock from Commonwealth countries.

As far as passenger activities went, the company spent considerable sums of money in an effort to improve their market share in holiday and ferry traffic. For example, the pier and port facilities at Weymouth were extensively remodelled. A new pier of reinforced concrete, three times the width of the old one, was created and duly opened by HRH Prince of Wales in 1933.

Unfortunately, the problems of taking passenger stock all the way down to the pier was still a long way from being resolved and it took a further five years before the tramway leading down to the harbour was upgraded to a satisfactory standard. Sadly, plans to improve the town station were deferred due to the outbreak of war. Work on modernising the two boats employed on the Channel Isles, the *St. Juilen* and the *St. Helier*, was, however, actually undertaken at Penarth in 1937, an action that was much to the appreciation of the travelling public.

The Irish Sea services were boosted in 1934 when the *Great Western* entered service to provide the GWR with a fourth member of the Fishguard - Rosslare fleet. Thankfully, these provisions and others led to an improvement in the company's shipping services in the 1930s. The heavy losses of the 1920s had now diminished, and in 1938 the group's profits had reached £23,500.

Unfortunately, the docks and canals continued to make losses, and by the time war broke out it can be seen that many of their facilities were no longer in the right place for modern traffic movements. Yet, with the outbreak of hostilities, times were coming when every piece of infrastructure would be worth its weight in gold.

As far as road transport is concerned, the GWR were already becoming masters of integrated traffic movement. The benefit of mechanising its horse-operated road delivery fleet was clearly perceived in the hallowed corridors of Paddington, especially as far as its London-based operations were concerned as fodder prices spiralled in the early years of the 1930s. Even so, the road delivery collection services were run outwardly at a loss, and as a result they were what accountants of modern times would see as being candidates that were ripe for disposal. Yet, it was rather an important part of a whole goods and luggage service and an indispensable one at that. In the modern vernacular, it was 'a highly effective loss leader'.

The same could be said of the company's catering and hotel services, which although profitable in some areas, were seen very much as a means rather than an end. Many of the railway hotels were however completely refurbished in the era, including the Fishguard Bay Hotel which the GWR operated but did not own. The same policy of refurbishment was true at station refreshment rooms all around the system, yet despite all this the GWR remained well behind the LMS and LNER in this area of ancillary business.

Finally, we could briefly mention the GWR's air services which commenced on 11th April 1932 between Cardiff and Plymouth. Aircraft historians, and readers of Neville Shute novels will appreciate that 1920s and 30s were a very difficult time for the embryonic British air passenger industry. There were many courageous attempts, and just as many significant failures because even the best of intentions came to grief in an economic climate that had not yet come to appreciate the rapidity of passenger air services. Safety, reliability and passenger volumes were all issues that still had to be addressed. For example, as far as capacity went, the GWR's Westland Wessex aircraft could carry only six passengers, but even so it was rarely run with a full load.

Extending the service to Birmingham helped, but this limited the aircraft to just one return trip each day and this was just as unprofitable. When the service came to an end at the onset of winter, just over 700 people had been carried. What followed in 1934, with a partnership between all four companies in the guise of Railway Air Services Limited did a little better, but the losses were still quite high and 'questions were asked in Parliament' about the railways' growing monopoly in the field of passenger transport. Still, the railways kept up their involvement to the start of the war, and but for this who knows which way a completely integrated, rail, road, sea, and air service might have gone. Whatever the case, we could expect that the GWR would have been doing all that it could to prevail and show that it really was **God's Wonderful Railway.**

In the 1930s the face of GWR freight transport varied immensely from its old goods locomotives, such as 2-4-0 No.3515 pictured above, to a fast developing road transport fleet. In 1936 they placed a substantial order for 412 road vehicles, but of these a batch of 16 Commer vans were cancelled, and replaced by an order for a similar number of Fords in 1937. The most useful vehicles were the three-wheeled 'Scammell Mechanical Horses' from Watford and the very similar 'Karrier Kobs' (built in Huddersfield). These were highly manoeuvrable towing trucks, which were employed at depots like Acton (pictured below) along with articulated trailers that could be picked up or dropped off with considerable ease. They were useful replacements for the labour-intensive horse delivery vehicles, and strangely enough they were readily accepted by the younger horse-drivers who were 'converted' to their operation. Even at big depots where horses were still in use, the 'mechanical horses' were used to replace chain-horses to draw heavy horse-drawn vehicles uphill at depots such as Birmingham's Hockley Goods Yard. As the 1930s progressed, joint motor vehicle services were operated with the other companies in competing areas, as part of a 'pool' arrangement of traffic sharing. In other districts, goods delivery and collections were centralised at certain depots, with the number of handling stations being reduced by two-thirds in both the West Midlands and South Wales.

Above:

This picture taken on a grimy September day at Wakefield's Kirkgate station, showing an ex-L&YR 2-4-2 tank engine, is quite representative of the type of services that the LMS inherited upon grouping. Whilst the WCML, Holyhead, and other fast express routes were the more glamourous workings, most of the 'Bread & Butter' duties fell to more humble engines. It matters not whether these were handled by ex-Caledonian, ex-Midland, or ex-North Staffordshire engines (to name but a few), they were the staple diet of many railway passengers who travelled local branch lines. Many of these pre-group locomotives lasted right through the LMS period and in to BR ownership. The Aspinall 2-4-2T shown here is a prime example of such engines' longevity for as late as 1958, eighteen of them were still in regular service although the class had been introduced as early as 1899. These radial tank engines, built at the Horwich Works were both ubiquitous and durable, and equally at home on passenger, freight and shunting duties.

CHAPTER THREE
The LMS Pre-war

The creation of a railway which stretched the length and breadth of Britain (running from the South Coast to the Far North of Scotland and from Southend in the east across to Kyle of Lochalsh and even stretching into Ireland via the Belfast & North Counties line) may, at the outset, seem to be a recipe for major success. In many ways it was, but the difficulties that surrounded the Grouping, the General Strike and the Depression which followed one another in quick succession all had their cumulative effects on the way in which the LMS could, and indeed would, develop. The biggest of their difficulties was however the internal 'politics' that surrounded the Grouping, and the continual jockeying for prominence and position.

Unlike the GWR, with its massive works at Swindon which dominated all the smaller works that were acquired at the Grouping, the LMS did not have one clear candidate to take on this role. Crewe, the mechanical headquarters of the old LNWR was probably the rightful candidate, but there were many in Derby who would (and did) argue that point. Both had a justifiable claim, but it was a fact that at both these works there was no-one who was the heir apparent to the title of Chief Mechanical Engineer. At Derby Henry Fowler had held the post for 14 years, and in some ways it was a pity he did not get the job straight away upon the Grouping. As it was, it would be two years before he achieved this honour and the late O.S. Nock once suggested that this was because the 'powers that be' had wanted to get well away from the Midland Railway's small engine policy. At Crewe there had been a succession of four great CMEs in the period from 1857 to 1920, Ramsbottom, Webb, Whale and Bowen-Cooke, but the latter had been succeeded in 1920 by Captain Hewitt Pearson Montague Beames.

The tenure of Beames' office was not a long one, and when the LNWR/Lancashire & Yorkshire merger took place on 1st January 1922, it was Horwich's George Hughes who took the post of CME. Indeed, despite its comparatively smaller size, it was L&YR men who took many of the senior positions in the new company. In many ways it was a succession of tragedies that had rocked the foundations of the new LMS, notably the death of Sir Guy Calthrop from the Spanish Influenza in 1919. Although just 44 years old at the time of his demise, he had already proved that he was a great general manager and who knows how this experience might have been applied in the newly formed LMS.

The death of Bowen-Cooke and the retirement of Sir Gilbert Claughton just before the LNWR/L&YR merger were the two other major factors in releasing Crewe's grip on control of the new company. The Midland influence, by way of contrast, had actually increased notably in the form of Sir Guy Granet the former General Manager of the Midland who became Chairman of the LMS in 1924. With Fowler as Deputy Chief CME and J.H. Follows as Chief Superintendent, Derby influence was soon keenly felt. Whilst the LNWR only had S.H. Hunt as Chief Goods Manager and E.F.C. Trench as Chief Engineer (civil engineer). By way of a contrast the L&YR had Arthur Watson as General Manager and R. C. Irwin as Company Secretary.

It is not difficult to understand that there was considerable discouragement amongst former Crewe supremos, who now found themselves demoted or moved sideways into lesser positions; for example it must have been galling for men like Beames to thereafter find themselves as mere Divisional Officers. Hughes did not remain in office for long so he did not have time to make his influence really felt, and upon retirement in 1925 he was eventually succeeded by Fowler. By now Derby had the upper hand, and for many years after this Midland influence was clearly evident. The path to harmony was not helped by the lack of appointments of men from the smaller companies into a position of prominence. Only D. A. Mathieson of the Caledonian was included in the list of Chief Officers in 1923, when he was appointed as Deputy General Manager for Scotland. This appointment did not suit rivals at the old Glasgow & South Western, and so more fuel was added to the fire.

Having talked at length with some of those who were junior members of the LMS HQ staff at that time, I have detected that a far from harmonious position existed, especially in Scotland and that as a result the decision to make largely autonomous operating divisions was taken. As a consequence three divisions came about, although there could have been as many as five, and each was controlled by a General Superintendent who, in turn, reported to J. H. Follows. The Western Division was ruled by A. Davies of the L&YR, but thanks to Mathieson's influence it was Caledonian men R. Killin and J. Ballantyne who had respective control over the Midland and Northern Divisions. Even so the old arguments continued, and O. S. Nock described them as 'the warring factions in which the two principal vendettas were the North Western versus the Midland and the Caledonian versus the Glasgow & South Western'. Understandably old company allegiances remained strong, and perhaps rightly so, but in times of change it beheld those involved to buckle down and make the most of the situation - unfortunately the sectarianism continued for many a year, and even down into BR days the pre-Group terms in regular use were to show where many railwaymen's allegiances still lay.

Above:
The path to amalgamation was not smooth either, and constituent companies like the Caledonian and North Staffordshire were so opposed to the merger that legal disputes arose surrounding the terms of settlement. Whilst these were resolved by the middle of 1923, the arguments undoubtedly boiled on under the surface. This was clearly the case in locomotive development where the ex-Caledonian men felt they had a case for a more prominent role in LMS affairs.

Below:
The epitome of elegance, the LMS branch line to Coniston in the beautiful Lake District. Pictured in the 1930s, the scene reveals a pristine little terminus, which is a million miles away from the grimy mill towns of the north or midlands, and the depressed slums of London which the company also served. Yet here in this beautiful area the Slump also had its effect, and traffic on this line dropped dramatically in the early 1930s.
Photo: Cumbrian Railways Association

All of this should have been prevented, as it indeed was on the GWR, but the sad fact remains that these were additional burdens that had to be faced by the LMS in what were the difficult years of the 1920s and early 1930s. As mentioned elsewhere, the loss of coal-traffic in the Slump was particularly worrying, and this was compounded by the general fall off in orders to firms engaged in heavy engineering and ship-building. Of course some areas were considerably harder hit than others, and on the LMS the former Furness section was especially troubled. Its iron-ore traffic from West Cumberland slipped away dramatically, whilst ship-building at Barrow ground to a virtual halt - even the picturesque branches penetrating the Lake District, once thronged with holiday makers in the season, were hit by the absence of families too impoverished by the Slump to afford the luxury of a holiday or even day trips to the country. That is not to say that things were all doom and gloom and no holiday traffic was run, of course it did, for people were determined to enjoy themselves and a cheap day trip to Blackpool, Rhyll or Coniston could be the perfect anodyne to the ills of life in the early 1930s.

However as far as the LMS went, their most positive move took place on New Year's Day 1932 when William Arthur Stanier was recruited from the GWR at Swindon and appointed as the LMS's new CME. Once again poor old Beames (by then Deputy Chief CME) probably felt cheated out of a position that Crewe men considered should have been his in 1923, but Lord Stamp (the new Chairman) felt that such an appointment would only rekindle the embers of the fires that surrounded the feuding of 1923 and his decision to appoint 'a new broom' from outside the organisation was probably the correct one. In the years that followed, the remarkable Stamp/Stanier team were, with their locomotive and rolling stock developments (as discussed later by David Jenkinson), able to turn the railway from being a collection of individual operations into a unified company with modern main-line stock. They thus inspired new confidence in the LMS which would carry it through the even more troubled years of war that lay ahead.

Above:
Testing achievement, Beyer-Garratt No.4999 undergoing trials with the ex-L&YR dynamometer car.
F.W. Shuttleworth collection

Far Right:
Two of the locomotives that did so much to improve the LMS image in the 1930s are seen here at Blea Moor, as Royal Scot class No.6109 Royal Engineer, *passes a waiting 8F freight engine No.8177*

Below:
Not all new technology was of benefit, and at Oakley junction in 1938 a new signalling system compounded human error and led to a fatal accident.

Train Services & Developments

Returning commercial confidence also came in the period that followed Stanier's appointment, and although coincidental it was nevertheless the break that the LMS had been waiting for. A new upsurge in business coupled with a new hand on the mechanical helm, so to speak, brought about the climate in which much needed changes could be acceptably made.

There can be no question about the generally recognised lack of punctuality on the LMS in the late 1920s, and one satirical cartoonist contended the initials stood for Lazily Moved & Slowly. In an attempt to address the situation the company launched a new magazine for members of the operating department which was entitled *On Time* and featured snapshots of employees or recognised their achievements in punctuality and recovery of lost time etc.

Speed of course was central to the new 'post-slump' business climate, and as industry struggled to recover, the quicker goods could be delivered to the consumer the quicker they would be paid for. Furthermore industry was less inclined to be as reliant on cheap labour in the 1930s, and the memory of the 1926 strike was still foremost in the memories of many 'Company Boards' who had been brought to the brink of ruin by the prolonged trade disputes. So, when a revival finally began to take shape, firms were more interested in mechanisation than the recruitment of staff. This attitude was also reflected in their demand for transportation services, and it is not surprising that the 1930s were a period of decline for Britain's inland waterways from which they would never commercially recover.

Speed was the answer, and the quest for it seemed to go to unbelievable lengths. However, there was still something of a shadow hanging over the West Coast Route from the troubled 'Races To The North' in the mid-1890s. As readers of my book *Trains In Trouble* will appreciate, the alarming accidents at Preston and the unexplained high-speed derailments at Aylesbury, Grantham, Salisbury and Shrewsbury had all placed a question mark on the appropriateness of express workings that were being scheduled right up to the maximum capabilities of men and machines.

Yet Britain was being left behind in the railway speed developments that were taking place on the long runs between principal centres in the USA and France, and it appears that in the quiet corridors of power, the railways were urged to make improvements as a part of the attempt to restore national confidence.

The Southern's efforts are discussed in this regard in a later chapter, but for now we concern ourselves with the Anglo-Scottish traffic and the goal to improve services along both main lines to a minimum journey time of eight hours or less. The LMS summer timetable introduced in May 1932 saw the Royal Scot timed at 7 hours 55 minutes and the Mid Day Scot at the prescribed 8 hours. Yet this was nothing more than a beginning of improvements and soon the Royal Scot was booked at 7hrs 40 minutes.

Even the difficult Settle to Carlisle main line was not immune from demands on service improvements, but how crews could be expected to maintain a schedule of just 94 minutes for the 86¾ mile mountain section between Skipton and Carlisle (pictured below right) seemed quite questionable. Yet maintain the schedules they did, and what is more they often took pride in being able to 'knock' a bit extra off them at times. Exciting and imaginative days they must have been, and I certainly wish that I'd been living in my house alongside the Settle & Carlisle Railway back then! Even more exciting must have been a journey recorded by the late Cecil J. Allen in the *Railway Magazine* in which he related an aggregate 64½ mph journey between Crewe and Willesden Junction - quite a remarkable performance on a 153 mile route which had many restrictions. The speed up of 1936-7 is recorded a little later, and it should suffice to say that we have felt it more important to record this in the section on remarkable achievements.

Acceleration of the timetable took a significant step forward in 1938, and in an attempt to stave off competition from Gresley's fast ECML services the Royal Scot working saw a reduction of 45 minutes in its Euston - Glasgow journey time. The journey was reduced to just seven hours, and whilst this was done initially with the aim of wooing traffic heading for the Glasgow Empire Exhibition, it was intended as a permanent measure. This was achieved by the reduction of just two stops, and the shedding of the Aberdeen portion. A new fast service from Aberdeen resulted in a 10 hour 25 minute working which, despite taking a route 16 miles longer than the East Coast Main Line, took just five minutes more to reach London than the LNER service. However, due to changing traffic patterns some long established express trains were withdrawn, but up in Scotland the LMS's principal cross-country express services were finally beginning to restore some of the sparkle of the pre-World War I railways.

On the former Caledonian route, the Aberdeen - Glasgow (Buchanan Street), was put in the hands of class 5 and class 5X 4-6-0s, and the timetable showed a 3 hour service for the 156 mile route. Even in the winter timetable, Jubilee class No 5727 *Inflexible*, belied its nameplates and did the run in 173 minutes 12 seconds on the 8-coach Bon Accord at the end of 1937. Royal Scot class locomotives operating the same service also performed well, particularly on the section north of Forfar.

Meanwhile on the suburban lines, particularly those out of Glasgow, a number of accelerations were noticeable. Of these the run from Glasgow to Largs saw notable improvements behind the standard compounds, and in 1938 the *Railway Magazine* noted Nos. 1179 and 1180 both making good runs despite the many adverse signal checks around Ibrox and Paisley. In each case a time of less than 55 minutes was recorded. The services to nearby Ayr were also benefiting from a number of accelerations following the introduction of the Jubilee class 4-6-0s, which were attaining speeds of up to 80 mph on some sections.

As far as freight traffic is concerned, the LMS were keen to take advantage of the improving situation which followed the troubled years of the 1920s and early 1930s The development of road-rail traffic interchange was very much on everyone's mind at the time, and having set the scene with the GWR's development of containerisation, we might briefly look at what the LMS was doing in this respect. To create a standardised container operation, the company transferred all building projects to the Earlstown Works in Lancashire, where new manufacturing facilities were provided in what had formerly been the wheel shop.

The new layout included extensive conversions, overhead cranes, high-frequency tools, better heating and lighting, and new staff facilities. It was capable of producing up to 1,000 containers per annum, and the company said it could then turn out a brand new container (painted in primer) in just two days. This would of course have considerably increased the LMS container fleet of 1938 then standing at 8,340 units, had it not been for the outbreak of war.

New Railways From Old

On 12th July 1938, one of the largest blasts ever to take place up to that time in Derbyshire's Peak District occurred at Caldon Low Quarries. Hardly surprising at a first reading, but when one considers that the blast was fired from the LMS Shareholders' Meeting Room at Euston Station by no other person than Lord Stamp, Chairman of the LMS, then this becomes quite a curious event. The link up between the Staffordshire quarry and London had been personally supervised by A. F. Bound, the Chief Signal & Telegraph Engineer, and it involved a telephone line connected to an electrical relay at Caldon Low. When the detonator was fired by telephone, approximately 100,000 tons of hard limestone came crashing down. The elaborate procedure was part of a planned rebuilding programme for Euston Station. The quarry had a long association with the railways, and it was connected to Froghall Wharf by a railway which was the second to be built in England under Parliamentary powers granted in 1776. In 1841 the Trent & Mersey Canal Company took over the working of the quarry, subject to certain royalty payments, and in 1847 the whole undertaking came into the North Staffordshire Railway. and thus to the LMS in 1923. In 1934 the LMS leased the quarries to Hadfields (Hope & Caldon Low Quarries) Ltd., but the close association between the two continued for many years to come.

Up in Cumberland, the isolated backwater that was better known as the Cockermouth, Keswick and Penrith Railway began to benefit from bridge improvements. In this exercise, the inverted bow-string girder bridges designed by Thomas Bouch were strengthened for carrying greater traffic levels and heavier engines. The largest of these was over the River Greta just east of Keswick, where a 114 foot long span was attended to. This led to the introduction of larger engines on the route and the ex-LNWR Class 2 goods 0-6-0 engines (Cauliflower's) were gradually supplanted by LMS Class 4 0-6-0 freight engines. Yet, the long term objective was to make the route accessible to a wider variety of traffic, particularly Class 5MT's and Jubilee Class 4-6-0s to take trains all the way through to Keswick Station pictured below.

New Ways & Works

We start this section not with a main line development, but the improvement of a minor suburban service on the south side of the Manchester line which was completed just five months after Stanier came to office. It was in fact the Manchester South Junction & Altrincham Railway which had been electrified as one of the first positive conclusions of the Weir report. Although jointly owned with the LNER, all the electrification work on the 8.5 mile long line was undertaken by the LMS and it was to prove an invaluable experience in the years that followed. It is not surprising that much of the expertise for the scheme, headed by F. A. Cortez-Leigh, was supplied by ex-L&YR men who had already achieved significant third-rail and overhead electrification projects to the north of Manchester earlier in the century. The MSJ&AR was, however, to employ 1500v DC overhead electrification in line with the Weir recommendation.

Other improvement schemes in those years were the quadrupling of the old London, Tilbury & Southend line for almost eight miles beyond Barking and the electrification of the line to carry 'Underground' trains to Upminster. New stations appeared at Heathway and Upney, whilst Becontree, Dagenham and Hornchurch were substantially improved. More importantly, at least in terms of railway safety, the line was given colour light signals and automatic train control.

The old North Midland main line also saw quadrupling to cater for the heavy traffic that was creating congestion between Ambergate and Duffield; interestingly this was the last major job for Alexander Newlands the Chief Engineer who retired from the LMS in 1933. Another massive and much needed improvement was the work undertaken to rectify the bottleneck at Trent Valley Junction south of Stafford. Commencing in 1938, the principle aim of the scheme was to improve the alignment of the up and down main lines, and the access from the up main to the Trent Valley section. Previously a 35mph limit had been essential, but to avoid unnecessary delays it was felt essential that the maximum permissible speed be raised to 55 mph. The smooth junction that resulted from these improvements meant that the deceleration and subsequent build up of speed that had hitherto been essential was now obviated, and the savings in fuel consumption over a five year period were said to be sufficient to actually pay for the entire cost of the work.

Of course these are just a few of the many developments and improvements, but I hope it will suffice to serve as an example of the work being undertaken by the LMS in the days just before the war. Furthermore, it was much needed work that was carried out in the valuable breathing space that was afforded to the nation by the 'Munich Agreement' concluded by Neville Chamberlain and Adolph Hitler. Whatever history might say about that concordance, it can be clearly demonstrated that it afforded the LMS (and the other members of the Big Four) much needed time to achieve the improvements that the railways clearly required if they were to sustain the nation in the time of crisis that would shortly come.

In other spheres of railway operation the LMS were making progress, and in one area in particular, that of safety, it drastically needed to do so. Although the LMS was far slower than the GWR in taking up the issue of Automatic Train Control (which it is said was a matter of some personal concern to Stanier) they were making moves in the direction of improvements. Their chosen option in the issue of safety had been to adopt the 'indirect method' of train control that was proposed in the Pringle Report, and thus their efforts were primarily centred on signalling improvements and track-circuiting. Colour-light signalling was the medium in which they placed greatest faith, and with a string of disasters taking place in the 1930s it was certainly about time that the LMS did something to address the panache for wrecking trains that they had seemingly inherited from the Midland.

Why the LMS had so many disasters is something of a mystery, but it remains an inescapable fact that their problems were seriously affecting confidence. I can not substantiate it, but a story was once told to me by a signalling designer with the LMS who said that Stanier and A. F. Bound the Chief Signal & Telegraph Engineer had a bitter row over ATC, and Bound criticised Stanier for trying to bring Great Western ways to the LMS. If this is true, it was timely as a wider dispute had arisen at that time and the 'Anti-Stanier Faction' were bending the ears of all and sundry, and there were those who certainly felt they could achieve their own ideas under the 'safety' of this situation. He also related that there was almost something of a similar dispute between Bound and R.A. Riddles who had been appointed as Stanier's deputy in 1933 and who subsequently made himself the unofficial chairman of the 'Back-up Stanier' campaign in an attempt to lessen the potentially catastrophic actions of the 'Anti-Stanier Faction'. Although the two maintained a cordial business relationship thereafter, it is said that neither very much trusted the other.

Station and infrastructure improvements in the pre-war period saw a number of new works being commissioned, particularly with regard to line improvements. For example the Wirral line saw much rebuilding in connection with the electrification programme, especially the stations at Hoylake, Meols and West Kirkby where complete rebuilding took place. However, despite the change to electric passenger traction, freight working remained in the hands of steam locomotives and a single steam passenger train ran daily between West Kirkby and New Brighton with a through coach for London (Euston). A major LMS development in that pre-war period was the Toton Marshalling Yard Mechanisation Scheme which became effective on 30th May 1939.

Toton, located in the Erewash Valley, had long been associated with the movement of coal traffic, and it was primarily involved with trains taking 'black gold' out of the coalfields in Derbyshire, Nottinghamshire and South Yorkshire. From here it despatched the loaded wagons to destinations such as London, Birmingham and the Eastern Counties. As early as 1885, the yard had been handling around 700 wagons a day out of 16 sidings; yet by 1938 the figure had grown to a phenomenal 5,000 per day from 35 sidings. Originally shunting was done entirely by horses, but in 1901 'hump' or gravity marshalling techniques were introduced.

The mechanisation of the yard in 1939 was yet another project that was clearly called for in its own right, but was probably funded through the Government's plans for improving those railway services which would be of direct assistance to the nation in times of war. A control tower was installed at the top of the hump, but it is ironical to note that the braking systems which it controlled were of German design and origin. Illumination was provided, but already in-built into the system were ARP cut-out and dimmer switches. Another practical arrangement given to the design of the yard was the 'ARP Ballast Visibility Plan', this witnessed concrete kerbs being laid just beyond the edges of the sleepers and thus boxed in the ballast which was a very light coloured granite.

This ingenious arrangement thus allowed the dark wagons to stand out clearly from the yard, even on the darkest of nights. Even so, to supplement the ease of operation, telephone links were provided between the control tower and various points around the yard.

Another decision which had already been taken with a view to ARP requirements, was that of the motive power that was to be employed in working the yard. If the hump shunters were to continue working, even in the black-out, it was evident that steam engines (with their tell-tale plumes of smoke or showers of sparks) were not really suitable. Therefore a proposal to further develop internal combustion engined shunters was given consideration, and the far-sighted approach to blackout restrictions did more than anything else to stimulate the development of the diesel shunter.

Below:
The design considerations of the new marshalling yard at Toton, (in addition to operational requirements), also had to consider the problems of 'blackout operations' as the white ballast shows.
Photo: LMS Official

Remarkable Achievements

Having mentioned diesel shunters at the end of the last section we really ought to elaborate on the LMS's remarkable achievements in the field of diesel locomotion. Whilst it might rightly belong elsewhere in the narrative of this book, we can say that these achievements followed Sir Harold Hartley's interest in a diesel shunting locomotive that was exhibited at the British Industries Fair in 1932. Coupled with this development was the appointment of Charles E. Fairburn as Electrical Engineer, a replacement for Cortez-Leigh who retired in 1934. Fairburn came to the LMS from English Electric, but he had also been closely involved with the NER's Newport - Shildon Electrification programme, and was thus eminently qualified to help the LMS pioneer its electric and diesel motive power programmes, amongst which the Wirral 650v DC electrification programme and the English Electric shunters were an important part.

In 1944 Fairburn would ultimately succeed Stanier as CME, but until that time his work on modernisation schemes was a significant contribution towards 'the new LMS'. By 1936 the diesel shunter programme was well under way thanks to Fairburn's stewardship, Ten were ordered from Armstrong Whitworth and ten from English Electric, and these were the ones that proved the strength of Hartley's argument, for they went on to become the fore-runners of a massive class of standard shunting engines employing the 6-cylinder 350hp English Electric engine. When the first of these was put into service at Crewe they were averaging up to 150 locomotive hours per week or, put another way, around a minimum of 20 hours per day, seven days per week.

Yet, when we consider what Stanier was achieving on the West Coast Main Line with his newly introduced pacific locomotives, even the important development of the diesel-electric shunters is put into the shade. Some could superficially argue that Gresley's achievements on the East Coast took prominence over Stanier on the West, but such argument takes little account of the fact that the LMS route was far more demanding. The steep banks of Grayrigg, Shap and Beattock were more than enough on their own, but the entire route north of Lancaster was so demanding as to prove an extreme endurance test for any engine.

In reality the accelerated services between Euston and Glasgow were roughly equivalent to those being run from King's Cross to Edinburgh by the LNER in 1936. However, it was evident that as the Coronation year of 1937 approached, there would have to be a general revision of LMS policy, specifically because they understood that the LNER were planning to introduce a non-stop 'Flying Scotsman' service which would do the run to the Scottish capital in six hours. Admittedly the load of the Silver Jubilee style trains would be strictly limited, but it was a bold and daring move that would undoubtedly take traffic away from the LMS. Accordingly non-stop runs were tried between London and Glasgow on 16-17th November 1936 behind No.6021 *Princess Elizabeth*, which was hauling a light load of just seven cars northwards and eight on the return trip south. The runs came in at 5 hours 53$\frac{1}{2}$ minutes and 5 hours 44$\frac{1}{4}$ minutes, and if the six hour schedule could be achieved in rough wintry weather, what could the engines do on the summer timetable? The trials were superintended by R.A. Riddles, as Stanier and Sir Ralph Wedgwood had been invited by the Crown Commissioners to make an inspection of the Government-owned Indian railways which were in a deplorable state.

Riddles actually rode on the footplate during the trials, and he noted that certain modifications could be purposefully made to assist continuous high-speed running. Undoubtedly this influenced thinking at the LMS, and for months it was rumoured that a six hour schedule would appear the following spring when the new summer timetable was printed. However, there was considerable disappointment when it was revealed that the schedule would be six and a half hours, and include a stop at the Border City of Carlisle. It was of course a very practical arrangement, and on the face of it not much of a sacrifice as it was far better to set a standard of service that contained sufficient leeway to allow for the inevitable delays that occur in daily operation. Yet, despite this 'set-back' for LMS supporters, a practical demonstration was given of exactly what the new Coronation class locomotives could actually achieve in the form of the Invitation Run on 29th June 1937.

As railway historians all know, a maximum speed of 114 mph was achieved and had the driver not been forced to slow down due to the nearness of Crewe, it might have gone up even higher. Yet it was not the maximum speed on this journey that really counted, rather the overall journey times. On the return run, the remarkable time of a minute under 2 hours was recorded on the final leg of 158 miles to Euston. Thereafter the Coronation Scot service despite its uninspiring coaching stock replaced Mid-Day Scot as the crack Anglo-Scottish train on the West Coast route.

Ancillary Services

Whilst locomotive developments of the 1930s would normally occupy the central theme of a book like this, even the most ardent railway enthusiast must recognise that the LMS were much more than just a railway company. The diversity of the company's operations was remarkable, and like the other members of the Big Four, the LMS entered into a variety of fields that it saw as being complementary to railway services. Notably, the most important development in this field was the company's shipping and dock operations. Whether these were deep sea docks, Lakeland pleasure steamers, inter-island packets, fishing docks, or Irish Sea terminals is rather immaterial, for in all these activities the LMS played a part. New facilities were provided at the docks; mechanised coaling equipment, new warehouses, lengthened docks, new luffing and traversing cranes and so on, whilst new boats were ordered for the services the company operated.

Just before the start of the period covered by this book, 1936 saw the launch of the turbine steamer *Marchioness of Graham* for the Isle of Arran service, whilst the diesel engined *Teal* was built at Barrow-in-Furness for the Windermere service. Actually, the *Teal* was not launched in Barrow, for there was no navigable connection between the Morecambe Bay and Windermere. Accordingly the LMS had the added complication of transporting prefabricated sections of the *Teal* by rail to Lakeside station where a slipway was utilised for the assembly of the boat and its subsequent launch.

In July 1939 the LMS substantially improved its Irish Sea services, with the introduction of the *Princess Victoria* on the Stranraer to Larne route. This modern diesel-powered ship had new facilities, notably the provision for the transportation of motor cars between Scotland and Ireland. Up to 80 cars at a time could be conveyed on the ferry, and the roll-on, roll-off principle was applied for the first time to this route. Previously cars being shipped between the two countries had to be slung onto the vessels by low-luffing cranes. New ramps were provided to allow for the drive on/off facility, but the two were completely different in their operation. At Larne the ramp was raised and lowered by electric motors, but that at Stranraer was a counterbalanced system which was operated by hand winches.

The roll-on, roll-off system took about 20 minutes to load the ferry, and in the war years which followed it was of considerable strategic importance as it provided a 'military road bridge' between mainland Britain and Ireland. In many ways, it is a good example of railway development funding that would later be applied for military purposes. The ship itself was capable of accommodating 1,500 passengers and had lounges and dining rooms for 1st- and 3rd- class travellers. The twin-screw ferry was the first really large motor vessel in the fleet of any British railway company and it served both railway and military needs with great dexterity throughout the war, but not many years after it returned to a solely peaceful role it was to be involved in a major tragedy when it was lost during a heavy storm which swamped the car deck and took the vessel to the bed of the Irish sea!

Above:
The view across Windermere taken shortly after the Teal *entered service. The vessel under steam however is the* Swan *which is just about to depart with a service to Bowness and Ambleside. Lakeside station was one of those truly magnificent LMS terminals and right at the very heart of the English lakes. Whilst Wordsworth, Cannon Raunsley and others who saw themselves as the guardians of this picturesque part of England may have argued against the advent of the railways and steamships, today environmentalists advocate public transport as the best way to visit the area.*

Below:
By way of contrast the picture below shows the Kyle-Kyleakin ferry waiting to leave the Kyle of Lochalsh with two cars bound for the Isle of Skye.
Photos: Both LMS Official

In passing we might also mention the road vehicle fleet of the LMS, for this had reached a massive 3,287 motor vehicles and over 2,000 trailers by the end of 1936. The subject is to be covered in a forthcoming book on the subject in the **Nostalgia Road** series jointly published by Atlantic Transport Publishers and Trans-Pennine Publishing, so we will not go into the subject at any great length, other than to briefly mention the validity for the LMS getting involved in such services. Under the terms of their formation, the Big Four railway companies were obligated to collect and deliver any traffic that was offered to them. Not all of this could be handled by rail throughout, so during the 1920s and 1930s many new linking road services were introduced.

Furthermore in order to arrest the transfer of freight to road haulage the railway road-vehicle fleets were

Above:
This picture is used for three counts. Firstly it is typical of the type of special services which the LMS were providing for some customers, in this case the David Brown Tractors company at Meltham Mills near Huddersfield; secondly it is a view taken in wartime, as will be noted by the camouflage paint-work on the factory buildings; and thirdly it shows one of the new VAK tractors that we discussed on page 17.

also strengthened as part of a constant move towards replacing the horse with mechanised transport. As horse operation was becoming less than economical, Mechanical Horses from the firms of either Karrier or Scammell were introduced. Such development was both significant and also timely, because whilst the horse had remained the main form of transport, only those places within a three to five mile radius of a station or goods yard could usually be offered a delivery service.

Yet, as the quality of petrol-engined commercial vehicles improved, this means of transport was used to open up new territory, particularly in rural areas. This became known as the 'Country Lorry Service' and they varied in their radius between 7 and 10 miles of a station, and thus brought about a far better service for farmers and outlying communities that were not served by railways. For the LMS this service had particular benefits in the remoter corners of Britain which the railways penetrated but did not really serve; for example the Peak District, Yorkshire Dales, North Wales, the North Pennines, Scottish Borders and the Highlands were all provided with new services which actually did much to arrest rural depopulation. Yet it was not just in cartage or express parcel deliveries that development was made, as considerable expenditure was also put into upgrading or acquiring bus fleets.

Below:
Outside the Appleby Creamery, with its slogan 'Milk For London', a 4-4-0 No.472 waits with a train of 12 6-wheel milk tankers. To the right of the picture a white fence will be seen to the edge of the field, and this indicates the course of the LNER's Eden Valley Railway which ran parallel with the Midland line at this point.

Although these operations were so beneficial to both the railway and the communities they served, we should make it clear that the Acts of Parliament by which the early railways were formed did not really envisage the movement of goods by road, so it was not until 1928 that the railway companies were legally in the clear to operate road vehicles. Yet once the road rail links were established, they were of major benefit and perhaps the best example of this is found in the movement of milk from farms to dairies. Just along the road from my house stands the Appleby Creamery, built by the Express Dairy Company in co-operation with the LMS. Private delivery siding facilities were provided and milk from the lush green pastures of the Eden Valley moved daily down to London in six-wheeled tankers. Eggs, cheese and other produce was sent this way and the close association of the dairies and the railways worked to the benefit of all concerned.

CHAPTER FOUR
The LNER Pre-war

In common with the sort of traffic problems already mentioned in the chapter on the LMS, the LNER were to suffer similar consequences in the late 1920s and early 30s. The year 1931 was the climax of these difficult years and by then the demand for coal was at an all time low, but this traffic was the life-blood of the railways - especially the LNER who serviced the coalfields of Central Scotland, Northumberland, Durham, Yorkshire, Nottinghamshire and the East Midlands. It was with coal that the origins of the railways had been cast on the Stockton & Darlington Railway in County Durham, and with the associated heavy engineering that sprang up in the same area in support of the mining industry. So many great technological advances had gone on from coal and railways into other fields of the rapidly industrialising world, and the North-east region had been at the forefront of this development - not least in heavy engineering and ship-building which sprang up along the banks of its three main rivers, the Tees, Wear and Tyne. Naturally when the Slump hit, this powerhouse of the industrial revolution was affected both immediately and dramatically.

The economic and political crisis which had affected the country meant that the region's industries were cruelly affected, few orders for ship-building were being placed, and the great steel works were producing only a fraction of this potential capacity. The Jarrow Hunger March is perhaps commonly perceived as the most evocative and harrowing demonstration of these times, but the troubled days still provoke bitter recollections in the memories of many old folk in Northumberland and Durham. Neville Shute's book, *Ruined City* also tells the tale of the North-east in those worrying times of gloom and depression. In turn all of this had brought a great recession in railway traffic, and as noted railway historian Michael Rutherford remarks; 'The LNER were the most affected of all the Big Four, it was a juggling act to maintain survival'. Even the formerly profitable docks on the East Coast were quiet and tall cranes stood on many a wharf like a gaunt, rusting skeleton silhouetted against the skyline waiting for ships that were never going to come.

The terrible conditions that existed in Europe at this time meant that the tonnages, both import and export, from these lands slipped away to little more than subsistence levels. All that could be done was a tightening of the belt and, as the saying of the day went, 'try and weather the slump'. In view of this critical situation, what actually followed in the way of advances and developments on the LNER was really quite remarkable.

Above:
An undated view of the Crouch End to Alexandra Palace push and pull service with LNER 2-4-2 No.7107 working a 2 coach formation. Note the assortment of shovels and firebox tools stored haphazardly on top of the side tank.
Photo: Real Photos

An Unlucky Tunnel?

The Mansfield Road tunnel near Nottingham's Victoria Station (LNER), gained the reputation of being something of an unlucky location during the year of 1938. On 31st March ex-GCR Director Class 4-4-0 No.5437 *Prince George* was derailed inside the tunnel. Almost six months later fourteen wagons of a freight train were to suffer a similar fate at the same location, resulting in a pile of debris which blocked the line for 18 hours. Finally, as the year came to a close, a passenger coach took both legs of the point-work at the tunnel mouth, and derailed just two days before Christmas when the station was at its busiest time of the year.

Train Services & Developments

Above:

In giving the public the Silver Jubilee and West Riding Limited services in 1935-6, the LNER had heightened passenger expectations, with the two-fold demands of speed and comfort being paramount above all else. Yet, in satisfying this level of customer expectation, the LNER had found unexpected advantages in the operation of its new faster services; for example the maintenance cost on the Silver Jubilee coach sets was considerably lower than they had anticipated, and the amount of 'down time' incurred by these sets was incredibly low. True, the service was only operated on weekdays, and the coaches could receive mechanical attention over a weekend, but in the period from the introduction of the Silver Jubilee to the end of 1937, the train had only been stopped once - in April 1937 when a hot axle-box had brought the train to a stand for 16 minutes. Yet this was a train which had made no less than 517 return journeys in the two years from 30th September 1935 to 9th October 1937; these journeys being booked at average speeds of between 70 and 75 mph. Sitting astride one of the new vacuum turntables that were ordered from Cowans Sheldon to accommodate the A4's No.2512 Silver Fox *is seen at King's Cross.*

Having discussed the Anglo-Scottish situation in the mid -1930s in our previous chapter, there is little point covering the same ground again. Yet it is well worth mentioning the May 1932 accelerations that took place on the LNER, in particular the new record timings of the Leeds Breakfast Car Express which, after leaving Grantham, was allowed just 100 minutes for the $105\frac{1}{2}$ miles to King's Cross.

So greatly improved were the train services of the mid-1930s that when Sir Nigel Gresley opened the 1937 'Model Engineer Exhibition' in London, he could centre his address on the issues of locomotive performance, design and construction. At this gathering he said, that 'although locomotives had reached their maximum size in Great Britain, he did not think they had reached their maximum power.' He further added that the limitation in the weight of streamlined trains in this country was only the limitation imposed by the power output of the locomotives already employed. From this speech, and others of a similar vein, it was evident that Gresley felt that the public demand for speed was far from satisfied and that there would be a demand for ordinary trains to be worked at speeds such as those attained by the streamliners.

It was evident that Gresley's concern to satisfy this insatiable public demand was going to impose considerable difficulties especially given the LNER's locomotive policy. For example, to give trains with heavy loads (like the Flying Scotsman service) speeds of the streamline trains, would probably call for far greater power output than the company's existing A4 Pacifics could provide. Yet this public demand had to be satisfied, and the LNER were duly forced to make concessions to a travelling public who had little appreciation for the technical considerations of the matter. Furthermore, as the reader will undoubtedly appreciate, it was now possible for times of 90 or 100 mph to be achieved on some sections of the route. Yet, despite such hard work, the train sets were proving more than adequate for the job. Gresley's speech concluded that 'by the development of special train sets for certain services, the LNER could achieve overall economies in operation, despite the higher capital costs.'

It was a similar story with locomotive performances, for it was discovered by rostering specific engines with top link crews, and using these combinations almost exclusively for the prestigious services, considerable maintenance and operation savings could be achieved. For example, the use of *Silver Link*, *Quicksilver*, and *Silver Fox* on restricted routes and services resulted in an aggregate of 70% of all the journeys being on time or ahead of it. Even then, very few of the journeys which ran behind time were due to locomotive failures, as only one or two breakdowns were noted en-route. Excluding one or two notable exceptions, where failure was caused by unavoidable circumstances, the average delay for the whole period was around just 2 minutes per journey. To cover for locomotive failure Gateshead shed kept *Silver King* in reserve, allowing it out for other duties only after the Silver Jubilee had departed on its way. This meant that its most useful duty was the 11.10am Newcastle - Edinburgh (5.10pm Edinburgh - York) run.

With all these engines, the period 1935-1938 had shown that a low coal consumption of 37.6lbs per mile was attainable, despite heavy loads and high speeds. For the average travelling passenger, this posed an interesting question; if the crack expresses could achieve such reliability and economy, why could this policy not be employed on lesser services? It was this philosophy which prompted much of Gresley's public comment in the last full year of peace, and it is an area where significant advances might have been made had it not been for the outbreak of hostilities in September 1939. Even so, it obviously had some bearing on matters, as through 1937, 1938 and the first half of 1939, things did indeed begin to improve remarkably on the LNER.

An interesting appreciation of Gresley featured in the *London Evening Standard* after A4 Pacific No.4498 was named in honour of the great man at London's Marylebone Station. I mention this because it just shows that we modern day writers are not the only one's to make the proverbial male hen-up, because this particular journalist revealed some real fascinating 'facts' about the life and work of this celebrated engineer; one was that 'after gaining experience at Crewe, he worked at Harwich under the famous Sir John Aspinall, who became manager of the old Lancashire & Yorkshire Railway', another was that 'he introduced the streamline principle to British railway engineering; the streamlined Coronation Scot being his creation.' Doubtless many readers were amazed to learn that Doncaster had absorbed Crewe, and that the L&YR had extended its influence down to East Anglia.

Speaking of East Anglia, the services there saw a number of improvements at this time, especially following the timetable changes of 27th September 1937. This led, amongst other improvements, to a respectable 65 minute booking between London (Liverpool Street) and Cambridge. Meanwhile a few ex-GER engines that had become surplus to requirements in the district were then sent much further north, and several played a surprising role on ex-NER metals in the North Pennines. High on the moorland wastes of the Stanhope & Tyne Railroad, and on the bleak crossing from Barnard Castle to Tebay and Penrith, Holden 2-4-0s were seen at work, whilst others became usefully employed in Scotland, especially in the Borders region where two were found working around Selkirk, Jedburgh and Roxburgh. Whilst one of these was working a St. Boswells to Reston freight it suffered the ignominy of a fractured driving wheel tyre.

Meanwhile, a number of class B12 4-6-0s were roaming even further afield, with examples being employed on the old Great North of Scotland Section after they were displaced in East Anglia by the newly-arrived B17s. Initially used on the Aberdeen - Elgin route, and fitted with ACFI apparatus, the class drew the nickname 'hikers'. In the winter months they were almost exclusively employed on the extensive fish traffic trains, but in the summer months their duties were both wide and varied - some were even temporarily transferred from Kittybrewster depot to Eastfield, in order to work excursion services on the Oban line. Those that remained on the old GER system were heavily employed in the war years that followed, working very heavy service trains, ambulance trains and troop trains. However, they also fought an increasingly rear-guard action until they were finally concentrated on just a few depots, Colchester, Ipswich, Norwich, Yarmouth (South Town) and, most of all, Stratford.

The 1938 timetable saw a continuing growth in the overall level of services, with some significant improvements in a number of areas, however few commentators thought that the LNER could trim much more time off the East Coast services. The principle development was the introduction of a new 'Flying Scotsman' service, which had restaurant cars for Newcastle and a buffet car service for Cleethorpes. Its modernisation owed much of its inspiration to American long-distance practice, and its internal refinements reflected this. For example, the buffet lounge boasted a coffee machine, ice cream cabinet, refrigerator and an automatic toaster. Decorations were in pastel shades, and much use was made of Perspex and Rexine for the first time. Passenger comfort was certainly paramount, and coupled with the LNER's streamlined approach to locomotive design (then being continued in a second batch of A4 Pacifics) we can see how the company was keenly striving to expand its customer base.

Now, although a speed up in services had taken place on the East Coast route, the Great Eastern and Great Central sections were, however, devoid of any major improvements although some Scottish services were to benefit. These developments were notable on the West Highland section where the brand new class K4 2-6-0, No. 3441 *Loch Long* was being tested. Meanwhile on the route from Aberdeen to Edinburgh the express services were also seeing a benefit from increased locomotive performance, as Class A3 4-6-2s began to trim an extra few minutes off an already tight 85 minute schedule. One of the best runs at the beginning of 1938, was undertaken by a combination of No.2796 *Spearmint* and 2-8-2 No.2004 *Mons Meg* which came on to the train at Dundee, and between them they turned in a time of just 80 minutes despite atrocious weather. At last, it seemed as though the LNER were turning the corner in Scotland and, in so doing, restoring public confidence after the awful accident at Castlecary on Friday 10th December 1937 in which 35 people were killed.

Above:
Although of hardly the best quality, this picture recently came to light during the 150th celebrations of the opening of the Lancaster & Carlisle Railway. It shows an ex-Great Eastern exile in far away Cumberland. For a short while No.7408 was allocated to the Eden Valley line, replacing the older NER types that had worked this route for many years. The exile is photographed in Penrith station in November 1937, whilst awaiting a turn to Kirkby Stephen.

Observing The K4's

At the time of the class K4's introduction O.S. Nock wrote in the *Railway Magazine*, 'Knowing the extent they [the LNER Class K2's] have to be opened out to keep time with their full 220-ton loads, I wondered how long *Loch Long's* boiler would stand up to the demand....... I was fortunate in selecting the 5.45am from [Glasgow] Queen Street to Fort William on a day on which the engine was loaded to within 14 tons of her rated maximum, which is 300 tons tare (80 tons more than a 'K2') so that the tare load of 282 tons and the gross load of 305 tons were a real test of the engine's capacity; and her performance was a triumphant success, the steaming was as near perfect as could be wished and no more water was used than is customary with the 'K2' engines when hauling two-thirds of this load - in fact there was a comfortable amount in the tender at both Crianlarich and at Fort William. This means that *Loch Long* was doing about 50 per cent more work on the same amount of coal and water as a 'K2'.

New Ways & Works

In the terms of fixed structures, the LNER began a number of improvements to its infrastructure in the latter half of the 1930s. King's Lynn Station was one place that received an improvement plan, as a modern booking hall and concourse were approved. Included in this scheme was re-electrification which saw the station lighting systems brought up to acceptable standards.

Elsewhere on the Great Eastern section, it was turntables that began to attract attention. In order to accommodate the new B17 4-6-0s which were introduced in 1936-7, larger turntables had to be provided. Most of the orders were placed with Cowans, Sheldon & Co. in Carlisle, but not exclusively so. London's Liverpool Street and Thorpe Station at Norwich were amongst the first to be attended to, which was particularly essential if the two streamlined B17s with the larger 4,200 gallon tenders (Nos. 2859, 2870) were to be turned at the end of their journeys.

On the freight side, the LNER undertook improvements to several pieces of infrastructure and it announced plans for a new 4.5 acre goods yard at Doncaster's Wheatley Industrial Estate. In April 1938 a major re-signalling scheme was implemented at Hull Paragon Station, at which time there was a complete switch from a traditional semaphore signal system to colour lights and electro-pneumatically operated points, all of which were controlled from a brand new signal box.

In 1934 the LNER inaugurated a number of improvements in the electrified service on North Tyneside, and also commenced the electrification of the 11-mile long Newcastle - South Shields line which was then carrying around five million passengers a year and thus ripe for development as a 'commuter route'. Ninety, out of the original 132 electric cars, were withdrawn and replaced by new, all-steel, twin-car sets. Yet, out of all the LNER's pre-war works, we must consider its Trans-Pennine electrification programme over the Woodhead route as being the most significant.

Here, for the first time ever in Britain, a substantial main line route was to be modernised and upgraded to operation by electric traction.

It was a daring and adventurous plan, behind which Gresley was placing a not inconsiderable part of his reputation. He had already looked at electric operation in Europe, especially Switzerland, and reported favourably upon it to the LNER Board. Encouraged by the Weir Committee Report, here at last came the opportunity to move British railways into the 20th century. The growing cost of coal through the 1930s had provided an impetus for the railways to experiment on a large scale, but it is most ironic that the main line where they chose to develop it was one that was founded on the carriage of large quantities of coal.

Following the Government's recommendations, a 1500 volts dc overhead system was proposed for the Manchester to Sheffield line and the Wath branch, but the steeply graded branch from Penistone down to the heart of the South Yorkshire Coalfield at Barnsley was not incorporated, although this is now the only surviving part of that system.

Ironically, whilst the LNER were pressing ahead with their new electrified Trans-Pennine line, the North Eastern Division was in the process of dismantling the pioneer electrified line which they had inherited at the Grouping. Built by the NER in 1905, the Shildon - Newport line had employed five Raven electric locomotives to replace over a dozen steam engines, and carried considerable quantities of coal from the centre of the South-west Durham Coalfield to the Teeside docks at Newport. Though an initial success, decline of coal production during the Slump, changing mining patterns and the construction of new steelworks on Teesside meant that the scheme was far less attractive by the mid-1930s. It was also felt that, having proved their worth in Durham, the five Bo-Bos could be used to good effect on the Manchester - Sheffield -Wath line.

The actual civil engineering work was instituted in various phases, but as the last summer of peace drew to a close, seven miles of overhead gantries had been put in place at Hadfield, Woodhead and Sheffield. Extensive work was being carried out on the 3-mile long Woodhead tunnel, with engineers taking possession of one or other of the single line bores from 10pm every Saturday until 4am on the Monday morning. At Darnall, near Sheffield, a new combined steam/electric motive power depot was being erected and a flyover bridge was under construction. When completed this provided a means by which locomotives could cross the main lines between the up side and the depot, without having to resort to a level crossing on what was then an exceptionally busy main line. Sadly, the outbreak of war was to bring to an end the complete electrification scheme, although some elements of it were to be completed as 'essential works' during the period of hostilities.

In the south, the LNER's electrification programmes were concentrated on two particular sections; the GNR North London lines and the Great Eastern route to Shenfield. By the end of 1938 rapid progress had been made on the North London line, with the new track being completed between East Finchley station and the junction of the New Barnet branch. A new bridge was provided to carry the Great North Road (A1), whilst East Finchley station had been completely rebuilt. New sidings were provided near Park Junction, Highgate and, at a very early stage in the proceedings, London Passenger Transport Board battery-electric locomotives were being stabled there. Another appearance in these sidings in May 1939 was what outwardly appeared to be a train of tool vans, but ultimately turned out to be one of the new emergency works trains which were being formed as part of the railways' ARP Programmes.

Meanwhile, on the former GER line, new platforms were being provided at Forest Gate and Manor Park, but the platforms at Globe Road and Bishopsgate had been removed in preparation for the new works. Another casualty of the programme was the former LNER sports ground at Stratford, which was dug up to provide siding accommodation. Yet by the summer of 1939, the company were reporting good progress with its scheme, and two miles of overhead gantries had been erected between Brentwood and Harold Wood, whilst the locomotive shed at Ilford had been demolished in preparation for the electrification. Like Woodhead, a lot of the work concerned with the Shenfield electrification was abruptly suspended by the Railway Executive Committee in 1939; yet in failing to complete the colour-light signalling programme, they actually left the way open for several serious accidents to occur in the years that followed.

**Improvements
At Sheffield Victoria**

With the planned conversion of the Woodhead line from steam to electric traction, the LNER took the opportunity to remodel Sheffield's Victoria Station. The improvements included a new booking hall and enquiry office, new toilets and refurbished waiting rooms. The whole appearance of the station was considerably smartened up, as much use was made of bright paint colours, ceramic tiles and stainless steel. A new entrance was provided from the booking hall to the Royal Victoria Hotel, whilst road vehicle traffic was accommodated by the extension of extra road space in front of the station and improvements to the station approach. This work also involved the relocation of the old Great Central Railway War Memorial to a new site within the booking hall. Ironically, this memorial had not long been moved before the clouds of war were looming once again over Europe. In fact, when it was being rededicated, British Foreign Office officials were in Munich arranging for Neville Chamberlain's [ill-fated] 'peace talks' with Adolph Hitler. In the months and years that followed, England's 'City of Steel' was to prove what it was made of as the Luftwaffe specifically targeted the area.

Left:
Like the development on the Woodhead line, electrification of the route to Shenfield in Essex was considered essential in view of the developing traffic and the recommendations contained in the Weir Report. The conversion came under the LNER's 1935 - 40 New Works Programme and a good start was made on the job before war broke out. By September 1939 two miles of overhead girders had been erected and the Ilford steam locomotive depot demolished. Contracts were placed for coaches with passenger operated press-button doors and all-steel bodies. Colour-light signalling was also to be introduced on the intensively worked lines from Liverpool Street and it should have become a most modern railway. As it was electrification was delayed until 1947.

The Most Remarkable Achievement

In August 1938 the late Cecil J. Allen wrote, 'When a record is broken, there is nothing like doing it thoroughly. And the London & North Eastern Railway, in its brilliant speed achievement of Sunday, July 3, carried its purpose into effect with such thoroughness as to leave the nearest British competitor some 11 m.p.h. behind' and with this he began a description of the most notable feat in the whole history of steam locomotion, namely the setting of a world speed record which has now stood unbroken for almost sixty years. The legendary events of 3rd July 1938 are now preserved for posterity, and have therefore been covered in depth by numerous writers, but no account of the Last Years of The Big Four would be complete without a summary at least.

It is perhaps ironical to note that the record was, in fact, a by-product of a series of important brake tests which required a succession of high-speed runs. Naturally, a fast section of the ECML between Grantham and Peterborough was used for these tests, as it offered the most advantageous ground. The engine chosen was A4 Pacific, No.4468 *Mallard*, which was formed into a train comprised of a dynamometer car and three twin-articulated sets from the spare Coronation train set. At the sharp end of the 240-ton train were Driver J. Duddington and Fireman T. H. Bray from Doncaster shed. Whilst the objective was the Westinghouse brake tests, there can be no doubt that Gresley wanted to use the occasion to try and better the LMS timings which had been achieved on the West Coast Route.

Gresley suggested to one of his assistants, Mr. N. Newsome, that the Westinghouse tests could be used to try and beat Stanier's achievements, and so Sunday 3rd July became the chosen date. A decision was therefore taken to reduce the weight of the test train, and a pair of articulated coaches were dropped from the usual formation of 8 coaches and dynamometer car (pictured top left). However, no-one told the Westinghouse people who were taking part in the tests, but as *Mallard* (pictured below) began her furious assault of Stoke Summit, there could have been few who were surprised with what was about to happen. The race down to Essendine was most remarkable, and the excitement in the old NER dynamometer car was quite intense, at first it was recorded that *Mallard* had peaked at 125 mph, but careful examination of the charts revealed that she had done that famous 126 mph for at least 144 yards.

However, it was not without cost and the three-cylinder engine developed trouble with its big end and it had to be 'stopped' at Peterborough. Sadly, all the reporters, photographers and newsreel cameramen were waiting at King's Cross and so the event did not receive the immediate accolade it so rightfully deserved. Yet within hours, this achievement was world-wide news, and this particular record was brought back to Britain where it has stayed ever since.

A trip into the main hall of the National Railway Museum at York will usually reveal *Mallard* in all her 'garter blue' glory and, unless she is away on tour somewhere, one can but marvel at this engine as it approaches its 60th anniversary. The bronze plaques on its side that bear testimony to this unique event are a fitting reminder to the balmy summer in the last year of peace, before the thunder of war rumbled across the country and set railway progress back so many years.

The Drake's Progress

'With my lovely blue streamlined engine, *Mallard*, we drew away from Grantham and I accelerated up the bank to Stoke Summit and passed the box at 85 mph. Once over the top I gave *Mallard* her head and she jumped to it like a live thing, then 108, 109, a hundred and ten. Go on old girl, I thought, we can do better than this; so I nursed her and shot through Little Bytham at 123 and in the next one and a quarter miles the needle crept up further. One hundred and twenty-three and a half, 124, 125 and then, for a quarter of a mile, while they told me that the folks in the dynamometer car held their breath, 126 miles per hour. One hundred and twenty-six, that was the fastest speed a steam locomotive had ever been driven in the world.'

Driver Joe Duddington speaking to the BBC on Sunday 3rd July 1938.

Ancillary Services

Whilst the LMS was promoting its excursion traffic in 1938, the LNER were developing another area of business altogether. Whilst it was not exactly forsaking the 'rest and change' philosophy of excursion and trip trains, it was the Train Cruises programme of the late 1930s which was seen as being a more profitable departure. For example the 'Northern Belle' was one of the most popular cruises, and it was very much an 'in vogue' form of holiday. It still offered rest and change, but it was also considered as a prestigious form of travel. Departures from King's Cross took place on a weekly basis, commencing on 3rd June, but for a 5s (25p) supplement Continental passengers could commence their journey at Antwerp, Flushing, or the Hook of Holland. Yet this service was not only aimed at the fashion-conscious middle class or overseas visitors, as special cruise trains were also run for a wide variety of special groups including at least two for the Boy Scouts organisation.

For those who wanted to travel to the continent from Britain, the LNER offered a special weekend cruise from Harwich on their steamer the *Vienna*. Yet the thing that has always puzzled me is why the LNER never really went for the development of an Anglo-Irish ferry service. It may not be instantly recognised, but the LNER did have a railway-served port on the West coast of England, from where its predecessors the North British Railway had operated its own shipping fleet servicing both the Isle of Man and Ireland.

The port was Silloth, located at the end of a long single track line from Carlisle, but one that was connected directly to the Waverley line and the route to Newcastle. What is more, this latter line was the shortest rail route across England and one on which European and Scandinavian traffic could easily have been moved to Ireland. Quite why they chose to route this traffic via the LMS owned ports on the Mersey remains an anathema to me, for properly developed Silloth could have been a significant asset for the LNER.

Another major ancillary area of the LNER services was the many hotels that the company owned. Of these a good many were substantial facilities, serving important cities like Aberdeen, Bradford, Edinburgh, Glasgow, Hull, Leeds, Lincoln, London, Newcastle, Perth, Sheffield, and York. They also had an eye for the tourist trade as well, and had hotels at places like Saltburn, Scarborough and Port Erroll. At the latter location the Cruden Bay Hotel was served by its own little tramway built to 3' 6" gauge, which conveyed the guests on the last mile of their journey from Cruden Bay station to a hotel originally created by the Great North of Scotland Railway. Not surprisingly the hotel catered mainly for golfers, and at the height of its vogue, there were around 100 local boys available for caddy duties.

In Oliver Carter's excellent book '*British Railway Hotels*', page 43 states 'All seemed set for a bright future, but the season was too short and the railway passed through comparatively poor country. As the years passed, the hotel simply, but gradually faded out of existence. First the railway line closed to passenger traffic in October 1932, then the tramway in March 1941, and finally the hotel on November 7 1945 after serving as a wartime hospital.' Many other hotels and facilities in the LNER's 'hospitality business' did not survive the war years ahead and by nationalisation the hotels at Lincoln, New Holland, Grimsby, Aberdeen and the Great Central in London had been sold, closed or re-developed for other purposes.

School On The Platform

In 1938 the LNER assisted the Argyllshire Education Authority by providing facilities for a new school at Gorton, which is situated in the wilds of Rannoch Moor. To relieve congestion at the small Rannoch school, a decision was taken to provide additional accommodation close to the West Highland line as many of the children at Rannoch were the sons or daughters of men employed on the LNER, (mainly permanent way staff). A decision was made to provide an old coach from Cowlairs Works, and this was taken to Gorton, lifted from its bogies and mounted on the platform. This platform was not used by the public, and it did not appear in the timetable, but platform it was nevertheless. As a consequence arrangements were made to stop the 5.50am Glasgow - Fort William Breakfast Car Train at Gorton, where it arrived at 8.34am bringing a few children and a teacher from the Bridge of Orchy. In the reverse direction, the 2.40pm from Fort William made an appropriate call to return the teacher and pupils, to their homes.

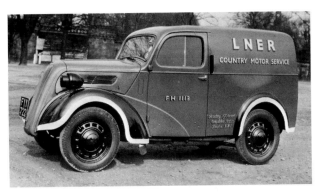

A study of a map of the pre-Grouped railways will reveal a certain unique feature evidenced in many of the companies which would be combined to form the LNER in 1923; in as much as three of the main constituents, the Great Eastern, North British, and North Eastern enjoyed a virtual near monopoly on the railway traffic in the areas that they served. To a lesser extent the Great Northern enjoyed its territorial advantages in Lincolnshire, and the little Great North of Scotland ruled the roost in the north-east of Scotland. It was an advantage that the LNER pressed home to good effect, but a continual erosion into both freight and passenger traffic came in the period after World War I. The railways countered by obtaining their own road vehicles, although until the passing of an Act of Parliament in 1928 their authority to do this (in the field of goods traffic) was rather questionable. Actually the GNoS had begun its road services when buses were introduced to link Braemar to Ballater station in 1904, and both the GER and NER started their own bus services soon after. By the latter part of the 1920s the LNER were taking full advantage of the 1928 Act and they rapidly expanded into road vehicle ownership, notably in the field of motor buses. Their association with British Electric Traction, Tilling's, and (up in Scotland) the SMT led to agreements being made into which bus companies the LNER would actually take shares. In view of the fears exercised about 'railway monopoly' it was important to note that the LNER did not normally take a controlling interest, but they were very important players nevertheless. Along with the LMS they also acquired part-ownership in the Halifax Corporation fleet, and shares in the Eastern Counties Omnibus Co. However, their biggest success was with the United Automobile Company which had seriously threatened the virtual monopoly of the railways in the North East.

The progress towards the Country Lorry service has already been highlighted, but on the LNER this one factor was for many years sufficient to stem the flow of traffic away from the railways. So, by the provision of a lorry or small vans (like this Fordson model pictured above), this desertion could be arrested and new business encouraged at the same time. Such new business was notable in the country districts and, as it will be appreciated, the LNER had a lot of those in its territory. Yet it was not only in the country that road vehicle services proved their worth, as the mechanical horses from firms like Karrier and Scammell were showing their value in town cartage. Meanwhile in other cities the LNER began acquiring existing large hauliers, such as Currie's in Newcastle. Yet another novel service was the LNER's special hire fleet which included vehicles like the AEC horse-box seen below. These vehicles were widely used in East Anglia and in other LNER districts in which horse racing or training was prevalent.

In the avenue of freight vehicle operation the LNER took an important step forward after the 1928 Act, and the slow (but sure) process of mechanisation in its cartage fleet was much in evidence during the 1930s despite the general fall-off in traffic during the early part of the decade. It should be appreciated that the general decline in the overall freight traffic was almost £10,000,000 between 1923 and 1932 or, put another way, a drop of around 27.5%. In view of these losses it would seem strange for a company like LNER to make such substantive increases in road vehicle operation, but it should not be forgotten that the introduction of these services often resulted in considerable economies and improved efficiency. Even the most basic lorry or van could outperform a horse and cart, and private hauliers were able to run rings round what was in danger of becoming a moribund collection and delivery service from the railways.

The shipping fleet continued to assume importance, especially those services that originated from Hull and Harwich, and plied the North Sea to the Continent. Amongst the vessels in the fleet, the new steamships *Vienna* (commissioned in 1929), *Amsterdam* and *Prague* saw the 1930s starting in style. Not only were the railway vessels widely appreciated by travellers on scheduled routes, but they also came to be enjoyed by thousands of tourists who booked day cruises at the weekends when the 'spare boat' was available for such duties. On the Clyde the former North British ships and ferries were strengthened in the 1930s, and the development of evening cruises also became a feature here. On the routes from the Humber, freight traffic became the order of the day, and despite the Depression, the LNER fleet had weathered the storm better than many of its independent rivals, thanks to the railway's ability to offer an all-inclusive service.

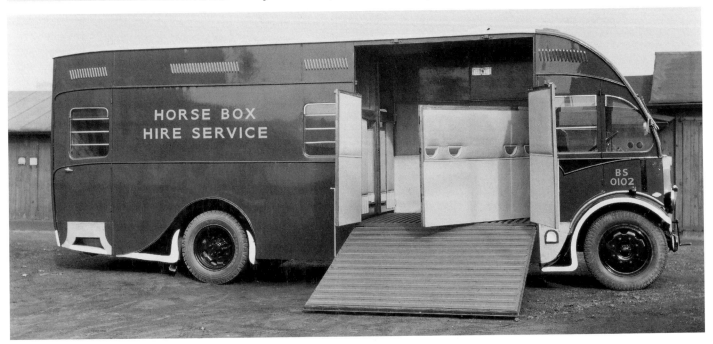

CHAPTER FIVE
The Southern Pre War

In having covered the larger members of the Big Four, it makes the review of the Southern Railway somewhat problematical, for its developments had by no means as great an impact as those on the GWR, LMS or LNER. Indeed, in fairness it has to be said that far more could be written about the other companies in comparison with the Southern and, as a consequence this chapter could be much shorter than those that have gone before. Furthermore in many of those areas where the Southern did make substantial progress, it was not what could be called revolutionary. This was, for no other reason, due to its very *raison d'être* which meant it was first and foremost a passenger carrying railway serving the commuter belt south of London! With its principle business of commuter flows and boat trains being supplemented by excursion, race and seaside traffic, it is hardly surprising to note that 75% of the Southern Railway's business was connected with the carriage of passengers! Couple this with the fact that (outside London) there were hardly any industrial towns on the entire system, the low percentage of freight is hardly surprising.

Yet all of this should not belie the company's importance nor, indeed, its achievements - specifically in the field of electric traction on its commuter and middle-distance express services. In this regard, much of the development can be traced down to the steely determination of one man, Sir Herbert Walker, whom we have already discussed in connection with his leadership of the Railway Executive Committee during World War I. Yet, from the outset Walker was faced with problems as the new company got off to a very shaky start while the three factions snapped at each other like so many angry animals.

From the very first day of its existence, the Southern Railway began to attract a very bad response from the popular press. One of the complaints was that much of its rolling stock used on mainline services was non corridor and not particularly opulent or comfortable even in first class. However, with the exception of a few trains whose speeds were rather indifferent we must emphasise that, taken all round, the three constituent companies were doing all they could under the difficult circumstances that prevailed in Britain after World War I. Yet months after the Grouping had taken place, the management of the newly formed Southern Group was not properly resolved. Indeed, it was not until July 1923 that a top level management team was announced and even then there was no clue as to who was going to be the new General Manager.

Above:
Electrification was the Southern Railway's most remarkable achievement and throughout the 1930's this was its most singular goal. In just five short years it had (in the most unassuming way) converted no less that 1,760 track miles to third rail electrification. It was not progress that could be placed in the same categories of the record-breaking fashion as the LMS or LNER, nor in the safety-conscious, efficient way of the GWR, but the Southern's electrification was efficiently quiet progress in more ways than one. In the pages that follow therefore, our appraisal of the Southern railway in the build-up to World War II does not contain accounts of record breaking speeds, vastly improved train services or other ostentatious displays of prowess. Rather it reflects a commercial confidence in developing the sort of services that the fare-paying passengers most needed. In many ways this was the real success of electrification.
Photo: SR Official

Above:

In 1925 the Southern Railway introduced a set of seven new Pullman cars onto the 10:50am service from Victoria all of which were named. The popularity of the service increased even more and it became necessary to add other vehicles to the train whilst additional Pullman cars were being ordered. Another step forward came in 1926 when the French railways inaugurated an all Pullman service by the name of 'la Fleche d'or', in other words the Golden Arrow. The train of this name did not take off in Britain until May 1929 by which time it had been decided to give Pullman passengers a ship of their own with all the appropriate furnishings and lavish accommodation that were to be associated with such travel. The vessel that was provided exclusively for this service, was the beautiful new turbine steamer Canterbury *which had been built in Dumbarton. The Golden Arrow was perhaps one of the most beautiful trains of any featured in this book, and it was certainly representative of what is now a bygone age of first class travel. The Golden Arrow was formed from ten Pullman cars, and also included a four-wheel baggage van and a six-wheeled truck for carrying containers with registered through luggage. The* Canterbury *with accommodation for 250 passengers took 75 minutes to make the crossing from Dover to Calais.*

Photo: SR Official

The three main constituents of the Southern Railway all had Chief officers of considerable ability, a fact that was signified by the knighthood of all three men. The senior amongst these was one Sir William Forbes of the LBSCR. Next was Sir Percy Tempest who had been the Chief Engineer of the South Eastern & Chatham since 1899 and who had gone on to succeed Sir Francis Dent as General Manager in 1920. The youngest of the trio was Sir Herbert Walker of the London & South Western Railway who had originally served the first 27 years of his railway service on the LNWR. Initially these three men acted jointly, each presiding over their own division, but upon the retirement of Forbes and Tempest, Walker was appointed to the job of overall supremo.

His task would be a hard one, because of the fact that the initial concept of three joint managers had perpetuated the old company ideas far longer than had happened on the other members of the Big Four. Despite the fact there were some organisational changes, the Southern basically remained as 'convoluted trinity' as Eustace Missenden once called it! The Eastern Section remained largely South Eastern & Chatham in both feel and flavour, whilst the Central Section was essentially based on Brighton practice, and the Western Section remained, to all intents and purpose, much as had been in evidence in the days of the L&SWR prior to 1923. Actually, many old railwaymen have commented that the further you got down the 'Long Withered Arm' into the west, the more antiquated the equipment, the more informal the ambience and the greater the impression given that you were still travelling in Edwardian times. Nowhere was this more keenly in evidence than at Padstow, the end of the line which one old driver described in 1935 as being like 'a trip back through 50 years in time'.

Using all the strength and energy that he had exercised over the Railway Executive Committee, Walker pulled all three disparate factions into a series of common objectives, not least of which was suburban electrification. Yet here too he faced a dilemma as his electrification programme could have easily set the Southern in as much of a state of turmoil as was evidenced on the LMS following the Grouping. The debate after 1923 was not whether to adopt electrification or not, but rather which of the two existing systems the new company should develop. Which ever course Walker chose, he would be sure to offend sensitivities in either the former LSWR or L&BSCR camps. The fact that he charted the company through these potentially troubled waters is a remarkable tribute to both the man himself and the high regard in which he was held by both his contemporaries and his workforce.

Walker's new management situation continued with only modest refinements until 1930, when another set of structural reorganisations came about, and these new arrangements were to last in their basic form until nationalisation in 1948. The new management style was one of combining operational responsibility with commercial judgement. Significantly it was a move that was to bring the Southern more into modern company business operations rather than the structures that were applied to conventional railways elsewhere. The Southern had thus taken a bold step forward, but it was certainly the right approach, and in many ways it put them in a far better position to recover from the effects of the Slump than their contemporaries.

As a commercial operation the Southern was to become one of the world's most efficient railway companies as its primary policy was both progressive and cost-efficient, and in reality this was to lead naturally to the electrification project. The aggressive policies of the old London & South Western were paramount in the new Southern thinking, and thankfully so; for heaven forbid what would have happened had it been the lethargic mentality of the impoverished old South Eastern & Chatham that had prevailed at the end of the 1930s. The Walker policies were to be more far-reaching than anyone would at first assume, and whilst his strong hand was clearly seen in the control of the Railway Executive Committee in World War I and the early years of the Southern, its legacy was also keenly evidenced in World War II. How so? Well, if Walker had not steered the Southern so well after its formation, one hazards to guess at what sort of state it might have emerged from the Depression. The fact that it emerged in a relatively good shape, although always a little impoverished, had laid down the basis for 1930s reconstruction and electrification. On this point the book, *The Great Days of The Southern Railway*, states 'One dreads to think how less effectively the Blitz, leave alone the great Dunkirk evacuation, would have been handled under latter-day philosophy.' The changes that Walker had started were soon making there mark, both on busy main line services and the more rustic parts of the network. Even on the ambling branch lines down in the far South-west, the Southern's policy of efficiency and smartness prevailed amongst its none-too-well remunerated staff, and their station work often put the neighbouring GWR lines to shame.

The very last locomotive to carry LNER livery was ex-GER 0-6-0T No.8568,
seen here at Stratford shed in November 1954. It was finally given BR colours in 1956.

Southern Railway (ex-SE&CR) 0-6-4T No.1597
heading a down train of SE&CR 'Birdcage' stock near Bromley South in June 1937

Air Raid Precautions & The Blackout

Following World War One, there had been an almost pathological fear of the use of gas as a weapon of war. With little wonder for, all over Britain, every town had its tragic reminders of this insidious form of warfare. Thousands had died, and many of those who had survived were destined to spend the remainder of their lives with ruined lungs. As early as 1935, the Air Raid Precautions Department had been alerting civilians to the danger of what an aerial attack by the enemy would mean. There had been a foretaste with the raids of the German Zeppelins and bombers during World War I, when locations as diverse as Derby Works and Todmorden Signal Box had been bombed. The year 1916 had been an especially bad time for the railways, but as the Royal Air Force improved its fighter aircraft, the 'Hun' could no longer strike with impunity at these civilian targets. The lessons that were learned from this period stood the railways in good stead, and consequentially they became one of the first major institutions to implement the Government recommendations. Obviously, pre-war forecasts had to be based on a great deal of guess-work, but the precedents of aerial bomb damage in the Spanish Civil War had been sufficient to indicate what a modern air fleet could do against lightly defended territory and Barcelona provided the most tragic, but most spectacular example of all.

To educate railway employees, mobile instruction units were constructed, the first of these being turned out by the LMS at Wolverton in November 1937. By the autumn of 1939, every member of staff on the Big Four had received ARP training. One area of this training involved how to work in a 'blackout', and this began in earnest with 'provisional regulations' introduced in May 1938. However, blackouts were at complete variance with normal railway operations which required plenty of light. When railways were worked at night, larger stations, goods yards and marshalling yards were provided with adequate lighting from overhead floodlights and the like, thus enabling 'round the clock' operation, Yet, such facilities were of necessity, no longer appropriate in times of war as they would act as a magnet for enemy aircraft. When experimental black-outs were ordered in the summer of 1939, RAF planes had been sent on practice missions against dozens of English towns. The RAF, and the Ministry of Home Security did not like what they had seen, and a further reduction in lighting levels was ordered.

This meant that, for the duration, railwaymen would have to creep around in the pitch darkness as they tried to carry on as normal. For some this saw a considerable worsening of their working conditions. Suburban train drivers often had an even harder time of things, as they had to ensure that their trains stopped within the length of the platforms, and not leave any coach doors overhanging great voids into which unwary passengers might drop. As a dispensation, a small red light was fitted to many station platforms, and this became a driver's aiming mark. However, drawing to a stop by a tiny, almost insignificant light was still very difficult, especially when it was raining cats and dogs. Another difficulty was noticed at stations which still had 19th century platform heights, as for example Stocksmoor between Huddersfield and Sheffield. At this location, one dark night in the early 1940s, an army subaltern alighted from his train and missed the step which the porter had provided. Two broken legs and a lot of correspondence between the War Office and the Railway Executive eventually resulted in the platform being heightened.

If it was bad for train crews, the blackout was even worse for railwaymen on the ground, particularly those working in marshalling yards, goods yards and carriage sidings. Here rails, signal wires, point rod and levers of hand-operated points all presented a serious impediment to mobility. In this environment men had to work without light, and all the time shunting engines might be taking 'cuts' out of the trains being marshalled and propelling these into other roads. As these 'cuts' were 'knocked' into their new trains, the shunters would have to chase after them in the dark in order to 'pin-down' the brakes or sprag the wheels in order to stop them colliding with the stationary wagons on to which they were to be coupled. In all types of weather, including snow and ice, the shunters worked with unremitting toil in poor conditions on what was one of the hardest railway operations ever carried out in the blackout. In gravity or hump marshalling yards, the task was even harder, as wagons came down the incline and over the various points in relative silence, passing the shunters and chasers like silent ghosts in the pitch blackness. The men who worked the wagon retarders were also in a position of great difficulty, as they had little indication of when the vehicles were passing. Only when the 'cut' came over the king points did they have a clue, for the juddering this sent through the rails soon became the tell-tale means by which they were alerted to their approach.

Under these difficulties, it is little wonder that trains were often delayed in getting away but there were added difficulties for platform staff when the station lights went out; reading luggage labels, getting people and baggage on and off trains, and avoiding tripping up over the 1,001 impediments which might be lying around the station was no easy task. Naturally accidents happened as passengers had to grope around in the dark and, with human society being what it is, a variety of unsavoury incidents also took place. The theft of baggage, parcels and other railway property also increased under the cover of darkness when thieves, black-marketeers, and spivs found the railways a relatively easy target.

A difficulty of ARP precautions for engine drivers were anti-glare screens which encased the whole footplate and turned it into a veritable hot-house in which they were placed for long, tiring and very stuffy turns of duty. Now the conditions these enclosed cabs generated were diametrically opposite to the requirements of alertness and vigilance which were called for in an engine driver. Beyond the spectacle plate, his world had also changed during the hours of darkness. No longer were there the tell-tale signs, the bright lights of towns, or the muted glow of taverns and farms that were passed en-route. Even the signal lights were dimmer than they had been prior to the war, with the end result that the line ahead not only looked different, but it felt different too. Drivers and firemen did not actually have to learn the road again officially, but that is exactly what they did in practice. One fireman, John Jones, related his experience of working the Somerset & Dorset Joint line, with its many tunnels, saying 'When we was wrapped up under the blackout sheets, it was like being inside a little watchman's tent, but with the brazier on the inside. Running down from Bath on warm summer nights during a 'red alert' was like being in a Turkish bath, my mate used to say it was hotter than Hades itself, but he wasn't the one having to do all the shovelling.'

At London termini, the strengthened wartime trains were often too long for the platforms, and this resulted in the added work of loading people into two portions of the train in different platforms before the train was joined together by the station pilot engine. This posed a considerable strain, as we will later show.

Signalmen were the most badly affected, especially in rural locations where the light from the track-side 'boxes spilled far and wide over the surrounding countryside. As good visibility is the main prerequisite for a signal box, it was inevitable that the windows could not be boarded up or curtained off, so something had to be done to reduce light emissions. There were some highly dubious schemes introduced to reduce the lighting to the required .002 candle-power, but the most bizarre must have been at Watford where a 'box was equipped with ultra-violet light and the signal levers painted in fluorescent paint.

Obviously the situation could not go on like this, railways and docks needed some light to operate by if they were to continue to work round the clock. As the demand upon transport services grew, the operators of these vital services had to appeal to the authorities for a relaxation of the blackout regulations if they were to play their part in the war effort. Accordingly three categories of 'permitted lighting' were allowed; of these Category A (Red Alert) meant no light at all; Category B (Purple Alert) meant you could just about see where you were going; whilst Category C was such as to permit a certain amount of illumination which, whilst far from adequate, was just about sufficient to do the job. There was also a sub-category C1, which came somewhere between B and C. In many places, these lighting relaxations only came into force after a master switch had been installed at a central control position.

At engine sheds, the problem of coaling and watering locomotives in complete darkness was bad enough, but the blackout compounded existing problems of safety in areas where inspection pits, turntable wells, ash pits and a profusion of rails presented numerous hazards. An even greater difficulty emerged in the handling of locomotives at the end of their duties, notably in the area of ash disposal. When ash was dumped from a firebox, it would often glow red hot for many hours, especially when winds fanned the embers. Such fires burning all around a steam depot would also act as a beacon for the enemy bombers, so special measures had to be taken to dispose of the ash.

One Divisional General Manager in Scotland came up with the bright idea of transporting ashes to a remote moorland siding, but the proposal upset the community in which the proposed dump was situated. Unwilling to have a target to guide the 'Jerry' bombers to their village, the canny Scots enlisted the support of the local Chief Constable who threatened to issue a warrant for the arrest of the DGM concerned. In most cases, the decision was taken to empty the ash-pans inside the sheds, even though this contributed towards an exceptionally unhealthy and very sulphurous atmosphere inside which was intolerable for the people actually working therein. For fitters who were, by the middle of the war, undertaking repairs in the shed that should (under normal circumstances) have been carried out at the various works, these conditions were often impossible. In ordinary times unions would have struck against these conditions of employment, but as these were not ordinary times the men carried on phlegmatically.

However, by this time there were far fewer members of staff to rebel against such things, and with increased railway duties being supplemented with service as ARP Wardens or Home Guard patrols, the time for such frivolities was strictly limited! In total 99,000 railwaymen came forward at the first appeal for volunteers, and at one time as many as 156,046 were enrolled in the Home Guard. Naturally, men on these home defence duties were often heavily involved with the protection of railway installations.

In the various company chapters that follow, we recall some of the worst bomb incidents, in which cities like London, Birmingham, Coventry and Liverpool all feature. However, it may seem strange to relate that the first German bomb to land on mainland Britain during World War II fell on none of those places, but at far-away Wick in the North of Scotland on the 10th April 1940. A few weeks later the railways suffered their first serious damage when Middlesbrough was bombed on a bright spring day in May. The first bomb to fall in the Home Counties landed in Addlington on 18th June, the night after France surrendered. It was what Herman Goering later described as an "armed reconnaissance mission".

On the 7th September, the first night of The Blitz began at 5pm and it lasted over 12 hours, starting nine major fires and almost 1,000 lesser ones. In its wake it left 430 men, women and children dead, and seriously injured a further 1,600. London was undoubtedly the worst to suffer, but throughout the rest of the war, one place after another was to suffer the devastating effects of high explosives, incendiaries, and later the rocket bombs of V1 and V2 classification. Where direct hits on lines were sustained, relatively quick repairs were instituted and business was soon back to normal. Yet, from the railways' point of view, the most frustrating types of enemy action were the Delayed Action devices and UXBs (unexploded bombs) which seriously affected traffic until such times as they could be rendered harmless.

Docks were a very difficult working environment, for precisely the same sorts of impediments that made goods yards dangerous. However, due to the fact that the docks were singled out by the Luftwaffe as a primary target, the electrical power supply was cut off immediately the threat of approaching aircraft was notified. Several dock crane drivers have recounted their alarming experiences on the railway-owned docks during air raids like those pictured below at Grimsby. For example, when the power was cut off, the cranes came to a dead stop, often with the open back of the crane poised high over the water in the dock, meaning that there was nothing between the driver and the black, open void behind him. In such a predicament, men often sat for hours on end whilst the enemy bombers rained down high-explosive around them. But there were added dangers, as the oily or coal dust covered waters of the docks in the blackout often looked just like dry land. In such conditions at the LNER's Hull Docks four workmen fell into the water one night and of these only one was rescued. At Portsmouth a car full of naval officers was caught a glancing blow by a moving train and it careened in to an empty dry dock without anyone noticing. Even men who knew their docks well got into trouble, and there are many tragedies recorded where dockers fell into coal hoists, dry docks, grain elevators and the like.

Oxford station, April 1939 showing GWR star class 4-6-0 No.4021 British Monarch *in the platform with a four coach local and Hall class 4-6-0 No.4988* Bulwell Hall *standing on the up through road.*

LMS (ex-Highland) Clan Class 4-6-0 No.14767 Clan Mackinnon *in utility unlined black livery at Aviemore in 1946, the last of the class to survive and the only one to outlive the LMS*

GWR 0-6-0ST No.2195 (formerly Cwm Mawr) *still retained its company identity
(and visible evidence of the 1939 removal of its nameplate on the saddletank) when seen on the dump at Swindon in September 1953.*

Double headed express at Reading , August 1937: GWR Star class No.4020 Knight Commander
and Castle class 4-6-0 No.4082 Windsor Castle

Above:
One of the emergency feeding stations provided for the returning BEF forces was at Headcorn station, where railway staff were assisted by members of the RASC and local housewives in the demanding work.
Photo: SR Official

Below:
In addition to the splendid work carried out by the Southern, the GWR also had a major share in carrying the soldiers to safety after Dunkirk.
Photo: Brad Leigh Collection

The Southern Stand-by To Repel Boarders

Ashford works were heavily involved in making armoured plate for the twelve armoured trains which were used on different railway systems around the country. The Southern had four of these, one was based at Canterbury, one at Tonbridge, one at Barnstaple and one at Wadebridge. The Southern also saw another form of armoured train in the form of Super Heavy Gun Batteries which were found at Aldington, Bishopsbourne, Adisham, Rolvenden, Shepherdswell, Eythorne, Staple, Poulton, Lydden and Martin Mill. In a number of cases these batteries were accompanied by a train converted at Ashford to provide living quarters. Normally diesel engines supplied by the LMS were used for haulage as the enemy had no smoke plume to aim their guns at. At a number of locations new sidings had to be made to accommodate the living trains, and a new connecting single line was constructed between the railway running from Canterbury East to Faversham, and the line from Canterbury to Ashford West.

Dunkirk

With the end of winter came the expected offensive in France, but the swiftness of the Nazi push through the Ardennes region caught everyone by surprise. This push and the fall of the Low Countries resulted in the BEF being caught in a pincer movement, and subsequently isolated and surrounded at Dunkirk. With the situation worsening, a decision was taken to evacuate as much of the BEF as possible, although no-one expected to be able to save more than a small portion of the force. On 26th May, Operation Dynamo, a plan designed to save the men from Dunkirk, began by transporting the BEF across the English Channel. One of the first ships to arrive at Dunkirk was *Mona's Isle*, which reached there early the next day, and in the days which followed it alone evacuated 25,000 troops. On 29th May, the Luftwaffe began targeting the evacuation proceedings at Dunkirk but, even so, 47,300 men were evacuated that day.

The next day, an additional 54,000 troops left for Dover and the south coast ports. Several ships were sunk as the Royal Air Force and the German Luftwaffe battled overhead, including three destroyers, many pleasure craft and a number of railway-owned vessels. On 31st May, another 68,000 men, including some French troops, were evacuated whilst the French 1st Army fought a rear guard action to protect the proceedings.

On the first two days of June a total of 89,000 men were taken to safety, even though the evacuation was restricted to the hours after sunset due to the Luftwaffe's continual strafing of the beaches. Unexpectedly, almost the entire BEF had been saved as Operation Dynamo rescued a total of 220,000 British and 120,000 French and Belgian troops. The evacuation at Dunkirk left only two British divisions in France, both engaged in action south of the Somme River, though an additional 120,000 men (including many railwaymen serving with the Railway Operating Department) were still engaged on the lines of communication in France.

When the BEF retreated from Dunkirk, the four main line railways supplied a pool of 186 trains and allocated these to the Southern Railway. In turn they ran a total of 620 train journeys from the seven main channel ports in just eight days. Conveying some 320,000 men from their landing ports the Southern worked the trains to places like Reading, Salisbury and Basingstoke, or reception centres in London such as Crystal Palace and Olympia. Once on to the LMS, LNER and GWR, the trains got the men to regrouping points although some of those which were heading to reception camps in the midlands and the north made use of special ablution and kitchen facilities at the LNER's Leicester London Road station. The LNER also ran eight evacuation specials of its own after a number of boats unexpectedly arrived at Parkeston Quay. Sadly one of these was bombed outside the harbour and the survivors, still covered in sea-water and oil, were put straight into one train and taken up to London. On emptying the train, the officials said that the state of the coaches had just got to be seen to be believed.

Less spectacular was Operation Aerial, the evacuation of western France. On this occasion the brunt of the work again fell on the Southern, but the GWR also played a significant role as ships landed with the evacuees at Weymouth, Plymouth and Southampton. As the tattered remnants of the BEF were moved to re-grouping points, the LMS and GWR were running trains to ports like Cardiff, Liverpool and Glasgow to meet ships carrying the Commonwealth Forces who were arriving to defend the motherland.

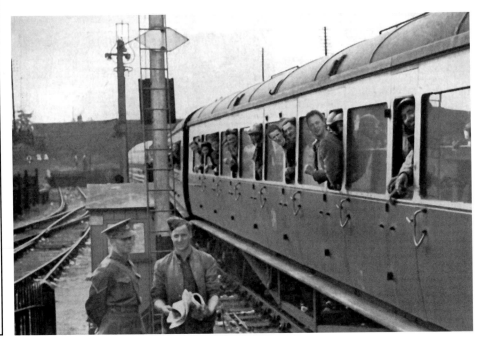

Awaiting The Invasion

The railways were also to play an important role in national defence, and trains were kept at readiness in order to rush troops to any place where an invasion might be attempted. During World War I, the fear of a German invasion in either Scotland or East Anglia had prompted the construction of British armoured trains. So as Hitler's Operation Sealion threatened to land troops in Britain within 6 to 8 weeks of the fall of France, a decision was taken to form armoured trains for service in Kent, Sussex, Devon, Cornwall, East Anglia and up the east coast to the north of Scotland. In May 1940, a meeting was held between Sir Nigel Gresley and William Stanier, when the plans for the make up of armoured trains was decided upon. The LMS took on responsibility for providing the trains, each comprised of two armoured trucks and two low-sided wagons, whilst the LNER said it would provide Great Eastern 2-4-2 tanks for the motive power.

As recounted from *Britain's Railways At War,* we note: 'For train crewing the Royal Engineers' Railway Detachment supplied the men (many of whom had just been repatriated from France), but the duties of manning the armoured train itself fell to the Royal Tank Regiment. Initially, just two officers and two NCOs from each train were sent to Shoeburyness, for they would then train the other ranks when the allocations of men and trains were assigned to their operating bases. All twelve trains were in readiness by July, and the allocations began. Six were earmarked for the Eastern Command, and six for Scotland - following on the principle of where the armoured trains were most needed in World War One. Of the Eastern Command trains, four were used in East Anglia and two in Kent. The Scottish Command quickly began to establish a country-wide patrol in view of the sparsely populated terrain, but one wonders why the units were used on seemingly secure stretches of coast line like that through Ayrshire. It had been hoped that as many as 20 trains would be built, but the orders for the remaining eight were rescinded and the Northern and Southern Commands began to clamour for their own trains. In fact, the Southern Command proposed working in collaboration with the Royal Navy for armoured trains mounting heavier guns. The War Office acted quickly, and the trains were redistributed so that each command had units at its disposal.'

Demolition Charges

After Dunkirk measures were taken to guard key railway installations, and prevent them from falling into enemy hands. At key places, water columns, point levers and coaling equipment were marked at their most vulnerable point by a splash of red paint. If the enemy landed, railwaymen were ordered to hit these paint marks with a sledge hammer and break them before retreating. As a final touch, a locomotive was to be derailed across the entry to important depots, engine sheds, goods yards and stations, and a grenade thrown inside the firebox. In many instances the duty fell to the commander of the local Home Guard Unit, but it was not unknown for senior railway officials to also be given the tools for the job. Special measures were taken to protect railway bridges across the Forth (as pictured above), Thames, Severn, Tweed and Tay, so most of these were mined.

Allocated to the LNER is WD 8F No.7659,
this Stanier designed 2-8-0 having obviously seen a lot of hard work.

A more typical LNER freight picture shows J25 No.5656. This design was introduced to the North Eastern Railway in 1898,
and with the abbreviated wartime livery NE once again appears on the tender.

The Railway Executive, learning from what had happened in the fall of France decreed that the priority for District Superintendents was to evacuate locomotives from the likely invasion area. In France they had tried to move whole trains, with the result that not all had got away due to the congestion and these in turn fell into enemy hands before their crews got a chance to destroy them. Clearly, the lesson was to get the engines away, as coaches and wagons on their own were quite useless to the enemy until he could bring over his own locomotives. Therefore, at the end of each day, locomotive depots in invasion areas were emptied of their charges, and these were stabled much further inland.

For example, LNER depots such as Harwich sent its engines to Maningtree, whilst those at Hull went to Selby and so on. By this time many members of railway staff were undertaking additional duties such as ARP Wardens or Home Guard patrols! Thousands of railwaymen came forward at the first appeal for volunteers in what was originally known as the Local Defence Volunteers, and it is appropriate to record that a great many of those who enrolled were actually employed in protecting railway installations.

Around the end of August the threat of invasion was at its height, and the defenders prepared for the almost inevitable code-word "Cromwell", which would signal that an invasion was imminent. On the night of Saturday 7th September, the warning was raised and the country went to readiness; around 11pm the crew of one of the Armoured Trains believed they had witnessed the start of the hostilities when the church bells of Stirling rang out to signify that parachutists had landed. This was, of course an error, but the train steamed out looking for the enemy for 12 hours.

At Lincoln the District Superintendent was hauled out of bed by two army officers with news that the enemy had landed in The Wash and he was ordered to take the specified precautions. This would have meant evacuating as much of the railway equipment as he could, and then order the destruction of all the vital installations in his District. However, and quite fortuitously, he refused to accept the word of these two officials and sought confirmation from the Eastern Command HQ who advised him that no such landing had taken place.

Thankfully no dislocation of the railway took place as a result, but the rumour did lead to some considerable alarm in the district and railway officials had a great deal of difficulty dissuading people who turned up to board evacuation trains that none were being run and that it was perfectly safe for them to go back to their homes. Even so, the railways waited and held their breath, and prepared to implement the Sunday timetable which would be used if a civilian evacuation of the south or east coasts proved necessary. Fortunately no invasion came, and on 10th September, Hitler postponed the invasion of Britain until the 24th. Four days later, it was postponed again until the 27th, the last day of the month that the tides in the English Channel would favour the Germans.

The Battle Of Britain & Beyond

Above:
Bomb damage at Charing Cross in the height of the blitz; thinking to bring the city to its knees and destroy major installations, the Luftwaffe flew 1,300 sorties in this offensive. The Germans, however, lost the Battle of Britain, and the outcome of the September air offensive over London caused Hitler to postpone the full-scale invasion of Britain indefinitely as his plans had been contingent on the establishment of German air dominance in the English Channel. The Luftwaffe lost approximately 1,880 aircraft in this phase of the war, as opposed to Britain's loss of 1,020 aircraft. By 12th October, Hitler had abandoned any idea of invading but his raids on Britain's cities continued throughout the winter of 1940-1941. Yet, despite the air-raids on almost every major industrial target, Germany failed to make a concentrated attack on the country's nerve-centres - the railway marshalling yards and bridges.

Travelling Post Office Service SUSPENDED

A major casualty of railway services during the 'Battle Of Britain' period were the travelling post offices. Lineside collection had, of course, been suspended at the outbreak of war but sorting still continued on many trains until this operation was withdrawn during the height of the blitz. Officially the service was withdrawn on 22nd September 1940 and with it some 387 railwaymen were released from their 'reserved occupation' status. It was the loss of men like these, plus stewards, sleeping car attendants, porters, plate-layers and so on that meant the railways would face severe staffing shortages in all grades when peace finally resumed.

The Battle of Britain began on the 13th August with the start of an offensive that was supposed to establish air superiority for the Luftwaffe. From 7th September to 12th November 1940, the Luftwaffe raided London 58 times claiming the lives of around 15,000 civilians; many more were injured and left homeless. The climax of the Battle was 15th September! Thinking that they had defeated the RAF and achieved air superiority, the Luftwaffe made a final offensive on London that early autumn night but they lost 58 aircraft against 26 RAF planes..

Having survived the onslaught, the next stage of the story came as the country re-structured itself. As every farm and factory went over to 'working for the national effort', it fell to the railways to move supplies and workers. From the docks and ports around the country, they moved large quantities of goods that were vital to both the civilian population and the military war-effort. Yet these goods were not arriving at the docks with ease, because on 17th August 1940, Hitler had declared a maritime blockade of Britain, attempting to curtail trade and choke the country into submission by use of lethal U-Boat packs.

In June 1940 Germany had begun the Battle of the Atlantic, using submarine warfare to cut Britain's overseas lifelines, particularly since they now had submarine bases in Norway and France. Undeterred by this threat the U.S. Congress passed the Lend-Lease Act in March 1941, appropriating an initial $7 billion to lend or lease weapons and other aid. By this means the United States actually hoped to ensure victory over the Axis without involving its own troops, but by the autumn of 1941, they were in a state of undeclared war with Germany.

In July, U.S. forces were stationed in Iceland and thereafter their navy took over the task of escorting many convoys between the United States and Iceland. In September President Roosevelt authorised ships on convoy duty to attack German vessels, and Hitler's threat of subduing the British by starving them out had been dramatically reduced. At the outset the Germans had only 28 submarines, but more were being built and these kept Britain in danger until the spring of 1943. Despite monumental losses from 'wolf-packs', the merchant marine landed huge volumes of supplies at British ports for onward shipment by rail, including vital fresh foods, timber, clothing, and no less than 3,000,000 gallons of oil each day. All of which had to be rushed away from the ports as quickly as possible by rail, to mitigate against possible destruction by the Luftwaffe.

By the autumn of 1942 the tide had begun to turn, and the 1st Army was taken to various ports for embarkation to North Africa; a task which involved the movement of 185,000 men, 20,000 military vehicles and 250,000 tons of supplies. On 26th October, the first British convoy of troops left the Clyde for Operation Torch, the invasion of French North Africa. The invasion was divided into two sections, comprising a Centre Task Force for Oran and Algeria and an Eastern Task Force to Algiers. On the same date a convoy of US troops, commanded by General Patton, set sail for Morocco. These convoys reached the Mediterranean on 5th November and heavy fighting followed, with substantial losses on both sides.

Victory was swift and decisive and French officials in Algeria and Morocco signed an armistice with the Allies on 11th November. Following the retreating Germans, the British 10th Corps recaptured Torbruk two days later.

In connection with this offensive, British railways ran no less than 700 military freights, 110 naval specials, 115 US Army specials and a prodigious 150,091 wagon loads carried in normal freight trains. During 1943 around 400 military specials were run as part of reinforcing the Allied campaign in North Africa, with the majority of these being destined for embarkation ports in South Wales and the Clyde. Yet, as intensive as this operation was, it was to pale into insignificance with what would happen in 1944.

D-Day

When the opportunity for opening up a second front became a reality, the railways moved men and equipment into the strategic assembly positions. By this time Britain no longer stood alone, and as these assembly points became established foreign uniforms and accents abounded. Railway controllers had been aware that 'something big was afoot' since January 1944 and a new phrase had been circulated as mysterious loads were being formed up and described as part of Movement O. The 'O' stood, of course for 'Operation Overlord' the secret code-name by which the invasion of France was being referred to by the Allied Supreme Command. More secret traffic began to appear, and as this slowly began to crawl toward the various embarkation ports it was clear that this was indeed the invasion build-up. It was especially obvious to men on the Southern and Great Western lines that ran along the south coast, as vast supplies of stores began to be consigned to stations serving tiny creeks, bays and inlets which had previously never sustained any type of 'port activity' whatsoever! Armoured tanks, military vehicles, tractors and earth-moving equipment, amphibians and small landing craft, were added to the loads of arms, ammunition, and stores.

In addition to these new embarkment areas full use was made of all the existing dock facilities, and in this regard the railway-owned ports around the country were widely used during the D-Day build up. Many of those had been facilities which had benefited from Government support in the 1930s. Of these, the roll-on/roll-off ferry service between Ireland and Stranraer provided a vital bridgehead to the army training grounds in Northern Ireland. Even so, this was not sufficient for the traffic which had to be carried, and a new military port was constructed at nearby Cairnryan.

It should be mentioned that railway links from the north were substantially improved, a task which included the complete doubling of 18 miles of single track on the Didcot, Newbury and Southampton Junction line. Other lines were also improved in connection with this work, including the provision of spurs between the GWR and Southern lines at Launceston, Lydford and Yeovil. These spurs facilitated an important flow of traffic towards the southern ports, particularly those in the West Country where almost every river estuary, inlet, and bay was packed with landing craft 'awaiting orders'.

One of the principal flows of traffic in the build up to D-Day was that of petroleum spirit. If one thinks logically about this, it will be appreciated that vast amounts of this stuff were going to be needed for both land vehicles and aircraft. It therefore flowed in great quantities across the Atlantic before being discharged into railway tank wagons or special pipe-lines. As the picture above (taken at Ipswich) shows, lengthy trains crossed from one side of the country to another. At the railheads these trains were met by road tankers, as shown below, which carried the fuel to airbases and army camps.

To allow the movement of this additional military traffic (such as that seen in the pictures on this page - which sadly have no identification due to the censorship of the day) new facilities had to be provided. Hundreds of lay-back sidings were converted into loops, whilst completely new loops were put in elsewhere. Many of these 'holding loops' were to be of limited use, with a short life expectancy, so they were made in a cost-effective way. Instead of sleepers, the track was mounted on concrete blocks similar to the practice employed by the earliest British railways. However, whereas the original railway sleepers were free-standing stone blocks, the concrete blocks of 1944 had the benefit of a cross-tie rod every third pair.

In the weeks that followed, these loops and sidings were to be packed with Stanier 8Fs, Austerities, S160s and even ROD 2-8-0s of World War I origin, quietly simmering at the head of up to 100 wagons per train. Meanwhile, flows of essential items were simultaneously arriving at Southampton and other ports such as the Clyde, Liverpool and those on the Bristol Channel. Many of these arrivals had to be quickly sorted, marshalled, and got out of the port areas (which were still under enemy aerial attack) and despatched to the various centres of embarkation. To assist this work, two large transit centres were built. One of these was at Micheldever between Winchester and Basingstoke and thus conveniently located for Southampton Docks; the other was near to London's docklands, being situated at High Meads near Stratford. According to US Defence Department Records, a third was planned near Chester to serve Liverpool, but this was never built and use was made of existing facilities. Generally transhipment was avoided by railway operators, but these sheds provided a vital function which enabled the incoming stores to be sorted into various orders of priority. Special, abnormal and out of gauge loads also began to run, and code names like Mulberry, Phoenix and Whale were common, but little understood military specials.

The main flow of the traffic began on 26th March 1944 which was the date for the initial movement of invasion trains - this was officially designated as the first phase. The whole second phase was a matter of great complexity, especially as a depot or factory originating supplies might be despatching items en-mass, yet in reality these were actually required in France on different dates. The only resolution to this was the sorting of goods, by which means 'blocks of commodities' were arranged for delivery overseas on specified dates. The third phase was simpler, as this involved the movement of reserves and stores that were needed once the 'beach-head' had been established. The movement of heavy stores was the next phase, and this began on 10th May and, by the day in question, some 24,459 trains in this category had already reached their destination. In total, the D-Day build up which had begun on the railways in March involved somewhere between 9,000 and 12,000 special trains up to the middle of June. But, in the three weeks that followed, this increased to about 3,300 per week. Other special train movements in the period show 12,000 tons of baggage, 436 tank trains and 817 specials carrying petrol and other fuels. Another extensive traffic flow, especially just prior to D-Day, were the supplies of bombs to the RAF and USAAF bomber-bases.

In the same period the railways conveyed around 230,000 men to embarkation points in the period up to August out of the total requirement of 300,000. Since it was planned to land 130,000 of these men in Normandy on the first day of the operation, followed by further waves of new troops as beach heads became established, it was essential that the lines of communication down to the embarkation points were kept clear of obstruction. Train controllers prepared well in advance, and they devised a system of moving trains which has close parallels with the modern merry-go-round system of coal movement. Even where lines were just a single track, careful control and the preparation of paths kept the routes free from congestion. So great was this 'O' traffic, that train crews were warned to expect to be away from their home depots for up to a week!

As the trains got near to the south coast, so the queues of traffic became denser and slower moving, especially at places like Bodmin Road, Chichester, Exeter, Fareham, Petersfield, Three Bridges, Truro, Winchester and Yeovil. On many routes trains were standing block to block on the running lines as they went south, whilst less important movements were often held for days on end in the sidings, just waiting for the code-word that would signal the advance. It was therefore not an uncommon occurrence for crews to be away from their home depot for days on end, and the railways had to make special arrangements for billeting and feeding these men. Station waiting rooms were commonly employed, and on the strategically placed Didcot, Newbury & Southampton Railway, women of the WVS did sterling work in caring for the railway crews who were waiting their turn to move on. To avoid build-ups such as these, from the spring of 1944 to the end of June, whole lines were to see severe curtailment of ordinary services or closed altogether. Some double track sections were singled and rearranged for working the invasion traffic; the line heading towards the south would be used by queuing trains, whilst the line running in the opposite direction would be rigged for single line working.

Learning From Gallipoli

On 18th April 1940 the War Office finalised its plans for the movement of goods prior to the invasion, in the guise of 'Stores Movement Instruction No.1'. This document envisaged several phases, the first of which was Pre-Stowage, this built up stores at convenient points for ship-loading. This phase took its origins from the fiasco surrounding the unavailability of essential supplies at the ill-fated Allied landings at Gallipoli in World War I, which resulted in troops being left stranded on the beaches whilst their ships scuttled back to Alexandria for reloading. When France was invaded this time, the hard-learned lessons of 1915 would not be forgotten. The second phase centred around materials that would be required at the landing zones on specified dates, and the ships carrying these across the channel would therefore have to be run to a very precise timetable.

Passenger trains were also much in demand, as large detachments of troops had to be moved from one end of the country to the other. From the Highlands of Scotland, the dales and the moors of Yorkshire, Cumberland, Northumberland and Wales, the training or transit camps spilled out their waiting soldiers. From the flat fen-lands of East Anglia, Lincolnshire, Somerset and the like, British, American, Commonwealth and free European forces moved into position. Some troop train flows followed the general north - south direction of the freight traffic, but many of these trains cut across the flow, by running east - south-west, thus causing even more headaches for railway controllers.

To move such large quantities of men and material on railways that were already stretched beyond capacity was no mean task. Engines, coaches, and freight stock had to be found, made up in to trains and then crewed by a depleted workforce. To this was added the complicated problem of finding paths for the specials in and amongst the priority traffic which was still having to be run, and this could only be achieved by the curtailment of normal, less urgent traffic and the amalgamation of other types of services. Who, before the war, could have imagined an ex-South Eastern Railway 4-4-0 drawing a mixed train of LMS and GWR coaches from Leicester to Peterborough; a truly combined 'Big Four' working that was reported in the *Railway Magazine*.

Elsewhere, as the pressures grew, civilian trains (both freight and passenger) were withdrawn without any explanation. Instructions were given to railwaymen to refuse to answer questions about the reasons why services had been curtailed, and the responses given by railway officials to members of the public varied from detailed facts about locomotive, steel and coal shortages on the one hand, to rather vague, stupid or unintelligible replies on the other. During this time security on the railways was at an all-time high, and the RAF paid special attention to the protection of railway installations from attacks by the Luftwaffe. On the ground anti-aircraft units and gun emplacements sprang up around key railway centres, whilst the Home Guard, Fire Guards and Civil Defence stood by on a constant state of readiness as their part of the defence of the railways.

In many ways this protective blanket was just like the one which had been thrown up around the railways and docks when the threat of invasion was at its height in 1940-1, but it was largely superfluous. Once again the enemy failed to take advantage of the tactical gains that were to be had in destroying key railway installations, either by aerial attack or by sabotage. It can also be revealed that, in high circles, there was a belief that there might even be a 'suicide raid' of a battalion of paratroopers who would be dropped on principal railway yards with the objective of ham-stringing the invasion build-up. Actually the German High Command does not appear to have taken the signs of invasion as seriously as they might have done, and many of the reports communicated back to Berlin by Nazi spies in Britain went unheeded. The only actual delay, as it turned out, was going to be the British weather!

The railways played their part in the invasion build-up unstintingly and often without regard as to who was going to pay for it all in the long term! The four weeks following D-Day were recorded as being the busiest period ever on the railways; 17,500 troop and store trains were run and a further 133 special mail trains were also operated. Sadly more than 300 ambulance train journeys were needed, and the bulk of these were handled by ex-GER Class B12 4-6-0s because of their high tractive effort to low axle-loading ratio. The crew for each train consisted of two drivers, two passed firemen, two guards and a fitter who carried a large number of spares as the engines were expected to travel long distances away from sheds where replacement parts could be reasonably expected. Even heavy repairs were carried out at foreign sheds, where the fitter would be assisted by local men. The crews naturally had to live in accommodation provided on the train, and when they ventured on to lines for which they had no route knowledge pilot drivers would be provided by the local locomotive superintendent.

There were also 865 special stock trains which ran 'single destination journeys', essential as they were carrying German prisoners of war to camps in Wales, the Lake District, Scotland and the West Country. Furthermore 4,000 block coal trains were run in connection with existing schedules that were extended as supplies were now required at the embarkation ports, where they would be stored in readiness for export to France as soon as the breakout from the beach-heads had been secured. To achieve all this extra running several hundred servicemen were loaned from the armed forces to the railways for a period of three months to make up crews for the extra locomotives that were being used. All these men were volunteers, and not all had previously been in the railway service. Most were put to work as cleaners, thus releasing cleaners to become firemen, and passed firemen to become drivers etc. The training and inspection process for locomotive crews was accelerated, and rapid advancement was made, and quite soon some of the servicemen were even passing out as firemen.

A total of 935 Austerity locomotives (seen above in a photograph at Reading taken by M.W.Earley) were built in advance of D-Day, and these may be viewed as one of the railways' most tangible contributions made in the offensive. However, these locomotives were not destined to idly stand in sidings awaiting for the invasion as they were intended to be employed in hauling the building blocks of the operation which became known as Overlord. About 450 of the Austerities were lent to the LMS, LNER and Southern railways, and a few went to the GWR. Meanwhile, a further contribution to the task at hand was the arrival of the US Army Class S160 2-8-0 locomotives (pictured below) that began appearing in the Autumn of 1942. As they were built to the British loading gauge, they too were available for use in this country before being sent overseas after D-Day, and the first was handed over to the GWR at Paddington on 11th December. The US Army also supplied a number of 0-6-0 tank engines which were well used at a number of ports, especially that at Southampton and the docks in South Wales.

Chapter Seven
The GWR at War

Whilst there is good reason for giving a detailed coverage of all that occurred on each railway during the war years, to do so would be a physical impossibility. Even recounting the highlights (and low spots) on each company would be an impossibility, so it leaves the author in something of a dilemma as to what to include and what to leave out; therefore the chapters that follow have been constructed in such a way as to give a flavour of what happened on our railways during World War II, with slightly different approaches being taken as far as each company goes.

For example, we will consider bomb raids on the LNER in much greater detail than the rest, and whilst this is (on the surface) unfair to the devotees of the other members of the Big Four it is not some prejudicial favouritism. Obviously our look at the Southern will reflect its rapid change from being (basically) a passenger railway, to one which ended up carrying equal amounts of freight and passengers by the end of the war. That of course was due to its special geographic position as the springboard used for the invasion of France. It was a role in which the GWR would have an important, albeit subservient role to the Southern, but nevertheless one which would see significant traffic down into the West Country and South Wales.

The LMS by contrast was a pipeline feeder, and allying itself with the GWR for onward transmission of the vital flow of goods from the industrial centres of the Midlands, North of England and Scotland. The LMS and GWR also played the most significant roles in the receipt of goods from overseas, and it fell principally upon these two railways to get men and equipment quickly away from the great receiving ports on the western seaboard, notably Merseyside.

In the pages that follow, we will look at how the GWR organised this traffic, and the ways in which it endeavoured to operate as normally as possible. In reflecting upon all these new flows of traffic and the ways in which the GWR coped with them, we can conclude that what happened in the safe movement of such trains was in no small part due to its remarkable ATC system which had been completed on most of its main lines just before the war. The superb safety system was indeed to play a major part in the carriage of the extra traffic, and this was clearly shown in the sad instance near Slough in 1940 when an 8F borrowed from the LMS (and thus not fitted with the warning apparatus) was involved in a serious fatal collision which would never have occurred had GWR engines been employed on both trains.

To show how the GWR set themselves up for one difficult time (e.g. the winter of 1941/2), we might refer to a bit of early propaganda which the company circulated to show its prowess in 'military terms'. It was in the depths of the severe winter that the GWR adopted 'military tactics' and rousing, propaganda-style talk to make sure its vital services of freight, munitions, troops and passenger trains got through. These essential workings were helped on their way by some 'new technology, including track detonators and automatic train control along with the more tried and tested methods of railway operation'; according to the publicity department who came up with the idea of likening the whole service to a military operation. The railway's 2,000 or so signal-boxes secretly became 'munitions dumps for a total of 350,000 powerful detonators - the GWR patriotically called them the '350,000-Bang Barrage' - which were intended to warn the drivers of trains of dangers ahead, especially when the snowdrifts of the severe winter concealed vital signals.

In the depths of war, the tracks were also well guarded against possible enemy sabotage, as well as having to be de-frosted. An army of 5,000 GWR 'line-side guardians' each one to stand sentry over a particular section of the route. 'Drilled to commando standard and with brilliant eyesight and acute hearing', they would be stationed at key signal-points and each man would check on the tracks in his area. They would also need to know everything about railway signal rules. Equipped with red, yellow and green flags, a tricolour hand-torch and his ration box, as well as a pack of 36 detonators as ammunition, the 'guardian' would assist the controlling signalman by laying detonators at strategic points to get the attention of train crews. Back at 'base camp' (the main depot), a precision plan meant each guardian got food and was relieved at exact times to help him through the day.

Technology that later came to be taken for granted was hot news in war-torn Britain in 1942. So-called 'siren robots' were making their debut on many newly 'converted' lines and a lot of things were expected of them. This was, of course, part of the GWR's pioneering system of ATC. Using electromagnets mounted in a sealed unit on the railway sleepers, the system backed up railway signals by triggering magnetic contacts fitted to the undersides of locomotives. For a 'Danger' signal, one of two electrical circuits would make a magnet trigger off a sensor to sound a very loud siren in the driver's cab, leaving the driver in no uncertain terms that he had to stop fast. Then again, unless the driver cancelled the signal, the train would stop anyway as this new system also pulled the automatic brakes on. For a signal showing a 'Clear' route, the other sensor would be activated, and a re-assuring bell would ring instead.

When the weather worsened and the blizzards struck, the GWR adopted military tactics once again. Thirty-two locomotives fitted with snow-ploughs were strategically-placed on its 2,000-mile network and kept in steam - waiting for the call from the company's band of 'weather spies'. Snow on the lines set the ploughs into action and they would drive through the drifts at speed just like 'an advancing tank force'. Even the worst drifts, chimney-height in the cuttings, could not take this onslaught as the ploughs barged through to clear the route for the vital services. In the worst conditions however, a nod from a high-up official in the London area was enough to start up a 'back-up' railway timetable that kept trains - and problems - to an essential minimum until things were back to something like normal. This was wisely done to prevent problems getting out of hand. Call it a bit of nonsense, overt propaganda, or just an amusing way of getting a message across during the dark days of wartime winter, but the whole package was part of the continuing safety development by the GWR and it was to help in all that followed.

Another thing that helped the GWR through the problematic war years was the decision (taken in conjunction with the Minister of War Transport) to increase the railway's line capacity over lengthy stretches of the company's tracks at certain known bottle-necks. The first, of "major importance" was the quadrupling of main-lines between Cheltenham and Gloucester to allow for movement of goods traffic. The works were completed within 6½ months of being authorised, instead of eighteen as had been estimated. Exceptional priority had been given to the job, which was spurred on by the GWR departments concerned and by the contracting firm involved, Sir Robert MacAlpine &. Sons.

The work was divided into two sections of approximately equal length and labelled "L" and "M", each linking up with existing intermediate and end sections of four lines. On Section L around 28,000 cubic yards of earthwork, mostly in embankment, were obtained almost entirely from borrow-pits on either side of the railway. The new embankments averaged 4ft. high and between 10 and 38ft in width. A layer of peat below the clay had some effect on the work, meaning not everything went according to plan. On Section M the works were much heavier, and this meant the use of mechanical excavating machines. There were no 'borrow-pits' to dig in this section, but 41,000 cubic yards of soil were removed from cuttings for use in the newly-widened embankments. The permanent-way for the new 'loops' consisted of second-hand 95lb rails on second-hand sleepers with new keys.

Above:
The development and extension of ATC was of paramount importance in keeping the GWR free from accidents. The system was based on Kemp & Rowell's patent device and included a fixed ramp located between the rails at a distant signal and a contact shoe on the locomotive; when the distant signal was 'clear' an electric current passed through the ramp and the shoe, sounding a bell in the cab. However, when the signal was at danger, no electric current passed through the ramp, but the ramp still raised the shoe, and this caused a warning device to go off in the cab.

Below:
Withdrawn at the outbreak of war the GWR's Vale of Rheidol Railway could have served a useful morale boosting role during the dark years that followed.
Photos: Both GWR Official

The second project was to improve a single-track connecting route, part of which was double tracked. Other sections of it were increased in capacity by the lengthening of passing loops, the addition of three new loops and improving the points and signalling operations on the line. With wartime reporting restrictions in place railway journals like The Railway Magazine, could give only a few scant details as far as this extensive work was concerned.

Even so they could give a few hints by saying that the 25-mile section was not used by heavy traffic, or even by very many trains at all. It had eight stations and these mainly served passengers, parcels and rural traffic. To allow trains travelling in opposite directions to pass, short crossing loops were laid at six of these stations. When the line was built in the 1880s, the engineers had enough foresight to build bridges and other features so that these could accommodate double tracks although they knew they were only building a single-track line. So from these details most railway enthusiasts would be able to guess that the anonymous line was in fact the Didcot, Newbury & Southampton railway.

Above:
The advent of war witnessed some startling changes on the GWR; for example the Didcot, Newbury & Southampton Railway changed from a quiet rustic backwater, to become an important artery from the Midlands to the port of Southampton.

Below:
Such was the shortage of staff on the railways in the war years that women were brought in to undertake a wide number of duties all over the GWR.

The fact that the DN & S had been built with sufficient room for expansion (in places) made the route ideal for conversion when it was needed for war traffic sixty years on. However, the parts that were not used for railway tracks had returned to wasteland and were out of shape for railway cuttings and embankments, so a lot of work still had to be done, and even then not all the original sections of track-bed could be used. New sections of track-bed had to be created to allow additional crossing facilities and other improvements. All the existing, 300-yard loops were extended to 550 yards to allow space for an extra engine and twenty wagons. The three new loops were 550 yards long as well. One of these was mid-way between two stations, and the new loops were planned so that the distance between them was no more than around 2½ miles.

In addition, two miles of the route at one end had been doubled, and the main line connection at the other end of the line was completely restyled and now crossed a GWR over-bridge to meet up with the SR line from Winchester. This new connecting line was around a mile long, and it went through a cutting, on a new embankment and over a new bridge. To speed-up its construction, all daytime traffic on the new route was suspended, except for trains bringing materials for the work. Only night-time trains used this normal route and the rest were diverted to other lines. For about 30 weeks passengers and parcels were taken by bus from station to station with no intermediate stopping places. The work was arranged so that excavation and tipping took place at an almost equal, balanced rate, and about 60,000 cubic yards of earth were moved. Some 11,000 cubic yards of ashes were used as bottom ballast, and 8,000 cubic yards of crushed stone formed the top layer of ballast. Around 6 miles of track had been laid and 2 miles of existing track slewed or realigned, as 52 new single connections and 15 runaway catch points were laid in. Water for the engines was provided by two water columns halfway along the route, and these were fed from a 15,000-gallon tank served by the local council's mains supply.

The old station signal boxes had become outmoded, so they were demolished and replaced by new signal boxes which were built at the ends of the loops. Though loop points nearest the stations remained mechanically-operated, new electrically-operated points were installed at the other ends of the loops. The motorised points were operated from the new signal boxes. The line was now being operated on the "token" system to avoid collisions between trains accidentally let onto the same section of single track at the same time. This special feature included the installation of auxiliary token instruments at the ends of the loops farthest from the signal boxes, and these instruments had a direct telephone link with the signal boxes. The whole upgrading of the line took less than eight months to complete. In the short-term the works were something of a puzzle to the inhabitants of the area, as 'their' railway was surely never so busy as to justify all of this work. Indeed after World War II, many of these temporary loops were removed and the Didcot, Newbury and Southampton line reverted to its relatively peaceful cross-country status after carrying so much traffic for the Invasion of France! It might not have been a long-lasting project, but it was one of those jobs that the GWR simply did, but did very well for as long as ever it was needed.

Passenger Train Services

In 1938 the originating passenger journeys on the GWR totalled almost 128 million, but throughout the war this increased substantially and by 1942 the figure had reached 169,000,000. At the same time train coaching miles were reduced by 9,600,000 on pre-war figures, and this clearly indicates that substantially more people were travelling on fewer but much larger trains (and even then their was considerable overcrowding). Amongst the GWR service casualties in the first autumn of the war came the passenger trains from Clynderwen to Fishguard Harbour, Newport to Merthyr, Stratford on Avon to Alcester and Uxbridge to Gerrard's Cross. Another closure, for the duration, was the narrow gauge line from Aberystwyth to Devils Bridge (although this was usually withdrawn in the winter anyway). It may have seemed little benefit in the carriage of freight or important passenger traffic, but several commentators wrote to the railway press stating that 'excursion lines', like this and the Romney, Hythe & Dymchurch served a moral-boosting purpose beyond all comparison to the actual cost and effort of operation. They were probably right in this appraisal, but in that first anticipation of war, such sentiments were not given very high priority in the hallowed corridors of power!

There were some very unusual passenger train workings during the war, some connected with the special war traffic, and others brought about by the consequences of enemy action. One such service was the Cornish Riviera Express. Under normal circumstances this express train would travel from Exeter to Penzance, via Truro and Bodmin Road, but at certain times during the war it was forced to make a lengthy detour at Truro and join the Southern in order to avoid Plymouth when it was being heavily attacked. From Boscarne Junction the re-routed train went onto Wadebridge (where a reversal was required) before it continued via Launceston and Okehampton, eventually rejoining the Great Western at Exeter St David's station.

However, the re-routing of this train was no easy matter particularly due to a steep gradient at Delabole which limited passenger trains on the North Cornwall line to a maximum of eight coaches and even then a 20-ton brake-van had to be attached at the rear. Great Western trains were often far longer than eight coaches and on many occasions they had a 20-ton brake-van at the front and one of 16-tons behind. So there had to be some means of rearranging the trains, and inevitably long delays occurred at Wadebridge (although these long waits were, however, useful to some people who would use the opportunity to go into the town to find food). The plan was initially in force from April 21st to April 26th, and again from 29th April until May 2nd 1940, although it was again employed in May 1941 when the Plymouth area came under heavy enemy attack. Finally the arrangement was again instituted in the summer of 1944, when it was felt essential to keep all unessential traffic away from the lines in the Plymouth area that were congested with 'Overlord' traffic.

To summarise the levels of the military passenger traffics we might consider just that which passed between the Southern and the GWR during the period of conflict, in order to give some impression of the overall scale of things. Personnel trains, numbered 30,890 carrying 9,367,886 servicemen and 582,005 prisoners of war. Ambulance train journeys were also staggering and these amounted to 1,797 workings starting at either GWR or Southern stations and carrying 408,051. The GWR also played a significant part in transporting a large percentage of the 6,269,160 service personnel that were carried on ordinary trains during the war, whilst special leave trains saw the carriage of a further 978,961 servicemen and women. Even more detailed arrangements were made for the transportation of USA Army personnel and stores that were joining the GWR at Birkenhead and the Bristol Channel ports.

Actually, the Americans had rather a forceful way of pressing their demands on the railways, who believed that the British railways (most often the GWR) should jump to their whims and orders at very, very short notice. They also had a way of announcing the arrival of military personnel at the ports, but these often tended to turn up with more baggage than would be expected of a British army unit, and so two or three times the number of trains and coaches had to be used to move the Americans to their new camps. The sudden demand for 48 special trains to be run in just three days pressed a heavy burden on the LMS and GWR, when American troops were to be moved from the Mersey and South Wales ports into the Midlands. On the 25th January 1944 the American authorities decided that (after just one hour's notice) a train load of soldiers which had been sent from Lisbon to Glastonbury had actually been sent in the wrong direction, and 50% of them should have actually gone to Bury St Edmonds. As a consequence a request was sent out to the Railway Executive to halt the train midway, at Gloucester, and make hasty arrangements with the Great Western and the LNER to divert half of the coaches through Oxford, Bletchley and Cambridge.

The differences in passenger traffic on the GWR during the war years is already covered in the text, from where it will be appreciated that the level of passenger numbers increased substantially. Whether these were express services down to the West Country like the one pictured above passing through Sonning Cutting, or a more humble working like the 0-6-0PT and two coach train which is seen below passing over the GWR's most impressive viaduct (at Crumlin), they all contrived to play their part in carrying the increasing number of people who needed to travel around Britain during the war years. In fact, it should be stated that the annual person's rail journey distance during the war years increased by a staggering 1100%.
Photos: Both GWR Official

Above:

A problem for the GWR in the early stages of the war was the requisition (by the Ministry of Supply) of a large number of Dean Goods 0-6-0's for use in France as the 'secondary goods' locomotive type on railways supplying the 'front lines'. In World War I, 62 GWR 0-6-0s had been sent to France, with 16 of these then later shipped to Salonika. By the start of 1939 many of the surviving members of the Dean Goods class that were still employed on the GWR found themselves being replaced by the new Collett 2251 class 0-6-0's. Even so it was 100 of the Dean Goods that were requisitioned and not one of the GWR's newer types. This left a tremendous shortfall of locomotives on the GWR and a variety of types were imported from other railways to fill the gap that the Dean Goods left. One of the companies that came to their assistance, by supplying 0-6-0 freight locomotives, was the LMS who loaned a variety of types including No.3196 which is pictured at Reading with a long freight train around 1943.

Photo: The late M.W.Earley

Freight Traffic

A special civilian traffic which came about because of the war was that of the Anderson shelters which we described in the preceding chapter. Whilst all the railways had a share in this traffic, a large proportion of it fell upon the GWR as two-thirds of the country's sheet steel manufacturing works were in areas served by the company. A large portion of the completed shelters went naturally to London, and by September 1939 1,303,401 shelters had been distributed from depots at Acton, Paddington and South Lambeth. In the local distribution the company's fleet of mechanical horses were strengthened by units from other towns, as air-raid accommodation capable of sheltering 8,000,000 people was trailed around the streets of the capitol. The extent of the growth of general freight traffic can be taken in comparisons between 1938 and 1942, for example in 1942 the GWR ran 725,000,000 loaded wagon miles, which was an increase of 165,000,000 mile, a significant rise of 30%.

In an earlier chapter we have discussed how the coal traffic fell away from the South Wales ports in the Depression, and only a modest percentage of this valuable export business had actually returned at the end of 1938. Yet, here were acres of dock and wharves which could be used to good effect if war actually broke out. In comparison with the ports and docks in the territory of the Southern and LNER railways, the GWR facilities were of limited naval use (although we should state that this is merely a generalisation as some docks did have specific applications in this regard). It was obvious that their use would lay in the handling of merchant shipping, and it was thus decided that the railways and docks in the Bristol Channel could be profitably employed in the handling of trans-Atlantic shipping, but the years of depression had taken their toll on the infrastructure.

For example, in the Newport District alone 164,000 new chair keys had to be fitted to replace those taken from semi-deserted lines and sidings by local people who were too poor to buy firewood. Fences and gates had similarly vanished, but it was the state that the cranes and wharves had degenerated to that caused the most concern. So, to handle the huge flow of imports that would be directed into South Wales, the GWR ordered 52 new cranes from both its own workshops at Swindon and from outside contractors. As a short-term measure other cranes were removed from ports on the Thames, or other semi-redundant commercial facilities on the eastern and southern costs. Floating cranes were also improvised from Thames barges which were paired up and then fitted with redundant quay-side cranes which came from a variety of locations. By 1943 one 60-ton and seven 50-ton floating cranes were busy alongside the single 100-ton floating crane which had been built for the GWR in 1938.

One of the new traffic flows that came to these ports was oil, and it came in progressively larger quantities as the war went on. Now to convey this substance from the terminal where it was unloaded at Swansea Docks to the refineries at Avonmouth, proved a major problem as there was a great degree of reluctance on the part of the GWR to take the frequent trains of block oil tank cars through the single-bore, four mile-long Severn Tunnel. As a consequence Operation Pluto was designed and construction of an oil pipe line from South Wales; it went along the bed of the Bristol Channel to North Devon and thus circumvented the vulnerable bottleneck. It was a task which was also aided by the Southern Railway who conveyed hundreds of tons of steel pipe to the shipyard at Appledore. In the meantime oil was sent by a variety of circuitous routes, and some of these were both lengthy and unusual.

Railway men had plenty of interesting things to do during World War II but GWR staff at Gresford were asked to do something that they wouldn't forget in a hurry - move mountains. Well, not mountains really, but practically all of a small, sandy hillside which progressively disappeared from near Wrexham as the war went on. Though people must have wondered how a whole hill could mysteriously vanish without trace, their tongues would have been tied because of the saying "Careless Talk Costs Lives".

In fact, the truth - when it finally came out - was almost as strange as the fiction. It turned out that the sand had been used as ballast for United States and Dominion ships travelling light while returning from the ports of Birkenhead, Liverpool and Manchester. A series of "special" trains were loaded with this sand - around a million tons of it in all - and hauled to Rossett, often at short notice. Much of the sand was left on foreign quaysides once it was dumped by the ships as they re-loaded, although some of it ended up being used in the construction of piers and jetties in America; in all a curious but very resourceful plan!

One of the big problems in the war was a great shortage of coal, not only was there less coal but it was worse in quality and steam coal virtually disappeared. Early in the 1940's firemen found themselves shovelling into the fireboxes of fast travelling express trains, rubbish that they would not have used pre-war to damp down the fires at home before they went to the cinema. It was a problem that grew worse during the war and, in connection with this problem James Milne is reputed to have wrote to a senior official in the Ministry of Supply (Coal, Oil and Fuel) 'the awful supplies we are receiving are compounding the difficulties of extracting speed and carrying heavy loads, and it is impossible to gain tractive effort out of the sweepings of the colliery floor.'

The problem was even more acute for the maintenance staffs (as badly burning engines developed more mechanical problems), and for the shed staff who had to rely on a great deal of skill to get the locomotives cleaned out or fired up and made ready to run again day after day. However it was not just coal that was at a premium, for almost every conceivable commodity was in high demand. For instance, wagon sheets and uniforms which had a normal life-span of up to five years were wearing out in under two, and most of the East London factories that had previously made supplies of both for the GWR had been destroyed in the Blitz.

An interesting element of wartime traffic certainly between 1940 and 1941 lay in the creation of special factories in which the railways were closely involved. The sites that were chosen had to be within an hour or two's journey of a major city, and preferably a distance that would make the running of special workmen's trains an easy task. In most cases railwaymen were actually consulted about the provision of services before a decision about a War Factory site was actually made. In some of the instances they actually protested and secured alternative locations, but in other instances they were not consulted at all, and it was usually in these locations that the greatest transport problems eventually arose.

These factories and a mushrooming number of satellite facilities began to grow all over the country in the early stages of the war. Somewhere or other the munitions that were going to be used during the war had to be made in vast quantities, and no site could ever be equal if all the objections were allowed to be given full weight.

We will look at the example of a factory that was built on the Great Western in South Wales, roughly between the stations at Pencoed and Bridgend. It was in a very good position for the supply of coal, and raw materials, such as steel, bricks, plus a variety of other items. Cardiff was just 16 miles to the east, Swansea 26 miles to the west and the chances of attack by air were (incorrectly) thought to be relatively slight. A good supply of labour was known to be in the locality, and this proved to be the case as 27,000 men and women eventually became the total workforce (plus a further 10,000 employed in ancillary work).

Building of the factory began when engineers started cutting out a hill some miles from the main line, with a view to creating an underground arsenal. Thousands of tons of bricks, concrete, steel, timber, tubes, pipes etc. all had to be brought to the site by railway owned lorries. That was until a branch line was completed so that they could come on the rails themselves. On the other side of the main line, another movement, involved the road haulage of 145,000 tons of material from railheads which began with the heaviest of cargoes coming from mineral trains and ended with light materials such as plumbing, glazing, lighting and heating equipment. The completed factories filled an area of four square miles. They took three years to build and absorbed twelve million bricks, 300 miles of cable, 20 miles of water pipes and 64 miles of drainage. They were provided with 58 miles of roadway and 24 miles of railway sidings. One can consider that 90% of all this had reached the Bridgend area in freight trains which all had to be taken through the congested paths of the railways at war.

However, that was not the end of the matter because after three years of construction new flows of traffic came on the railway. As we have said 27,000 employees had to be taken to and from their work at the start or end of each day. A new station with four platforms was therefore created with up and down loops, two signal boxes, and screening walls to protect the men and women from machine gun attack by aircraft or bombing. Production began at the factory in early 1940, and by the time it was fully operational it required the running of five workmen's specials a day. But by 1943 58 specials a day were needed, ten of which left at two minute intervals.

They were calculated railway fashion in passenger journeys, but this figure amounted to eighty million people per year. Yet it gives little idea of the actual accumulation of traffic which built up considerably two or three times a day, and when one train departed it was immediately replaced by another. Sixty-four wagons came every day with raw materials, 14 with coal and 51 left with finished munitions. When you consider that every industrial district in Britain contained some larger or smaller equivalent of the Bridgend factory, and perhaps often less conveniently sited, we begin to realise the railways had enough to keep them busy for weeks and years ahead.

Military Traffic

It goes without saying, that all the railways carried large quantities of special military traffic, often very odd trains run at very short notice. Troops, supplies, vehicles, armoured units, ship-wrecked mariners, supplies of bombs, aviation spirit and so on. In fact the list is endless, but as we progress through the next four chapters, we will look at some of the special traffic carried by each company and trust that this will be indicative of the type of work the railways were doing on the Government's account. One of these new types of traffic were patrolling armoured trains which the GWR witnessed in Devon and Cornwall. The armoured trains were conceived as problems grew in Europe and the threat of invasion became a distinct possibility for the British.

As this scenario became increasingly likely, the War Office turned their attention to protecting the country from invasion and the Home Command had to hastily construct new defences. To do this they began to requisition former naval gun barrels that were in store, as well as purchase a number of weapons from ordnance depots in the USA. However these antiquated relics of World War I were of only limited value, and emplacements had to be made to carry them as their former carriages or mountings had long since been scrapped. Yet, constructing a fixed emplacement was a major problem, as this could give a limited area of coverage, and there were simply not enough guns to give total protection of the entire coast line. Therefore a decision was taken to provide some of the guns with a mobile carriage which could get them to the 'invasion area' as quickly as possible.

Unfortunately the tanks that were then available in Britain were mostly equipped with just machine guns, and thus useless against the Nazi armoured divisions that would inevitably be sent across the Channel in support of an invasion. Accordingly, a suggestion was made that armoured trains be formed up as they had been during World War I, and these then sent to the likely invasion areas. At the time the army's Southern Command felt that, in addition to the channel coast area and East Anglia, the most likely place for invasion would be the West Country so three trains were transferred to patrol most of the secondary lines in Devon and Cornwall.

As stated in *Britain's Railways At War* 'It was of concern to the officer commanding the South West, Lt. General Alexander, that the Germans might make an attack on the river estuaries which bit deep into both the northern and southern coasts of the isthmus. A successful raid by a relatively small force could easily have cut off the slender road and rail links, providing the enemy with a toe-hold in Cornwall which it would be difficult to remove them from.

Of particular concern was the Camel estuary, so the line between Wadebridge and Padstow became a major patrol route. Another danger point, the Fowey River was less easy to patrol due to stabling difficulties, but at least once a week the Wadebridge train made an extended trip on the GWR line through Bodmin, Lostwithiel, Fowey, Par and St. Blazey to Newquay. In Devon Train A was ready for action up the Teign Estuary or between Brixham and Kingswear, whilst Train F was up at Barnstaple, running regularly between Ilfracombe and Torrington.' No invasion came, but the trains continued their patrols until the danger eventually passed.

Concrete Sleepers

Concrete sleepers were still in the experimental stage at the start of the war, but the timber shortage led to a search for alternative materials to lay British railway tracks on. Steel had been tested but the steel shortage soon put paid to that idea, so both the GWR and SR began to develop the idea of concrete sleepers. Reinforced concrete was easier to get, and many miles of sidings were re-laid with either concrete through-sleepers, whilst sleeper blocks were used elsewhere (such as in the DN&S expansion scheme). Although these new sleepers were seen to be heavy and difficult to work with, they were thought to be worth having if they had a much longer life-expectancy or lower maintenance cost than traditional wooden sleepers. It was assumed that some designs would probably suit secondary lines, or sections where train speeds were not high, and the likely cost in purchase and maintenance of the new sleepers would be the governing factor in their use. The average weight of a wooden sleeper was 237lbs, but a ferro-concrete sleeper, complete with its two chairs and bolts, was 550lbs (more than twice as much). However, the GWR's design of reinforced-concrete pot-sleepers weighed 246lbs, not much heavier than a traditional wooden one.

Evacuees

Below:
Bearing the official caption, as approved by the Government's Censorship Department, the picture below shows 'the evacuation facilities provided for the Great Western Railway staff. The railways carry on as normal from the safety of an English racecourse station.' The office was in fact provided at Newbury in one of the GWR's attractive excursion coaches. Each member of staff was provided with a table and four seats allowing adequate room for their work. The luggage racks became filing cabinets and blackout curtains were provided on the windows.
Photo: GWR Official

The extent and scope of the evacuation of London is detailed elsewhere in this book, but it should be said that the GWR played a major role in getting vulnerable members of society out of the city. It was not only people who moved in the evacuation however, as meat, butter and tea were shifted from warehouses and docks in the Port of London. We can also reveal that, just as in World War I, once again it was the GWR that became involved in the conveyance of much of the nation's valuable resources, including some 'special' packing cases that were sent to South Wales where they were taken down into disused coal mines. If any one can shed light on what these valuable and secret traffics were, a number of financial historians would like to know. Hospitals were also evacuated and 34 quickly improvised ambulance trains were used to move casualties and the long term ill to clearing stations out of the enemy attack zone.

On 19th June, 1940 the Government decided to demilitarise the Channel Islands, and the RAF and Army packed up their equipment and returned to England (mostly via Weymouth and Portland). This was followed by a voluntary evacuation scheme for women and children, and by 28th June the evacuation was completed. The GWR's Weymouth boats were supplemented in this work by five Southern Railway cargo steamers from Dover, and these vessels enabled 8,000 people to leave Jersey; 17,000 from Guernsey; and 1,500 from Alderney. Another flood of refugees arrived on the GWR and Southern railways in August 1940, mostly at Southampton and Plymouth, this time coming from as far afield as Gibraltar where civilians were repatriated back to the United Kingdom. The Southern railway had initially been given the responsibility of moving these people to safe reception camps in Essex and Suffolk, a task in which the GWR would have had little involvement. However, before the ships arrived it was decided that these zones also were in a danger area and that passengers should be re-deployed to the Midlands and Wales.

What became known as the 'second evacuation' was a task in which the GWR were heavily involved, and it came about after the threat of invasion became a real worry for the authorities. Naturally they decided to relocate evacuees from potential trouble spots on the south and east coast, and these were to be moved as far west as could be arranged. The evacuation took place in June 1940 and it required the removal of 48,000 children into the West Country, Wales and the Midlands. Eight days later an even bigger move was announced, as 100,000 children from London were removed to Berkshire, Somerset, Devon, Cornwall and Wales. These were to be carried between the 12th and 18th June. The Southern carried some of these along its 'Long Withered Arm' which reached down into Devon and Cornwall and they were asked to move 42,391 children in 84 trains beginning at Waterloo, Vauxhall, Clapham, Junction, Earlsfield and Wimbledon. However, many of the trains were handed over to the GWR at the same interchange points that had been used in the Dunkirk evacuation traffic. It was a precision operation in railway terms, and far more logically arranged than the initial evacuation of 1939, even though far less 'official' planning had been put in to it. In fact, along with three Southern Railway clerks who had, in peace time, been responsible for organising race meeting specials, it was the efficiency of GWR traffic planners that made the whole thing work so well. Indeed, on the back of one train from Reading carrying 317 children and 32 adults was chalked the slogan 'Leave It To The Railways'.

Another form of evacuation noted in the south-west of England, and particularly on lines served by the GWR, was the removal of large numbers of people from their homes, farms and businesses in the Devonshire countryside. With the American's demanding even more manoeuvring grounds and training areas, families had to sacrifice their homes and a great deal of baggage and furniture had to be relocated. Where farms were evacuated the machinery, horses, cattle, pigs and poultry were moved en masse. Now the area from which the relocation was taking place was not intersected by railways, and in the first stages of migration a lot of the work was affected by road lorries belonging to the railway companies. However it threw a great deal of the burden of traffic onto the branch line at Kingsbridge, and the main line from London to Plymouth, particularly where it passed through the section between Totnes and Brent. This transfer was accomplished quite rapidly, and only a few rebels remained, but they were soon packed off to grumble elsewhere; in their stead the deserted fields and beaches began to tremble to the roar of Sherman tanks and the crashing sound of American artillery.

Defence Programmes & Air Raids

One of the most outstanding features of the war was the way the railways kept on running, even during heavy air raids. Commendable efforts of footplatemen and shed crews are recorded on all the railways, but as the GWR handled the problem in their usual efficient way, we might consider how sheds on this system dealt with the blackout and still kept their engines in steam. Normally sheds and adjoining yards would be illuminated brightly during the hours of darkness, but in times of war this was clearly impossible. Subdued lighting systems were therefore introduced, but even these were controlled by a master-switch which could be 'pulled' at a moment's notice when danger threatened. Naturally, this threw more of a burden on to shed staff members to carry out work in daylight hours, and many boilermakers, fitters and cleaners who had previously worked nights transferred on to daylight shifts. Most worked appreciably longer hours.

For those who had to work at night, groping around a darkened shed was no easy matter, as obstacles and pitfalls were literally ever-present. The problem was partially resolved by painting doorways, window frames, steps, inspection-pit edges and so on with whitewash. This was all right whilst it was fresh and new, but the paint soon became dirty and obscured and the men resorted to groping around until the next time the paint brushes came out. Another problem of the blackout, particularly in London depots, was an almost total paranoia about the exposure of any naked light, therefore elaborate lengths were undertaken to extinguish all the little fires which occurred naturally at a steam locomotive depot. For example when a fire was cleaned out, and hot ashes dropped on to the track, standing orders were in place for the resulting glow to be quenched by buckets of water.

Oddly enough, it was not London or Birmingham that was to suffer the first surprise raid on the GWR, but the port of Swansea in South Wales. At 10am on the morning of 11th July 1940 a group of men were working on the King's Dock, when they saw a French aircraft approaching low over the waters. Thinking it to be an ally the men waved in salute at its approach, but on its passing the German crew of the captured bomber had slaughtered eleven of those unsuspecting workers and injured several more. Swansea was frequently raided in the months that followed and it seems to have been almost purposefully singled out by the Germans. (In fact it was the only one of the South Wales ports that was heavily attacked despite the strategic value of the many places along that particular coast). The raids in February 1941 caused even more devastation, with the main stations being cut off completely from the outside world.

Another unlikely location to receive the enemy's attention was the station and engine shed at Newton Abbot in Devon. In August 1940 a sneak evening raid by three aircraft bombed and strafed the railway before the alarm had even been raised. So severe was this bombing that 0-6-0PT No.2785 was that badly damaged it had to be cut up on the spot; an even more serious loss might have been sustained to No.6010 had not a bomb that landed nearby failed to detonate. Fourteen died in the raid, four of whom were railway staff, but the relic of Brunel's broad gauge railway, the locomotive *Tiny* which stood on a plinth on the station platform, escaped unharmed.

We could talk at length about the effects of the Blitz on London, but as we will later concentrate on this in our overview of the LNER and Southern lines in the capital, we will pass over the subject with almost indecent haste for the moment. However before doing so we could at least pay some attention to Paddington station which had been the subject of extensive air-raid precautions in 1939. For instance, the large overall roof had been denuded of its glass sheeting just before the hostilities really began; it was fortunate that such works had been undertaken, because a stick of three bombs landed outside the station in October 1940. Coming down in Praed Street, by the company's hotel, at least one penetrated into the London Underground station on the Inner Circle line below causing severe damage and many casualties.

As the war drew on, Birmingham (by this time the nation's second city) acted as a magnet for the German bomber crews, and the city was deluged with bombs over a prolonged period. The raids which started in the autumn of 1940 were almost continuous through the dark nights of the winter and into the spring of 1941, with lines being severed and services disrupted with frequent regularity. On the night of 24th-25th October the GWR suffered some of its heaviest losses of rolling stock and road vehicles during the war, with 75 goods wagons and 24 horse-drays being destroyed in just one night. Then, just five days after the infamous raid on Coventry, it was the turn of Birmingham to be blitzed on the night of 19th-20th November 1940.

A remarkable escape was the best way of describing the circumstances which followed the explosion of a bomb directly ahead of a passenger train which had come to a halt at Keyham signal box near Plymouth on 4th March 1941. As the crew waited for the boards to come off, they heard the tell-tale whine of a bomb falling from above. They jumped clear just in time, for as the bomb landed it blew the engine and tender clear from the tracks. Unbelievably, the train of coaches behind it were not in the least harmed, except for a few cracked or broken windows. Some sections of the GWR were relatively free from enemy attack, even though they were located in districts heavily bombed by the German Luftwaffe. For example, Bristol Temple Meads station was never seriously troubled nor traffic substantially disrupted, despite the cruelly devastating attacks which destroyed large numbers of houses in the poorer parts of the city.

Tragedy At Exeter

Whilst hit and run warfare was making life in Kent, Sussex and the south of England very difficult at times, cities like Exeter in the far west seemed relatively secure. However between 1am and 4am on the morning of Monday, 4th May 1942 this historic cathedral city was badly damaged and sorely wounded as the town centre was gutted. Quite a number of bombs fell on the town including several oil bombs and incendiaries.

Fortunately only very few actually fell on the railway itself. The first two of these were however delayed action bombs and they buried themselves outside St Thomas' station near City Basin Junction. The military authorities ceased traffic, and it was two days before they were able to resume it. Meanwhile GWR trains from London and Taunton had to run to St David's and then run back onto the connecting line at Cowley Junction to be able to reach Plymouth and the west. The third bomb that landed on Exeter's railways came down on the Southern's line between Exeter Central and Lion's Hall Halt, it too landed at 1:15am in the morning and although it narrowly missed a tunnel mouth, it severed both the up and down main roads. A very tragic example that happened during this particular time was an incident that took place at 6:05a.m. the same morning, a woman porter (who had been booked to start duty at 6am) came to the Station Superintendent to say that 'her brother had been killed when a bomb had hit her home in the city and she was very sorry to be five minutes late for duty because of the delay.'

Right:
A typical war-time scene on the GWR as 0-6-0PT No. 3727 approaches London in March 1942 carrying loads of timber for use in the 'Emergency Housing Repair Scheme' that was implemented for the restoration of the fabric of houses lightly damaged in the Blitz. To the rear (right) of the picture similar wagon loads of wood will be seen in the goods yard, whilst an emergency breakdown train is seen on the left near the engine sheds.

The nearest the railways of Bristol came to mass destruction was on 24th November 1940 when heavy raids rained down high explosives and incendiaries. The ticket office at Temple Meads was destroyed after one flammable device lodged behind a clock and went undetected until it set alight all the buildings alongside Platform No. 9. An exceptionally large bomb struck an embankment on the line to Bath, and it caused such devastation as to block the line for a period of no less than three weeks. A few days later (on 6th December) a moving train was bombed as it headed from Bristol to Salisbury behind a Churchward mogul.

Whilst mentioning the blitz, we should also recall that on many occasions drivers on the GWR (and elsewhere come to that) continued their day to day operations even in the heaviest of attacks. It was general policy to keep trains moving, goods at 10 mph and passengers at 15 mph at night, and 15 mph and 25 mph respectively in daylight hours. Naturally this was the logical thing to do, as a moving target is obviously harder to hit than a stationary one. Experience showed the value of this policy, and generally speaking the attacks on moving trains (or incidents of damage occurring in front of them) were the exception rather than the rule.

Ancillary Services

As with all the other members of the Big Four the Great Western Railway continued to maintain a large number of services auxiliary to the main operation of actually running railway trains. These might be divided into three principal subheadings: first of all came road activities, then hotels and catering, and finally shipping. The air services which the railway operated, had (of course) been withdrawn at the outset of hostilities. Turning to road vehicle activities there were quite evident problems at the start of the war because petrol supplies were at something of a premium and as a consequence of this there was actually a fall in the number of vehicles employed by the company between 1939 and 1945. Yet the GWR were actually something of an anomaly in this respect because the road vehicle fleets of all the other members of the Big Four increased on their pre-war totals, with the LMS and LNER doing particularly well in the expansion of its cartage by purchasing more and more mechanical horses.

We move now to the subject of hotels and other catering services offered by the railway, for here the GWR was to suffer a very mixed bag of fortunes. As will be appreciated all the restaurant cars were originally withdrawn at the start of the war, and whilst there were some partial restorations of catering services a few months later, by the end of December 1941 almost all these services had been withdrawn again, and this time for the duration. Travellers still had to eat however, and as a consequence a great deal of thought was put into station catering services.

The GWR's shipping fleet during the war were to provide a continuation of the pre-war service even though many of the vessels were requisitioned for war use. Obviously a number of the services that the company operated before the outbreak of hostilities, could no longer be continued whilst war was progressing. Notably affected were those to the Channel Islands which ceased completely from the 28th June 1940, and did not resume again until the autumn of 1945. Of the vessels that had previously plied between Weymouth and the Channel Islands, the *St. Julien*, had been requisitioned as a troop carrier (but was later converted to a hospital ship). The *St. Helier* was initially transferred to the Fishguard route, but it was shortly afterwards taken over for Government service and it operated from Southampton carrying troops across to France, notably to the ports of Cherbourg and Le Havre. At the same time the vessels *St. David* and *St. Andrew* were transferred from the Irish Sea and were also converted into hospital ships.

At the time of Dunkirk all these four ships were involved in the evacuation of the BEF along with the cargo vessels *Roebuck* and *Sambur* which had also been employed on the Channel Island cargo services. During that May/June the *St. Helier* made around seven trips to Dunkirk and was involved in two collisions in the English Channel during the operation. Another vessel that set out to assist in the Dunkirk evacuation was the tiny little vessel *Mew* which was usually employed on the River Dart between Dartmouth and Kingswear. However by the time she had arrived at Dover the evacuation was virtually complete and the authorities decided it was safer for her to stay in home waters. After Dunkirk the *Roebuck* and the *Sambur* were actually employed in Operation Aerial (the evacuation of Brittany) but on their approach to St. Valery both vessels were engaged by enemy gunners and badly damaged as a consequence.

The *St. Patrick* returned to the Irish Sea services after its short period as a troop transporter and worked the service between Fishguard and Rosslare. For most of the time this went without incident but twice in 1940 she was attacked by enemy bombers. Whilst this did not result in serious damage, on the morning of the 13th June, 1941, it was far less lucky. As the vessel neared Fishguard at the end of a journey from Rosslare, it was dive bombed and sunk. Out of the large compliment of crew and passengers, there were just 66 survivors. Although closely associated with the GWR services across the Irish Sea, the *St. Patrick* was in fact owned by the Fishguard & Rosslare Railways & Harbours Company. Another vessel on the Irish service was the *Great Western* which operated to Waterford until April 1944. During her service she was twice attacked by enemy aircraft but managed to keep safe until her call up for use as a D-Day troop ship.

We have already mentioned that several of the Great Western's vessels were converted as hospital ships, and during the summer of 1943 three of these were moved to the Mediterranean Sea where they were used in connection with the Italian and Sicilian campaigns. Unfortunately on 24th January 1944 the *St. David* was bombed and sunk whilst approaching the beach head at Anzio. Fortunately the *St. Andrew* was nearby and she went to the rescue of the survivors. Yet the *St. Andrew* did not escape unscathed from this campaign either, for in the summer of 1944 it was damaged by a mine and only just able to reach the port of Taranto from where it was patched up and returned to Britain for repair.

Finally we move to the Normandy invasions where once again three Great Western vessels were used by the Allied forces during the invasion of the beaches. The vessels were the *St. Helier*, *Roebuck* and *Sambur*, of these the two former Channel Island cargo vessels were used extensively by the Royal Engineers in connection with the building of a temporary harbour near Arromanches. Finally we might mention the *St. Julien* which was employed in the English Channel after the D-Day invasions when her role as a hospital ship was invaluable in repatriating the wounded from France. During this service the *St. Julien* was twice damaged, on both occasions quite badly, once by a mine and on the second occasion by a collision with another vessel.

Above:

By 1939 the GWR had already worked miracles in developing mechanisation in its road services, so it is understandable that its total of vehicles fell by around four hundred during the period from 1939 to 1945. Yet despite the diminishing number of vehicles, the actual work of the fleet was considerably enhanced. One of these activities was the transportation of Anderson shelters from factories in Wales to major cities like Birmingham, London etc. At first it was felt that the railways had been given an unfair advantage in being awarded this traffic, and the road lobby succeeded in getting a question asked about this in Parliament on 23rd March 1939. Yet, on investigation it soon emerged that large-scale shelter distribution could only be fairly and effectively achieved by the railways.

Photo: GWR Official

Emergency Canteens

Early in 1939 the railways identified a potential problem in feeding members of staff, particularly those involved in breakdown or war damage work which might require their being away from home for a long period of time in order to get traffic moving again. Accordingly the GWR, along with a number of other companies, introduced emergency mobile canteens. These canteens were provided in two guises, one of which was based on a mechanical horse that carried a container converted as a mobile kitchen, the other was in an old clerestory coach which was lettered as 'emergency canteen' and provided with gas lighting and all manner of items that were considered essential to feed the men in the field.

Workshops At War

It is very difficult to generalise about the variety of work that was undertaken by the railway workshops on the war account. The list of orders is endless, and things made for the armed forces at even just one factory or workshop could have run into hundreds or thousands of items, plus the conversion of standard parts for other purposes. The numbers are rather wearying to the mind, for example the Southern Railway made 360,000 tank components, whilst another LMS factory produced something like fifteen million cannon shells, and so on. At one period during the war the 35 railway workshops, who were undertaking work for the government, had nearly 20,000 members of staff engaged on this work. However it is perhaps of interest to report that a lot of the war work was in fact started well before the outbreak of war itself.

Roughly speaking factories during peace time, and this includes railway workshops, can reckon on working both men and plant for between eight to ten hours a day. Some may work up to sixteen hours a day, and out of the twenty-four this leaves a reasonable margin of time for expansion by adding another shift. However as for the railway workshops, by 1940 most of them were working twenty-four hours a day. All of them were directly needed for war purposes, so they were using up their reserves of both time, energy and machinery. They were therefore absorbing three to four times as much raw materials and turning out the equivalent in increased production, but this situation could not last for long. The railways were working to full capacity, seven days a week and, the margin of unused time was exactly nil. The GWR works could therefore, only carry on by using up limited time and resources which meant that other essential railway work (such as repairs) might build up to nightmare pressures. But build to nightmare pressures they did, and when it is considered that tanks, midget submarines, landing craft, guns, bombs, searchlights, aircraft parts, naval guns and all manner of other items were produced it is hardly surprising that essential railway work suffered.

Some of the more interesting items made at Swindon works included cudgels for the Home Guard. These were actually pieces of old boiler tube that were filled with lead and beaten at the end and fitted with a small rubber handle, which was in fact a bicycle handle bar grip. Another problem that Swindon resolved was the lack of keys for American aeroplanes which were arriving in Great Britain for use by the RAF. Unfortunately the Americans had decided not to send any keys to open the doors on the aircraft, so one of these doors was promptly removed and sent to the Swindon works with an RAF officer, and a master key was cut and these were than repeated by the score and sent to the Royal Air Force for circulation. Again amongst the other odd things was a new chain for a dough mixer that was used in making bread for the army. Meanwhile repairs were carried out to a New Zealand forestry unit's machinery and, oddest of all, battered dodgem cars from a funfair which was part of the 'holidays at home' programme.

Freight Traffic

In the space available it would be absolutely impossible even to recount a small fraction of the LMS freight activities between 1939 and nationalisation. Indeed, the huge increase in freight traffic placed a considerable burden on the LMS during the war years, and in common with our view of the other companies we can show the extent of this growth in traffic by comparing figures for loaded wagon miles in 1938 and 1942, for example in 1942 the LMS ran a massive 1,713,000,000 loaded wagon miles, a substantial jump from the last pre-war annual total by 435,500,000 miles and an increase of 82$\frac{1}{2}$ million on 1941's figure. Around 300,000 rail wagons were being used each week in the LMS area alone during the war, to move the freight starting its journey in that territory. Freight locomotives were kept really busy in 1942, doing 121 million miles that year, again an increase of 3$\frac{1}{2}$ million miles on 1941 and all of 19,000,000 miles up on 1938 when not as much vital freight had to "get through". We can give one specific example of how great traffic grew on the LMS, when we consider the case of Liverpool. Despite the severity of the enemy action against the port, which we mention in a little while, it can be revealed that in 1944 the city was handling four times the amount of freight traffic that it had in 1938.

An other interesting facet of war-time freight traffic was noted in the way trains were handled at Carlisle. Prior to 1939 it had long been the practice to make up Anglo-Scottish freight trains as rough sets, which were then sorted at one of Carlisle's many goods yards. This was a time-consuming practice, and it meant that much sorting and inter-yard trips had to be made between the various yards as had been done prior to 1923. Grouping had made some changes to this practice, but it had hardly dented the problem until wartime rationalisation and block trains, coupled with the pooling of private-owner wagons, made much of this sorting a thing of the past. Thereafter trains were made up in sets at their originating stations, and sent through Carlisle to their destination. Despite an overall 345% increase of traffic through the Border City, shunting miles actually decreased by 15% on pre-war totals. However, there was something of a counter side to this saving in effort, as the LMS had to spend around £350,00 on improving accommodation for enginemen at Dumfries, Kilmarnock and Law Junction, as through working increased the demand for overnight lodging and crew refreshments at these locations.

As the war progressed a series of problems to do with the logistic supply of food stocks arose in the country. One of the biggest difficulties was the supply of milk and it was found that with the increasing population in Britain, which was swelled by the American and Commonwealth forces, there was simply not enough of it to go around. As a consequence of this a substantial volume of milk was brought over from Northern Ireland. This averaged around 20,000 gallons a night to meet the needs of milk in Scotland. It was a supply of traffic that was carried on the Cairnryan ferry and brought into the military port there. However, it was a flow that was also prejudiced by the heavy build-up of war materials, military stores and personnel that were coming in via the same route. So at an early stage in the supply of this produce, it was decided that the problem necessitated the establishment of a new district control centre at Stranraer, along with new lines, signals and improvements to the junctions with the lines to Dumfries and to Glasgow.

Whilst in Scotland we should emphasise the exceptional levels of freight traffic which the LMS handled on Clydeside as part of its receipt of 'foreign aid' (both civilian and military), which was over and above the troop movements mentioned earlier. Freight traffic on Clydeside was equally shared by the LMS and LNER and both faced the same problems. The movement of traffic between ship, lighter and rail on the Clyde had, for many years, meant the use of horse and carts. However, with the coming of hostilities the problem of cartage was acutely felt in an area that was both densely built up and very hilly in places. The narrow streets and steep banks between the docks and the main goods depots or stations was a major problem, so motor vehicles were increasingly utilised as horses were unable to cope. Accordingly, all the mechanical horses and trailers that could be spared were sent to the city. Furthermore the LMS and LNER purchased or hired every motor lorry they could get their hands on, as they struggled to carry an annual 1.2 million tons of freight that were previously transhipped by horse wagon or local shunting trips.

Another of the major problems which the LMS began to face during the war was the amount of extra parcels traffic that they had to carry. In wartime economy is at a discount and as one official report said, 'Manufacturers, traders and commercial enterprises tell themselves that if they save small sums of money they will only lose them in excess profit duty, and so the extra costs that were involved in sending packages by express parcel train rather than by the more normal wagon load or sundries freight of train services soon became epidemic.'

Above:
A scene at Toton Marshalling Yard on the eve of the Second World War, showing the top of the new 'hump' and the control station located there,
Photo: LMS Official

Below:
One of the prime freight movers on British railways during World War II was the Stanier 8F, which was picked by R.A. Riddles as the War Department's standard heavy freight locomotive type. Although there were many who viewed this choice as a partisan action by Riddles, his decision was clearly justifiable as the 8F proved itself adequate in every respect. Here doyen of the class, No.8000 is seen just before the outbreak of war in an official picture.

By mid 1941 railway stations all over the country (and particularly on the LMS) had parcels were stacked up on platforms awaiting trains that were already overloaded with increased passenger numbers. The result of this state, at least in commercial circles, had reached the aforementioned epidemic proportions by the end of the year. At this time about a quarter of the platform space at Crewe station was permanently closed to passengers and used for the stacking and sorting of parcels which frequently reached the weight of one ton in place of the regulation one hundred weight that was allowed in the guards vans of carriages that were travelling on the main lines.

By the end of the war in 1945 the guards vans of virtually all passenger trains had been filled to the maximum load possibly permitted, and this necessitated the railways running extra trains (as a second part) if the stock, locomotives and paths could be arranged. Often one or another (and sometimes all three) proved to be impossible, so it resulted in an overall increase of 17% in the size of existing trains to carry this extra parcels traffic. By 1945 this extra 'parcels' traffic had reached 25 to 30 trains a day passing through Crewe alone and in hindsight we can see that Crewe was in no way exceptional. Every large junction station in Britain was experiencing similar problems and many of these difficulties were still in evidence as late as 1947-8. This increase in passenger parcels, however astonishing it may be, was only one of a small number of problems that were nibbling away at the railway's slim margin of rolling stock, running lines and labour. Furthermore, at this time that margin was already being rapidly eaten up by larger scale increases in the transport demands of the military. Yet as 1943 progressed orders were issued from the H.Q. at Euston, that all non-essential traffics be halted and those facilities that were not remunerative be closed, withdrawn or suspended.

Euston were, of course, privy to the classified information regarding the movement of 'O' traffic although they had little idea about the whole D-Day plan at this early stage. Even so what they did know occasioned the withdrawal of a number of ancillary freight services at the end of 1943 or early in 1944. There was nothing for it, something had to give, but few District Superintendents were willing to make sacrifices in their domain, many rightly considering that enough had already been pared away in the lean years of the 1930s. As Britain geared up for the 'second front', the LMS really had to prioritise their efforts in order to maximise their effectiveness. So a number of non-essential services and facilities were abandoned or mothballed including the LMS's trans-Pennine waterway, the Huddersfield Narrow Canal, which paralleled the railways below the hills at Standedge. Although its loss was not a severe one at the time, the lack of maintenance in the years that followed would create severe problems in the autumn of 1946 as we shall relate further on.

Yet, despite all this damage and devastation all services were fully restored by the end of the month (but the town was to suffer another serious raid the following April). So serious was this bombardment that it created a massive degree of dislocation, commencing when two exploded bombs landed in the path of the 9:45pm train from Manchester as it was heading between Nuneaton and Rugby (see inset box). However, five days after the first Coventry raid, the Luftwaffe struck Birmingham and five days after that it was the turn of Bristol. Like the GWR, the LMS facilities in Birmingham were under a continual state of siege in the months that followed. For example, two days after the raid which destroyed the large number of railway wagons and horse drays on the GWR, New Street station was hit on 28th October. The signal box was badly damaged and offices destroyed, and in the following month, platforms at the station were put out of action.

In December, Manchester suffered its worst attacks over the nights of 22nd and 23rd December, and in the midst of this stood the two LMS stations of Victoria and Exchange, between them having the distinction of what was then the longest platform in the world. The raid of high-explosives, delayed action bombs and incendiaries played their part in creating havoc. Approaching Manchester that night was Ken Fretwell who was working as a fireman from Mirfield shed at the time. As his train came down onto Victoria a signalman came out and waved the driver through, despite the fact that all signals were 'on' and a red alert meant that a minimum speed limit had to be obeyed. At the approach of the train, which was carrying a rake of petrol tankers, the 'bobby' came out on to the veranda of his 'box and told the driver to 'open her up and get the h**l out of here'. Just then the first incendiaries began falling, so the driver responded with a will and increased the speed on his ex-Midland Railway 0-8-0. As he cleared the bottom of Miles Platting Bank, the first of the bombs began exploding at the rear of his train, showering the guard's van with pieces of red-hot shrapnel. Unaided, the heavy train assaulted the bank as though the devil was on its tail, and they kept on going through Miles Platting, Thorpes Bank and out into the northern suburbs of Manchester. Railway enthusiast, Peter Hughes, recalled the same event and remembered how the fires that started as the train pulled away quickly consumed everything that would burn.

With the raid now intensifying, the signalmen kept the train moving in order to get it away from the danger zone, and it had green lights all the way to Sowerby Bridge. On reaching t'other side of the Pennines, the crew found that they had come over the summit at an average speed of 40 mph. and the smokebox door was glowing red-hot. Back in Manchester the bombs took out a large section of the roof at Victoria, destroyed the Divisional Control Room, and smashed a water main leading from a reservoir. Water cascaded from the severed artery and flooded out the control room and station, forcing clerks to get out through the emergency exits.

During that same Christmas week 800 enemy aircraft raided Manchester and Liverpool over a seven night period, with uncontrollable fires from the first raid serving as beacons for the enemy as they flew over the Pennines and Manchester to cripple the Mersey. With the railways broken in so many places, and the city completely cut off at every railway exit on two separate dates, nothing could have kept Liverpool running had it not been for the emergency bus services which the railway companies swiftly introduced. As an example of the ferocity of the attacks on the 22 miles of Mersey water-front, we might mention the fire which took hold of the munitions ship SS *Malakand* one evening as it was berthed at Huskisson No. 2 Dock; at 7pm the following evening the fire reached the holds, and the most fearful explosion took place and the whole bow section of the ship was blown through the air for a distance of 2,500 feet (763.36 metres) until it came to embed itself in the rook of the LMS North Dock Goods Station. The dock was completely destroyed, and in the end there was no alternative but to fill in this vitally needed facility.

The Delayed 9:45 From Manchester

Before this train had left the north it had been decided to send it beyond Nuneaton and turn it eastward on the line to Wigston and then south again to Rugby. If you look at your railway map this shows that the journey would add some extra twenty miles and this would be accompanied by a corresponding loss of time; by normal standards this should have been about an hour. But unfortunately this line of diversion was already overburdened with a lot of other military traffic and specials. Even so a path was made for the express train and when it arrived at Edwinstowe it had seats for all its passengers, and it was only eleven minutes behind time. However by this time two more unexploded parachute bombs had been found on the alternative route between Nuneaton and Wigston, and Royal Navy bomb experts had been to look at the problem and forbidden traffic. So there was nothing to be done except to draw the train back to Stoke on Trent and find a new path through Uttoxeter, Burton, and Leicester. The stopping and return to Stoke caused a delay of another hour and a half, and then further diversion was going to add more time to it. Progress according to the newly improvised plan was satisfactory but then another exchange of engine, fireman and driver was not easily managed. When the train finally approached London, there was news of another raid in progress as it came near to Watford and it had to reduce speed to the regulation 15mph, so it was hardly surprising that there were further and prolonged delays. It was even less surprising that the train, that was twice forced from its scheduled path and held up at various places along the way, should have been rushed by a large number of passengers that could be comfortably accommodated in the coaches of other trains just behind it!

Left:
Clearing up at Coventry station, after the raid, necessitated (in the weeks that followed) no less than 105 trains to carry rubble out of the city to a special recycling dump in the West Midlands.

On 10th May 1941, the London terminal station of St. Pancras suffered a devastating enemy raid during broad daylight. Six roads were severely damaged along with five trains and three platforms. Yet despite the devastation shown in the picture above, trains were running into St. Pancras in less than nine hours. A week later the station had undergone temporary repairs, and whilst this foreshortened three of the platforms it was back to business as usual. However, the severity of the raid so dramatically affected the Railway Executive Committee that the official censor was asked to withhold the publication of pictures showing the damage.

Lineside Acres Aid Food Production

One LMS policy which was introduced during the very first year of the war was the permission for farmers (and others) to use areas of lineside ground for agricultural and horticultural purposes. In 1940, for example, the LMS allowed 440 farmers to cut hay on railway embankments. It was an excellent scheme which not only reduced the workload on railway labourers, who would have had to cut or burn long grass growth, but it was also described by the Railway Executive as 'another nail in the enemy's coffin.'

When a bomb struck the Manchester Ship Canal at the city's Canada Dock, the nearby goods station stables were flooded and the goods yard was swamped to a depth that reached almost to the top of the wagon underframes that were standing there. When the water eventually subsided the goods depot was covered in stinking mud, an assortment of curious fish, and a huge steel barge which had later to be cut by welders using oxy-acetylene torches. It was the turn of the Clyde to suffer a devastating raid in March which destroyed no less than 40,000 houses in the poorest parts of the district between the ship yards and the docks. Yet, despite the destruction and mayhem, the city's railways escaped practically unscathed. In many ways, it was an air-raid on 16th April 1941 that was to cause the LMS its greatest blow, despite the fact that it was at Shortlands in Kent in the heart of deepest Southern Railway territory.

To explain this statement we should elaborate that Shortlands was the home of Lord Stamp, the Chairman of the LMS, who had vowed that he would never move from his home whatever the risks. He was often heard to joke that it would take a Nazi bomb to shift him, and that is precisely what happened. His loss was sadly mourned, for Lord Stamp was a national figure of whom it was said 'he was an instance of that very rare phenomenon, a man trained and distinguished in other walks of life, who became a railway expert in middle age.' In the book *Time Table for Victory* Evan John states 'A Civil Servant and statistician, he had no direct contact with transport problems except in the Marine Department of The Board of Trade, until he joined the LMS. He became its Chairman, and combined the post, with that of President of its Executive.'

Yet war marched on, and during the morning of 4th May 1941, it was again the turn of Liverpool to suffer, as over 100 incendiaries fell on the huge marshalling yards at Edge Hill. At Breck Road sidings, about a mile and a half away, the same type of devices had started a large fire in the middle of around 100 wagons holding ammunition. Fortunately, due to the bravery of four railwaymen, an exceedingly dangerous shunting operation succeeded in dragging away whatever could be saved. Yet all this took place in a maelstrom of exploding British ammunition and falling German bombs.

Before leaving the account of the German attacks on the LMS, we might return to an unusual event which occurred on 14th October 1940, and ended a most peculiar dispute when a Nazi bomb landed at London's Broad Street (High Level) station. For over 60 years a piece of left luggage had been in the care of the railway company, in the shape of an eight feet tall fossilised man named Ossian, but called 'Patrick' by the railwaymen, it was the subject of much controversy. Some said the relic, which had been 'discovered' in Ireland was a real giant, others still thought it to be one of the 'nephelim' (or the fabled men of old) that are spoken of in the Bible, yet it was generally accepted that it was a fake carved out of stone in the days of Victorian credulity. As the fake or fossil was starting on a 'Barnum & Bailey' style exhibition tour of Britain, its two 'guardians' became involved in a dispute over ownership. When the matter became an issue before the courts, 'Patrick The Giant' was made a ward of Chancery, and left in the care of the railway company at the Worship Street Goods Depot alongside Broad Street station. However, during the blitz the three ton 'fossil' was smashed beyond repair, and his remains were duly used to fill in one of the bomb craters left behind.

Ancillary Services

The LMS steamers, ferries and cargo ships had a brilliant war record, with most being pressed into useful service in one form or another. On the Clyde the motley assortment of ships were used for all sorts of duties and in addition to minesweeping, they were also used as tenders, to bring ashore tens of thousands of troops from liners anchored in the Clyde. Many of these ships served in the evacuation of Dunkirk, and the 33-year-old *Eagle III* was actually beached for 12 hours so that waiting troops could board her. The *Queen Empress* and *Caledonian* were both credited with bringing down enemy aircraft. The *Duchess of Fife* had steamed over 100,000 miles in war service, including four Dunkirk trips and a spell of minesweeping. Later she was used as a training ship, turning out fifty officers and ratings a week.

The *Duke of York*, from the LMS Heysham-Belfast link, was renamed *Duke of Wellington* for war service which included being an assault ship in the raid on Dieppe. Early in the war she had been used as a troop transporter. At St. Valéry, when in company with the *Princess Maud* evacuating troops under enemy fire, her Chief Officer Mr Williams picked up a live shell that had fallen on deck and threw it back in the sea. This brave act earned him the LMS "Stamp" Medal, and he was also "mentioned in dispatches".

The LMS shipping fleet played an important role in the D-Day landings for example, the *Princess Maud*, which normally served the tranquil Stranraer-Larne route, set sail on 5th June with 380 United States Army engineers aboard, along with twenty tons of explosives and detonation charges that were to be used against enemy beach obstacles on occupied France's northern coast. The *Princess Maud* was the last ship to leave Dunkirk in 1940 - and also the first troop ship to enter Ostend four years later. Up to 6th October 1944, four months after the Invasion, she had carried 16,211 troops to the Normandy beaches. Her master, Captain Clarke, was another LMS officer "mentioned in dispatches".

The *Princess Margaret*, another LMS steamer normally on the Stranraer-Larne service, served as a Commando ship in the "D-Day" Invasion and sailed on a special mission to destroy heavy coastal batteries. Her compliment of commandos landed at dawn on D-Day plus one - 7th June 1944 - and also brought in the staff and nursing sisters who would set up one of the first medical units in Normandy. The Prime Minister, General Smuts and Mr. Bevin watched from the gangway as men of the 2nd Battalion Canadian Scots Rifles climbed aboard the *Duke of Argyle*, which was used as an Infantry Landing Ship at the invasion. Normally this ship worked the Heysham-Belfast service, but in addition to trooping work it had served as a wartime Hospital Carrier ship. The *Duke of Lancaster* and *Duke of Rothesay*, also from the same Heysham-Belfast route, were commandeered as Hospital Ships and brought injured soldiers "Home to Blighty"; between 8th June 1944 and 10th March 1945 the *Duke of Rothesay* sailed 12,697 miles in 62 trips to bring 23,960 casualties home.

Below:
In the main text we have not paid much attention to the railway catering services during the war years; so we might purposefully address that by presenting this picture of the LMS 'Rail Bar' which was provided at Euston station from the start of January 1943. The new facility served tea, coffee, sandwiches, buns and pies as well as cold drinks and biscuits. Capable of serving more than 60 customers a minute from its long counter, the ample provision of staff ensured that travellers were quickly fed and sent on their way. This was just one of the LMS contributions in catering for the comforts of the travelling public and servicemen during the war year. Another was the conversion of part of the St. Pancras hotel into a special restroom and canteen. Put at the disposal of the Salvation Army, the facilities also included a shower room, reading room, games room and quick service counter which also supplied 'take-away' food. As from 10th February 1941, special buffet cars were also provided for the armed forces in trains to and from Scotland. These were situated in the 10am and 1pm trains to Glasgow on Mondays, Wednesdays and Fridays, and in workings at the corresponding times from Glasgow on Tuesdays, Thursdays and Saturdays.

Above:

Despite the diversion of a lot of railway workshop capacity during the war years, a number of railway projects were completed. One such project was the Coronation Class, and our picture here shows No.6244 King George V*, on 27th June 1940 as workers at Crewe prepare the engine for its re-naming ceremony after a change was made from its planned name* City of Leeds *(this name was later given to 6248 which was turned out in 1943). Other members of the class to be turned out in 1940 were* City of Coventry, City of Edinburgh, City of Lancaster*. There then came four members of the class in 1943 and a further quartet in 1944. The five last members of the 38-strong class were turned out after the war, three in 1946, one in 1947 which was named* Sir William A. Stanier F.R.S. *after its designer, and finally No.6257* City of Salford *came out in 1948 after nationalisation. In a period of 15 years, from the introduction of 6200* The Princess Royal *in June 1933, the two main express locomotive classes had been introduced by the LMS. With 50 members being built in total, despite the fact that 40% of this time span was during the war years, it was a significant achievement by any standards!*

Workshops At War

It will be recalled that during the First World War a considerable amount of the Railways Executive's workshop capacity was put aside for the manufacture of munitions and other essential items at the Government's request. Four years of war showed that there had been a considerable pressure placed on this capacity, and above all the ability to do normal railway repair work was severely limited, so it was evident at the start of the Second World War that a similar situation could not be allowed to develop in 1939-1945 as this would prejudice the operation of the railways. Even so in the Second World War the total turn out of munitions alone from the railway workshops was estimated at around £18,000,000 in value.

The size and complexity of the LMS workshops were to ensure they would play an important role in what followed, and as early as the mid 1930s, 'armament projects' were being considered and contingency plans were introduced for the acquisition of railway workshop capacity for military purposes. This diversion of energy was recognised at the time to be a rather dubious one, because the more non-railway work that took place meant that it became harder to keep pace with normal repairs and running work. Official reviews of the position in 1915-16 suggested that there was a risk of this balance being upset and the total effort suffering. However, the output from Railway Munitions Workshops was not reduced, even though there were many that believed that it should have been in the interests of better military transport. It is not difficult to grasp therefore that, when the War Office placed an order for tanks with the railway workshops of the LMS, in 1937, adaptations were made to the way that military equipment was constructed. For example in modern military tanks built in the late 1930's, it will be seen that the turret ring had exactly the same dimensions as many a railway engine's driving wheels.

Actually, the work that the LMS undertook on tanks was quite significant, and although much use was made of standard railway manufacturing machinery and working practices, the railway works became polished producers of these weapons of war. The fact that many of the tanks made by the railways were of dubious functional ability is another matter, for the design principles were imposed on the railways by higher powers. At an early stage in the war the Covenanter tank was being produced in quantity at Derby, and Horwich was working on the 'waltzing' Matilda tank, in fact it actually went on to make 406 of the unwieldy brutes during the course of the war. When it came to the Mk.V Cruiser tank it was something of a different story however, and most of the design work was placed under H. G. Ivatt who was Principal Locomotive Assistant at Derby Works. A section of the drawing office was set aside for the work and a special team of draughtsmen and designers got together under J. W. Caldwell (who later went on to become the company's chief draughtsman). The actual manufacturing of these tanks was initially allocated to Crewe Works, and four per week were being completed by the start of 1941. A constant visitor in the early days was Dr. Merritt who was involved with tank transmissions at the David Brown factory in Huddersfield. This company were served by an LMS goods yard and priority supplies were conveyed on special trains to Crewe, Derby and Horwich on a semi-regular basis.

A large proportion of York's output went to the Navy, including several sixteen-foot motor dinghys (which were tested in the works' static water tank), pontoons, floats and waterproof battery boxes. As D-Day neared, production was switched to components for Horsa gliders that were then delivered to nearby Slingsby; other aero production included parts for Lancaster bombers and Bothas. Sadly part of the carriage workshops were badly damaged by an accidental fire and the facility was not fully repaired until well after the war. Finally, the wagon works at Dukinfield were completely reorganised and fitted up for re-forming old shell cases as well as producing new ones. It should be mentioned that during this period the standard workshop week was in excess of 56 hours, and from 63 to 69 hours on the night shift.

Locomotive construction was confined solely to freight and mixed-traffic types on all the railway companies according to Government instructions, and the LNER was no exception to this. Very early in the war the company received an order for Doncaster and Darlington works to construct over 100 2-8-0s to Stanier's 8F design. However, before long the needs of the LNER began to demand that the production of a new class of reliable mixed-traffic engines would be needed to meet the increasing traffic demands, and the LNER had to decide how it could balance this with the Government restrictions and its occupation of workshop capacity in other war-work. Early in 1942 the prototype of the new 'Antelope class' B1 4-6-0 passed through the works, and shortly afterwards the class L1 2-6-4T emerged for both passenger and freight duties. Over 200 B1s were built between 1942 and 1946, and they were an important step in the LNER's aim for standardisation, as they used the wheel centres of the V2 class and the boilers of the B17's. The L1 was also seen as a first step in standardisation, and Thompson planned for 1,000 of these engines to be built, but this was a dream still-born in the nationalisation of the railways that followed the war.

Meanwhile, the construction of the V2 2-6-2 mixed traffic engines continued, but a series of minor derailments began to occur in regular service which were not fully understood until 1946 when it was found that serious track imperfections were combining with a design fault in the engine's leading pony truck. This reacted seriously with track defects, especially where track cross-levels were out of alignment so all the members of the class were gradually rectified and the class officially relegated to the mixed traffic work they had been designed for.

Below:
October 1942 and work is underway at Darlington on an unidentified member of the B1 'Antelope' class, as the boiler, cylinders and frame of another 4-6-0 come together inside the North Road Works. Interestingly these engines were well liked by the Chief Civil Engineer, especially on the former GER section, where their 'low-hammer blow' was a significant improvement on the B17 class that Gresley had built.

Disasters & Difficult Times

We begin this section, not with an accident but with the loss of a great leader. The LNER was to sustain such a loss at the worst possible moment, as Sir Herbert Nigel Gresley passed away at the age of 64 on Saturday 4th April 1941. Born on 19th June 1876, Gresley was the youngest son of a clergyman and he was educated at Marlborough College before serving an apprenticeship at Crewe. His contribution to the development of the LNER locomotive fleet needs no documentation here, but it is significant to point out that his far-sighted approach to main line traction went far beyond his graceful A4s, the workmanlike V2s, and the many mixed traffic designs that he produced. Just a short time before his death, one of his latest creations, Bo-Bo electric No. 6701 had just been out-shopped and displayed at York station along with *Bantam Cock*. To succeed Gresley, the LNER appointed Mr. Edward Thompson OBE, and transferred the headquarters offices of the Mechanical Engineering Department from London to Doncaster.

Fortunately, the LNER had been free of any major disaster since the terrible accident at Castlecary, and the last reported 'major incident' had been on 1st June 1939 when an ex-GER 'Claude Hamilton' had been in collision with a motor lorry at Hilgay Fen. The next serious incident was the previously mentioned collision at Harold Wood on 10th February 1941, when the 10am express from Liverpool Street to Norwich came to a halt on a 1:100 gradient due to a combination of a heavy load and poor coal supplies which were making steaming difficult. The engine in question, Class B17 No.2828 *Harewood House* was still building up steam when its train was struck in the rear by Class B12 No.8556 which had overrun signals whilst working a Southend express.

On 28th April two special coaches carrying schoolboys back to Ampleforth College were added to the back of the 12.45pm King's Cross - Newcastle train. As the train was running at 55 mph, the communication cord was pulled 8 miles north of Grantham and when the train stopped, the crew found the second of the two coaches to be well ablaze. Fanned by a strong draught from open windows the blaze quickly spread throughout the rear three coaches, and these had to be uncoupled for the rest of the train to be drawn ahead. Sadly six schoolboys lost their lives as these coaches were burnt down to their frames, the consequence of some of the boys carelessly flicking matches around the 3rd class carriages.

The disaster at Harold Wood (shown in the pictures on this page) was a particularly unfortunate event, as it occurred on a line which had been fitted with colour light signals and track-circuiting. With the exception of fitting ATC systems that sounded some form of warning to the driver, it would seem that little else could have been done to prevent this. However, some have suggested that the signalling, which was hurriedly finished off, was badly wired and prone to faults that could mislead drivers.

The following year a serious collision took place at Cowlairs East Junction on 30th January, and twelve days on from this a wagon loaded with steel plates ripped open the side of a passing passenger train at Beighton. Both of these incidents had 'blackout conditions' as one of the contributory causes, and each incident claimed 14 lives, with 71 seriously injured in total. The year continued to provide even more trouble as a bad derailment occurred on the old NER section at Pelton on 20th April and a fatal incident took place in Falkirk Tunnel on 18th June when a group of platelayers were struck by a train. The next year it was the turn of the seaside towns to suffer serious collisions, with the first occurring at Scarborough on 8th August and next at Whittlesea on 11th October. Both of these incidents have, however, been most elusive when it has come to finding photographs.

The year 1944 was one of several severe incidents, the first being a boiler explosion at Thurston on 12th January, then there was the serious collision at Ilford just four days later. As mentioned earlier, the area of Catterick saw a major disaster on 4th February 1944 as a number of wagons containing incendiary bombs, shells and ammunition caught fire in the yard. The indescribable explosion which followed razed the station buildings and the nearby Railway Hotel to the ground, killing the stationmaster and his two female clerks and injuring everyone else in the vicinity.

However, the worst of all was the well known ammunition train explosion which occurred on 2nd June at Soham. Three weeks later yet another ammunition train exploded as it made its way down to Whitemoor Yard, this time it happened as the engine was passing through the Yorkshire countryside near Selby and a number of 500lb bombs exploded, killing the driver of a passing train. The year continued with a derailment at Wood Green on 29th August, a boiler explosion the next day at Sudbury Hill, and an awful collision at Romford on the 29th December. Just seven weeks later, it was the turn of King's Cross to suffer, as a run-back and derailment occurred. Mind you, this was eventually bound to happen sooner or later because of the extreme pressures placed upon the railwaymen working that station, the only wonder was that it did not occur earlier or more often. Even so, as the war came to an end, it left behind it a legacy of worn-out engines, poorly maintained rolling stock and life-expired track which was all to combine with fickle whims of nature and human error, and be part of the process which turned Victory into Defeat.

Both pictures on this page show the result of the tragic accident at Soham in Cambridgeshire, after a wagon load of bombs caught fire and exploded as they were being taken through to White Colne Yard. Despite the bravery of the crew in trying to get the burning wagon away from the rest of the train, which was similarly loaded with high-explosives, it exploded just as the train began to draw away. The fireman and the signalman were both killed and the tiny town was devastated as 14 houses were completely destroyed and 36 more damaged so badly that they were made uninhabitable.

Two faces of the Southern in the 1940's : Pictured above light Pacific 4-6-2 No. 21C154 Lord Beaverbrook at an unrecorded location just after its introduction; meanwhile below a picture of Feltham Yard presents a busy wartime scene with a yard packed with a variety of freight wagons, many of which would be connected with war work.
Photos: Both SR Official

CHAPTER TEN
The Southern at War

As we have already stated the Southern was basically a passenger railway but all that was soon to change, as the balance of traffic increased to something like 50% freight, 50% passengers during the war. From this it will be appreciated that freight increased enormously but this was not at the expense of passenger traffic, which after a slight drop, eventually recovered to post-war levels. In fact so great was this overall increase that it reached a point where it almost overwhelmed the Southern Railway system, or at least threatened to, although it never quite did! Like the other members of the Big Four, it was prudent that the Southern should move its headquarters out of the vulnerable centre of London for the duration, and so it was they came to be located at Deepdene, near Dorking. From there they ran a massive operation which, according to O.S. Bullied, 'kept growing like Topsy as the military traffics were thrust upon us'.

The sheer volume of this traffic makes it somewhat difficult to present the story in precisely the same format as we have done with the previous three war accounts, particularly in the field of freight because military and civilian traffic became intermingled to such a large extent that it is often difficult to unravel the two. Yet the fact that freight traffic increased to such very high levels will serve to indicate the fact, that the Southern bore the brunt of Britain's war traffic.

Passenger Train Services

Of all the Big Four companies, it was the Southern that would have most intimate contact with the war and thus thereby face the greatest dislocation of services. Whilst none of the companies were to have a light time of things, the Southern had to face the three main periods of military movement, the BEF embarkation, Dunkirk and D-Day. It was also the railway nearest to enemy territory, and thus more likely to be affected by aerial attack. It also had the greatest number of naval and military bases on its territorial area, and also a fairly high percentage of the RAF's pre-war aerodromes. These facts were, therefore, to have a major impact on how the company operated and what services were run. After the early curtailments of the emergency timetable in 1939, the Southern managed to get its principle express workings restored when the new timetable was introduced on 1st January 1940.

Unfortunately, almost as soon as it did so, the system was to be severely disrupted by the wintry weather. Whilst it was not as bad as it was in the snowbound north of England, on Saturday 27th January 1940 the Southern began to suffer what became known as 'The Silver Thaw'. This came about as fine rain began falling on the South-east after a prolonged period of bitterly cold weather and as a result the railway began to experience numerous difficulties as ice caused havoc. Points froze and electric conductor rails began arcing (a difficulty which would appear again in 1941), and by early Sunday morning large parts of the system were at a complete standstill. Although many special trains were fitted with scrappers and anti-freeze sprayers, the temperature of 7 degrees Fahrenheit ensured that their work was to little avail.

All over the Western and Central sections trains came to a grinding halt between 27th and 31st January, and steam trains were reintroduced on a number of electrified lines on the 29th, but it was by no means a complete restoration of services. Nevertheless, the sight of electric express trains arriving at London termini headed by steam locomotives varying from 4-6-0 Atlantics to 0-6-0 goods engines and 0-6-2Ts had to be seen to be believed. The chief purpose of this arrangement was to prevent the EMU sets from stalling and assist where ice prevented the collector shoe making contact with the third-rail. Drivers of the steam engines kept in contact with the motorman by hand-signals, and when possible the motorman collected power to operate lighting, heating and brakes in the normal way. The Eastern division was less severely affected, but it was to have its share of troubles in the rapid thaw which followed.

Initially passenger journeys on the Southern fell from 360,795,107 to 230,220,993 as services were curtailed or completely cancelled for the duration. The loss of boat trains, seaside traffic, and the reduction of many commuter services into London having a severe effect. Yet this was soon replaced by hundreds of additional passenger journeys which came about because of the war, leave traffic being a prime example. In 1942 the journey figures had reached 292,575,449 and they continued to grow throughout the war so that by 1945 they had almost regained their pre-war totals.

By 1940 many of the trains operating down to the West Country had been increased to considerable weights, with the Waterloo - Bournemouth workings often comprising 17 or 18 coaches behind a 4-4-0 Schools class, whilst King Arthur and Lord Nelson class engines were handling 14 to 16 coach trains to Salisbury, even the re-built 'Paddlebox' 4-6-0s were doing excellent work on the specials to Southampton Docks, and this was just the start of things!

However to take passenger traffic in isolation from all the other events during the war years, would not show a true picture of the levels of traffic carried; it therefore beholds us to move quickly from normal passenger traffic to military movements. To do this it is best to consider such movements chronologically (and in conjunction with freight traffic) so that the fuller picture can be given.

This Page:
By the start of the war the Southern Railway was essentially a system of two distinct types. Whilst steam working remained on the bulk of the network, as shown above, electric traction was fast developing on the important commuter and cross country services. Thanks to the electrification programme, a large part of the network had been converted from steam working although many of the sets employed on the converted lines did not give as comfortable a ride as before.

Freight & Military Traffic

As mentioned at the outset, the distinction between ordinary goods traffic and military freight is not easy to state. The fact that much of the Southern's pre-war freight traffic was connected with Cross-Channel or Trans-Atlantic shipping will explain why there was a dramatic fall-off in what the SR considered 'ordinary business'. It was, however, soon replaced with other traffic flows, but these flows (even where the consignments were clearly for civilian use) were often directed by the military; food and coal for France prior to Dunkirk, 'lease-lend' from America, and 'Dominion Aid' all spring to mind as specific examples. As the war progressed, rail-born goods that in peace time would have been used for civilian purposes were being used for military ends. Now whilst the same could be said about any railway in Britain, it was far more evident on the Southern. Only coal could be seen as being the one major traffic that retained a 'civilian identity', but it too was used in large quantities by the military. So, the appraisal of freight and military traffic might best be considered under a single heading.

We have already mentioned the Mobilisation of the BEF and its despatch to France, the bulk of which traffic fell squarely on the shoulders of the Southern, so we might purposefully move on to what followed. Throughout the autumn a large steady flow of traffic was sent over the Southern to support the BEF, a great deal of it being consigned from Richborough, Newhaven and Southampton. The Southern handled it in a quiet efficient manner, but the difficulties of finding sufficient wagons was always a headache, and as a consequence 2,000 former private owner wagons (many from Scotland) were allocated to the SR from the Government's wartime pool.

Even so it was barely enough and matters came to a head during the bitter winter of 1939-40 with the shortage of domestic coals. A suggestion was made in the national press that this might best be resolved by cancelling all Sunday passenger services, and then operating coal trains to relieve the congestion. The Southern's traffic manager immediately replied, saying 'A little more alacrity on the part of the [coal] merchants when it comes to wagons would considerably improve the situation! Sadly many merchants have the knack of leaving an odd ton or so of coal in wagons, and we have then to shunt these to release other wagons which may be standing further up the sidings. The Company would certainly welcome a little more co-operation on the part of the coal merchants and other large users. By such means we can ensure that as soon as wagons are emptied, they may be promptly removed and replaced by loaded ones.' Yet as winter turned to spring, more serious worries were looming on the horizon, or at least on the other side of the Channel. By early May consideration had been given to what would have to be done if France fell, as it was clear that the burden of repatriating troops would have to be borne by the SR.

Sending Them Off

Above:

This typically posed press picture of 2nd September 1939 shows a scene 'Somewhere on the Southern Railway' as the BEF embarks for France. Oddly enough other pictures in the same series carry an official caption which proclaims the date to be June 1940, which was clearly impossible as France had already fallen; and was therefore just another piece of propaganda.

Below:

The boys are back! This time it is June 1944 and the scene is Waterloo station just prior to D-Day
Photos: Both SR Official

Dunkirk

It is surprising to relate that even as late as the thirteenth of May military traffic was still going outwards from England via the Dunkirk ferry, even though the Germans were sweeping down across Northern France like a swarm of locusts, and no less than four days later all the ports in North-eastern France would be closed. Three days on from this the service between Havre and Southampton was also cancelled, and on the 23rd Boulogne harbour closed. On the evening of the 27th the ominous code-word Operation Dynamo was issued, and for a fateful nine days the massive evacuation of Dunkirk began.

As the seriousness of the situation in France had become known in Whitehall, the Southern's Superintendent of Operation and the Superintendent of the London East Division were summoned to the Metropole Buildings where an urgent military conference had been convened. At this meeting the railwaymen were told that a very large number of troops could shortly be landing at ports on the South Coast stretching from Margate to Littlehampton, but they had no information as to dates, times or landing places at this stage. At first Whitehall said that approximately 300,900 men were to be expected, and trains would have to be ready for them.

Few of the trains could be sent through the London area, and no destinations were specified. Above all, the operation had to be undertaken in complete secrecy which fact made it an operational nightmare for any railway. Fortunately, at a meeting of the Railway Executive Committee the next day, the secrecy condition was reduced to a 'need to know basis', so the support of other professional railwaymen could now be enlisted. The demand for rolling stock and locomotives could not be clearly estimated in view of the uncertainty of when and where troops would be landing, and once landed where they would be going. In the end the Southern had to find sufficient motive power and stock for the operation, and this would entail using a total of no less than 186 locomotives.

Some 55 trains, carrying a total of 24,108 men, were actually run early in the mornings for a week prior to the evacuation officially beginning. Then, at 5pm on 26th May, a telephone call signalled that Operation Dynamo would commence at dawn the next day. On Monday 27th May the railways in Kent went on to a Sunday service to facilitate the extra movements and 7 trains with 3,386 men were handled, the next day 14,054 soldiers were carried by 31 trains. This was however, just the tip of the iceberg as these preliminary flows of soldiers and civilian refugees were just the beginning of the mass exodus that would follow.

Bringing Them Back

Above:
The emergency feeding arrangements that had to be implemented on the return of the BEF after Dunkirk was another well organised railway accomplishment. Elsewhere in the text we have mentioned the feeding stations that the Southern Railway established on the platforms at Headcorn. This close-up view shows local people, military personnel and railway staff all 'mucking in' together.

Below:
Receiving foreign evacuees at Margate during the Dunkirk crisis.
Photos: Both SR Official

Emergency Canteens

At the Dunkirk evacuations food was served at Headcorn and Paddock Wood stations, where staff were suddenly faced with the prospect of feeding 145,000 troops. Assistance came from 40 men of the Royal Army Service Corps, even so it was not enough and an additional 40 to 50 ladies from the neighbourhood came along. Between them they worked round the clock for nine days in shifts of eight hours, although some of them were on duty for a consecutive twenty-four hours. The catering headquarters were in a large barn on the edge of the village, from where the food was made up and carried across the fields to the up platform. One local lady cut so many sandwiches she declared at the end of it that she never wanted to eat a sandwich or anything else ever again. Oceans of tea and coffee were provided as 19 stoves were brought into use to boil water, but there was such a shortage of cups it seems that tin cans were employed. When it was time for a train to move on the RASC sergeant would walk down the platform shouting 'sling them out' and a shower of tins rattled onto the platform as the train puffed away. At Tonbridge the station master began a local collection to raise money to buy the food for the soldiers; on the first day £25 was raised, on the second day £125, and by the time the evacuation was over they had collected over £1,000.

In the week that followed this first stage of the evacuation, the first block of trains that had been provided by the Southern was to be eclipsed by the veritable flood of personnel that had to be carried as Operation Dynamo swung into force. The sheer number of trains was quite astounding as the following table shows.

Day	Date	No. Trains	Personnel Carried
Wednesday	29th May	76	38,479
Thursday	30th May	88	44,938
Friday	31st May	107	56,282
Saturday	1st June	110	59,147
Sunday	2nd June	45	25,123
Monday	3rd June	51	27,344
Tuesday	4th June	50	26,195

Most of the boats went either to Dover (200,000 men landed), Folkestone (35,000 men and 9,000 refugees landed), Margate (38,000 men landed) and Ramsgate (43,000 men landed), but Newhaven, Eastbourne, Brighton and Littlehampton were not immune from the events. Yet, even at the height of the operation, no Government official could supply times of landings or the eventual destinations of the men. Even within the Southern system, the distances which some of these trains ran was quite excessive. In fact a large number carried French troops down to the West where they were refreshed, re-equipped, and re-embarked on transports heading for Brest and other ports in western France. This added complication saw trains being hastily provided from Kent to Southampton although others went further west to the ports of Plymouth, Devonport, or Weymouth.

In addition to this 283 military or naval specials were run to various destinations, as equipment had to be moved to various points on the system in case of the enemy launching an immediate attack across the Channel. Ambulance trains were also operating on a regular basis from Dover Marine station's No.3 Platform (pictured below left), and the nearby Customs Shed had to be turned into a mortuary. Hordes of stray dogs came with the men from France, many being 'evacuated from the Boche' by French and British soldiers alike. Rabies control, it seemed, went to blazes in those mad days and a special railway lorry service had to be introduced to collect these animals. Food and clothing also had to be provided, and the railways rushed in large supplies of both, using Dover's old Customs Shed as a temporary supply store.

On Sunday 2nd June, 70 additional trains had to be run to move children away from what were now potential invasion zones. In all 40,000 youngsters were moved long distances inland, including many who had been evacuated from London the previous autumn. All this extra work meant that railway personnel of all grades were continuously employed for very long periods 12, 14, 16 and even 18 hour days were common; some men never went home at all during a two week period, and they simply managed to snatch a few hours sleep where they could before returning to the task at hand. As the human resources of the railway were sorely tested, so too were the physical elements.

As might be imagined the phenomenal level of traffic caused a series of major problems for the Southern, not least in the shape of additional coaling, ash removal and the supply of coaches in the evacuation area. Accordingly a large load of coal was brought in by a special convoy of trains running from Betteshanger colliery, but this commodity was always in short supply at the

ports, as supplies were needed for both locomotives and the many coal-fired vessels that were plying the Channel. No-one kept an account of the coal supplies that were taken by special trains, but we can gain a rough impression from the fact that at the end of the operation 300 tons of spent ash had to be later cleared away from Redhill engine shed.

The actual movement of repatriated men required some 2,000 coaches but the Southern could only provide sufficient stock to make up 55 trains, so the balance of the trains were made up as follows GWR 40, LMS 44, and LNER 47. Junctions where the trains could be handed over to other railways were also quickly arranged, as it was evident that very few of the trains could be handled exclusively on the Southern system. Redhill was made the strategic centre for the operation, with Reading assuming a secondary role. Both stations were cleared of ordinary freight and passenger traffic, Redhill was closed completely as far as the public were concerned, with civilian passenger trains being directed to Earlswood station and a shuttle-bus service introduced to bridge the gap.

In reality the evacuation routes from the Channel Ports were something of a puzzle as very few drivers were clearly aware of the ultimate destination of their trains when they set off and typical instructions would be 'Stop at Guilford, and ask them where you're going!' Even so the whole process between 27th May and 4th June went like clockwork, train after train drew in, filled up and drew away again; each was packed with tired, grimy and smoke-stained men, most with a bun in one hand and a bit of fruit in the other. Twenty minutes after a train had rolled away, another took its place. Interestingly the Southern's pre-war excursion traffic enabled them to manage the Dunkirk evacuation with magnificence and splendid action.

This was perhaps based on its experience of handling special traffic for Twickenham, the Naval review, the Schnieder cup, Ascot races and so on. In such instances there had been no element of the unexpected and by a great deal of advance planning a highly detailed timetable would be evolved with all its complexity of

engine working, pathing, carriage provision, and special staffs. It was different with Dunkirk for there was nothing to go on, and a different method was obviously needed. Improvisation, word of mouth and telephone calls were the order of the day. However, thanks to the Operations Superintendent, a Mr Wheeler, the Southern were able to cope with the traffic that Dynamo occasioned. The Divisional Superintendent at Orpington and his assistants should also be mentioned for, as soon as the problem was brought to them, they set up sub-control officers at Dover Marine, Tonbridge, Ashford, Faversham, Chatham and Dartford. Additionally inspectors were also placed at both of the stations in Dover, both of the stations at Folkestone and at Ramsgate, Ashton, Headcorn, Paddock Wood and Faversham. There were also sub-control offices at Haywards Heath, Chichester and Shalford. Meanwhile empty trains heading for the Channel ports were stabled at Queenborough, Faversham, Margate and Ramsgate.

Despite all of this, ordinary everyday life went on for the railways, and although some trains were cancelled elsewhere men and women still went to offices or factories and had to be carried. There was little easing in the labour's of many railway staff during that period of time, as the daily suburban traffic had to carry on somehow, and during that period the Southern Railway carried 20 million passengers and six million tons of freight. When it was all over the General Manager, Eustace Missenden, wrote to the staff saying "Now that the task of conveying the BEF on its homeward journey is over, I want to express to you all my unbounded admiration for the way in which this work has been planned and carried out. The long hours and devoted service of thousands of railwaymen and women have enabled this difficult operation to be brought to a successful conclusion, and I feel sure that every one of you who has taken part in it will always remember it with pride and thankfulness as I do. THANK YOU!"

After the fall of Dunkirk, a large proportion of the Southern's freight traffic suddenly disappeared again. Freight to and from the Channel Ports vanished almost overnight, as export traffic died away with dramatic suddenness. Even the major port of Southampton, with its massive dry dock, was affected by the blockade of Britain which Admiral Doenitz's U-boat fleet began to impose. With the added threat of fast German motor torpedo craft known as E-boats, the Dover narrows were becoming far too dangerous to pass through, even in well-protected convoys! As a consequence the south and east coast ports became virtually unsafe for commercial ships, and shipping was mostly concentrated on the western side of Britain.

Overall freight traffic saw a considerable growth on pre-war totals and we can illustrate this by taking a comparison between 1938 and 1942, when the Southern ran 192,000,000 loaded wagon miles; though this was substantially lower than any of the other three railways, it was still an overall increase in pre-war totals of 30.5%. This meant that they soon came to an acute shortage of suitable locomotives, and this was to lead to some radical developments as David Jenkinson will later recount - notably so in the creation of one of the ugliest, but most effective 0-6-0 tender engines ever designed for a British railway in the 20th century, namely Bullied's Class Q1. The introduction of the Southern's first main line electric locomotive in June 1943 was however, also a very significant development in the economic handling of goods on the electrified lines. These locomotive developments were to be sorely needed, for inside a few years a new flow of traffic began to appear on the Southern, namely that for the invasion of France.

Above:

A major difficulty in receiving the soldiers, British, French and Belgian, was the fact that many had eaten very little during the previous few days, so refreshment facilities had to be quickly established. Throughout Kent and South London, bakers, confectioners and railway catering staff all around Britain worked day and night providing refreshments for the tired soldiers that were arriving at the Channel ports. The picture shown above was taken at an LNER works canteen. There is no exact date to the picture and we are not saying it actually dates from Dunkirk but in more ways than one it is just too delicious a picture to omit. Indeed few railway books ever show such views of railway staff, yet nevertheless the railways employed bakers, confectioners, pastry cooks and so on. During the war many of them were called up for service with the armed forces, but those employed at the works canteens (in particular) were retained in view of the vital work that they undertook. When the bakers at the LNER's canteen at Stafford Works were asked to prepare food for the returning remnants of the BEF that were landed at Harwich, it is reported that some extraordinary sandwiches and pastries were produced. When told that nothing elaborate was needed, the principal cook is reported to have said 'nothing is too good for our brave lads'. Photo: LNER Official

D-Day and Its Traffic

Above:

Micheldever is a small village in a rural part of Hampshire that prior to 1939 was perhaps only nationally known for the very strange reason that in a corner of the local church yard there stood a grave on which it was reputed that no snow would ever lay. However, that was soon to change for Micheldever became a well known name to railwaymen and military stores personnel as during the war a large depot was created near the village station. Irreverently named Woolworth's, it used to be able to supply anything that was needed by the Military, from field dressings to tank parts, from railway wagons to push cycles. Whatever the Allies needed in the field, Micheldever could supply from stock in a very short time. In turn they despatched the goods to Southampton docks where they would be sent abroad to support the invading armies. The creation of new marshalling yards and additional sidings at rural stations was very much a case of the Ministry of War Transport deciding not to put all its eggs into one basket and just before D-Day approximately 35,000 tons of stores and munitions for the American army were sent to sidings at Launceston, Tower Hill, Whitstone and Halwill. Additional sidings were also provided at Lydford which became an auxiliary yard to Plymouth.

As far as D-Day went the Southern began to witness its first bulk movements as early as December 1943 and Longparish on the little-used branch leading off the Andover-Romsey line was one of the first stations to get these 'specials'. Inside a month it had received no less than 478 wagon loads of blockbuster bombs, and by April of 1944 the number had risen to 1,451. Another remote depot that saw much traffic was that at Dinton, near Wilton, which required an extra goods loop and siding to be added. Meanwhile an inordinate amount of traffic was witnessed at the little creek near Bosham, and to help this flow of traffic much use was made of the old line from Midhurst which had been closed to general passenger traffic in the early 1930s. It was only thereafter used for the occasions of the Goodwood race meetings, although a small amount of goods traffic had been maintained and by 1940 the tunnels on the line had become a stabling ground for wagon loads of ammunition that were being stored after the Fall of France. However, by 1944 these had been taken away and the line was used as a storage area for American wagons that were also intended to be used in the forthcoming invasion.

Petrol was another D-Day traffic that began early and, because of the obvious need for secrecy, little was written at the time about a series of pipelines which were established to convey oil across England; two of which were on Southern Railway territory. The first of these was the 72 mile long pipeline from Walton-on-Thames to Lydd on which construction work commenced on 12th June 1943; by the end of July the railway had conveyed 8,000 tons of pipe, in sections each 40' long, with a further 459 tons of similar pipe being taken to Appledore. The second pipeline ran from Paddock Wood to Port Victoria, and this involved the carriage of 1,357 tons of pipes which varied in length from thirty-five to fifty feet. A large number of motor lorries, tractors and cranes were also imported by the railway to play their part in the building work. Though the trains carrying these civil engineering vehicles were few in number, the movement of military vehicles by rail was overwhelming. Everywhere the overworked staff faced up to this extra traffic with a mixture of efficiency and improvisation, although it is said that the station master at Winchester declared that he never wanted to hear the name of a tank again.

To relieve the problems that all this extra traffic was creating, new marshalling yards were erected at Micheldever (seen above) and Brockenhurst to compliment the existing ones at Eastleigh and Feltham. Plans for another new depot at Lockerley (near Romsey) were implemented in 1943, and a rail connection was provided to the depot from the Salisbury line. The signal box controlling the new junction was in place as early as October that year, and it served the four reception roads that were provided. However, in planning of the new depot provision was made for a further additional eleven stabling lines which would then provide a total of 14 miles of track. Once opened the entire complex came under the control of an American Army 'Sergeant Yard Master', and in the next seven months no less than 19,600 tons of war materials were moved through this location. At Eastleigh the railway depot by the main line was also brought into use as a concentration and marshalling point for material that was going to be sent to Europe and to this end a large section of the huge yard was segregated for 'military stores only'.

In addition there was also a large number of locomotives that the American Transport Corps were storing for use on French railways after the invasion. Yet even with all this extra provision, by early in 1944 many of the dumps and stores on the Southern system were full to capacity.

Those freight flows that were being moved into the Southampton area in 1943/4 were quite often moved into the New Forest where they were stored in relative security. Sometimes these supplies had to be divided and sent on in smaller lots to other destinations, so reloading often took place at tiny stations. Places such as Brockenhurst, Christchurch, Lyndhurst Road, and Beaulieu suddenly had greatness thrust upon them even though the staffing difficulties were most acute. A larger proportion of the consignments were ultimately destined for the various 'Stores Loading Points' around the district, including Marchwood on the west bank of Southampton Water. At Fawley a petrol storage

installation was built, and another was put on the opposite bank of the water at Netley. The Americans, meanwhile, made their main oil depot west of the New Forest at Poole in Dorset. But everywhere from the New Forest to Plymouth the petrol, stores, munitions and arms were building up on sidings which 'could barely accommodate another wagon'. Yet more was to come, and as the pressure grew upon the staff who had to handle this 'secret' traffic, a stirring message was sent on 19th May by the General Manager at Waterloo, who said: 'To all Southern Railwaymen and women the hour of greatest effort and action is yet approaching.'

The railways were the conduits to the ports, and the size of this traffic might be demonstrated by the fact that at any one time during the D-Day period no less than 3,000 wagons might be loading or unloading at Southampton docks. Even the small ports at Poole and Hamworthy received heavy traffic (mostly in petrol, diesel and flame-throwing oil), which began to arrive in the middle of May at the rate of around 700 tons a day. The little slipway at Lymington had to be doubled so that tank landing craft could be loaded simultaneously. The port of Littlehampton was busy loading ammunition, and early in May nine 'supply barges' were taken into the river and 2,700 tons of ammunition were loaded on to them; by the end of August some 18,000 tons of ammunition had been sent from this one port alone.

After the freight, the troops followed. They came from all over England, Scotland, Wales and Northern Ireland in vast numbers to temporary billets in staging camps in the south. Many came by lengthy journeys in the backs of army lorries, but they mostly travelled by rail. By the end of May they were moving to the ports and the numbers involved were quite staggering we might use as our example the town of Newhaven. The port there had closed to normal commercial shipping in July 1940 and reopened the following year for the conveyance of coast-wise coal traffic but in 1944 it became a point of embarkation for no less than 62,000 men in the first assault and a further 100,000 by the end of July. In total the following number of soldiers were dispatched from Southern ports: British 364,350; American 2,165,883; whilst in the opposite direction came 310,113 prisoners of war.

As soon as the beach-head had been secured in Normandy, there had to be sent all the additional 'support', this traffic, including a massive quantity of locomotives and rolling stock that would be employed on French railways as soon as they were liberated. These were shipped from Southampton and Richborough, as 279 locomotives, 674 American wagons and 269 other vehicles (including six ambulance trains of fifteen coaches each) used the three train carriers. In addition several railway cranes were also loaded up and sent across the Channel. Yet this was still not enough, and landing craft were organised to carry two more locomotives, and 6,821 wagons from Southampton and Lymington.

Above:
The Southern's new electric engine had travelled 40,000 miles on 'operational trials' after its introduction, and in an answer to a Parliamentary question Mr. P. J. Noel-Baker (Parliamentary Secretary to the Minister of War Transport) said this 'offers the hope of electrification under conditions which would allow maximum use of the fixed equipment.'
Photo: SR Official

Below:
Loading an Austerity 2-8-0, No. 78250 onto a 'Landing Craft Tanks' in Southampton Water in July 1944. Whilst the majority of locomotives for France went by the train ferries, landing craft were also employed on two occasions as this poor quality but equally interesting photograph demonstrates.
Photo: SR Official

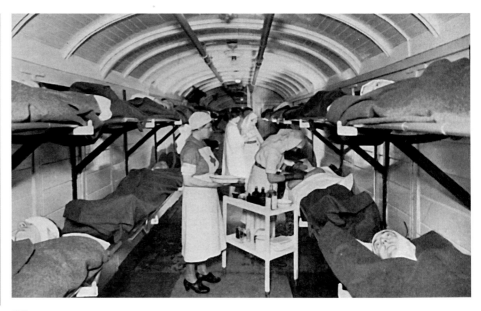

As the two pictures on this page show, it was not merely children that were evacuated from the cities as hospital patients, the elderly and infirm (with certain illnesses) and young mothers with their children were all considered to be at risk and were thus moved to safe areas in the country.
Photos: Both SR Official.

Evacuees

Before war actually broke out the plans had been put into place to clear the cities of the most vulnerable members of society, but the thinking behind the mass movement was more to do with the fear of gas attack, rather than the rain of high explosives that eventually followed. However, as it turned out the numbers wishing to leave the cities were not as great as initially anticipated by the government. When the evacuation began on 31st August 1939 it was not merely moving people out of the London area but also from places like Southampton, Gosport, Portsmouth and the Medway area. London children were not allowed to use the mainline termini, and as a consequence suburban stations were used at Richmond, Wimbledon and New Cross Gate. To reach these Southern stations London Transport buses were used to convey the children, and in total 5,895 passenger vehicles were used to convey 345,812 passengers. The railways made provisions for 225 special trains running at the rate of 75 trains per day, but the full numbers of evacuees never did turn up and many trains ran with less than full capacity. On the 1st and 2nd September a minor evacuation took place at the Medway towns of Rochester, Chatham, Gillingham and Rainham. Even Borstal prisons had to be moved out bag and baggage on the 2nd and 3rd. Then on 5th September 13 more special trains took 2,600 people from Belvedere and Erith to parts of Kent. The evacuation of the Southampton and Gosport area took place on 1st and 2nd September when 127 trains took 30,000 people to safe-havens in Hampshire, Dorset and Wiltshire. A further 18 trains ran from Southampton, Portsmouth and Gosport on the 27th and 28th. Another evacuation in which the Southern Railway was involved was that of the Channel Islands which took place in June 1940. However, at this very point of time much of the Southern's area found itself in a potential invasion zone, and so a second movement of evacuees was needed to get them further into the west, Wales or the North. For instance the famous Roedean School was evacuated to Keswick up in the midst of the Cumberland mountains.

Defence Programmes & Air Raids

As stated earlier, in many ways the Southern bore much of the brunt of war, for it was the only British railway that was within reach of all four means of attack available to the German forces: viz. land-based guns, aircraft, rockets and ships. A high percentage of all the aerial attacks on England necessitated enemy aircraft flying across Southern territory and as a consequence, loads of bombs were often 'tipped' on SR territory when the Luftwaffe planes could not reach their targets. For the Southern, the serious raids began on 19th June 1940 when the Engineering Depot at Redbridge was to receive a direct hit, and a large quantity of valuable permanent way materials were destroyed. On 10th July a moving train was bombed near Newhaven, killing the driver and injuring the guard. Thereafter attacks on railways around the Solent became more frequent, and on 16th August 1940 the station at Malden received a direct hit killing staff and passengers. On 7th September came the most memorable night thus far, as Waterloo, London Bridge, Holborn Viaduct and Victoria all suffered problems. At Waterloo a driver was killed and two firemen injured, whilst the viaduct crossing the Thames to Vauxhall was badly damaged. Although all eight lines across this structure were undermined in such a way as to completely disrupt traffic, two lines were returned to service after 10 hours (thanks to assistance from the Royal Engineers) but the whole viaduct was not reopened until 1st October. Unfortunately these problems were compounded by bombs hitting Hungerford Bridge, Nine Elms and Waterloo Bridge on the night of the 10th September.

The area was raided again on the 19th, and on the 23rd all the signals and mechanical points were put out of action at Waterloo. The night of the 25th was another bad time for the Southern, and the 29th was even worse. On 8th October four high explosive bombs landed around Waterloo, and five days later Nine Elms was hit; in this raid a huge crater was blown open and in its maw 18 wrecked trucks were later found to be piled one on top of the other. Early November witnessed bad raids on 5th, 7th and 9th, and the goods depot at Blackfriars was destroyed. Included with this loss was the bonded warehouse which contained large quantities of spirits and champagne.

A month later a succession of land-mines were dropped along the Thames in Central London, one of these festooned itself around a signal box at London Bridge station, and there it stayed until Royal Navy experts came to defuse it, yet despite the all too obvious dangers the signalmen carried on at their duties. In the infamous fire raid of 29th December, London Bridge station was hit again, this time by showers of incendiaries. Those that fell on the station were extinguished, but others set fire to nearby houses and flames from these threatened to engulf the station and the railway bridge. Cannon Street, Charing Cross and Waterloo all had a hard time of it, and it was not until 5th January that all the damage was effectively patched up. Yet that very night, another large bomb fell on Waterloo, destroying the offices and blocking the entrance to the underground station.

On 8th March 1941 a series of raids were directed in the area around Waterloo and Clapham Junction, and by 9pm on the Saturday evening all the roads through Clapham were out of action. Rapid repair work followed with cranes coming into service at 1.50pm on the Sunday, and normal traffic resuming at 4pm on the Monday. After a series of heavy raids in March, the night of 16th-17th April was another bad time for London, in particular Charing Cross. The events started around 1.50am when a high-explosive bomb landed on Charing Cross Hotel, along with over 100 incendiaries on the station; fires broke out everywhere, including the roof and underneath No. 4 platform.

The following morning it was the operating staff who needed courage, coupled with a fair amount of resourcefulness as Charing Cross, Holborn Viaduct, London Bridge, Victoria and Waterloo were all closed to traffic. As train services were gradually restored, more hand-signalmen were pressed into service; and, undaunted by a terrible catastrophe that killed several of their colleagues at Blackfriars, most were actually working 12 hour shifts up to 26th April.

Below:
This really is a period picture taken at Waterloo station in August 1939, and not a 'still' of Captain Mainwaring from the television comedy series 'Dad's Army', but you'd be forgiven for thinking otherwise. Again the official caption on the back simply states 'New shade for reading lights in corridor compartment. Note the ordinary blue lights at the top.' Coupled with blackout curtaining, and the painting of some compartment windows, these measures were to make the coach interiors exceptionally dark. A series of unsavoury incidents, mostly assaults of various kinds on female passengers, which took place in non-corridor compartments led to a serious re-think on the levels of permitted lighting. Instead of the blue bulbs 15watt clear bulbs were ordered in some quantity.

Right:
Pictured on 11th May 1941 the wrecked Schools class, No. 934 St. Lawrence stands outside Cannon Street Station having been struck by a German bomb. The cab is completely devastated and the tender has been blown apart.
Interestingly the locomotive's nameplate lays like so much rubbish amongst the debris on the permanent way below.
Photo: SR Official
Courtesy Kent Libraries

Seaside Bomb Attacks.

The seaside stations at Dover, Folkestone, Brighton, Sandwich, Eastbourne, Hastings, Seaford and Newhaven all had several attacks, mostly hit and run raids. Folkestone was actually bombed and shelled throughout the whole of the war, but the stations at Folkestone and nearby Shorncliffe were exceptionally lucky although the station master's house was to prove the exception to the rule.

In May 1943 five bombs fell on the viaduct at Brighton's London Road and completely destroyed one of the brick piers but left the rails defiantly suspended above the gap. Eastbourne had a number of hit and run raids, but ironically it was on the 16th September 1942 that the most tragic raid occurred during the demonstration of a motor fire pump by an Inspector who was engaged in ARP training. At the time of the demonstration an enemy raider flashed over and when it had passed several of the staff and the Inspector were dead and the fire pump totally wrecked.

Canterbury endured 445 high-explosive bombs, and in one raid alone during June 182 of these fell along with 8,000 incendiaries. Then on one of the last days of shelling from German guns across the Channel, Dover's Priory station was directly hit on 13th September 1944. Several people were killed and more injured but it also produced 'much courageous achievement on the part of the staff.'

On the night of 10th-11th May incendiaries and bombs showered down on Cannon Street, and during this raid the only irreparable Southern Railway locomotive casualty of the war was sustained. As two engines, Nos. 934 and 1541, were being moved out of the station a bomb struck No.934 and blew it over on to its side. Fortunately the driver and fireman escaped in the nick of time, but 934 had to be written off. Interestingly, although this was the only total casualty of enemy action, another 189 engines were damaged to a lesser extent.

Outside London the primary targets on the Southern system, at least from a strategic objective, were the major ports and naval bases to be found at places like Chatham, Plymouth, Portsmouth and Southampton. German maps captured after the fall of France in 1944 show that these locations were targeted by the Luftwaffe, and the fact that they were not destroyed beyond redemption perhaps had more to do with poor German aiming than the state of British defences. Even so Southampton was to suffer badly, with its commercial and residential districts decimated in the constant attacks, yet damage to the railways was comparatively light. Speaking of the city, *Timetable to Victory* states:-

'It was evidently put on the list of harbour towns to be assaulted in the last months of 1940, and one would have imagined that either the railways or the docks would have been the principal target. There was little damage at the docks, rather more to the cold store, warehouses etc., but this does not appear to have been the main point of attack. What was gutted, and horribly gutted, was the High Street and the shopping centre, with a circumjacent area that did not quite reach the Central Railway Station (or for that matter the great electric power-house that lies short of it) nor the Terminus Station on the other side, beyond which lie Canute Road and the docks.'

The first alarm raised at Southampton came on 16th October, 1939 when a confidential message foretold an air-raid. Fortunately, no attack came although the Marines Officer stood by all night. In fact it was to be nearly a whole year before bombs were dropped to any great extent, and the first really serious raid came on 13th August, 1940 which, in turn, caused a large fire at the international cold storage building at the docks, and also severed the mains water supply was severed. As a consequence the fire brigade were not able to attend to the fire and it was still raging on the 15th. In all some 2,000 tons of meat, and 2,400 tons of butter went up in smoke, and only on the 20th did the fire come to its end.

The enemy bombers came again with a vengeance on the night of 23rd and 24th September, but this was followed by a temporary lull. They returned on the night of 23rd November when the station was ringed with fires and the sports club badly damaged. The docks were pock-marked by 40 large craters, but somehow or other no railway stock was destroyed and only the track suffered minor damage. However trains had to be diverted away from the Southampton area, and it was two days before the services properly resumed. A really dreadful weekend came over the period of 30th November and 1st December, and the vital business districts of Southampton were severely dislocated. Two warehouses were destroyed on the docks, and serious damage was done to the Post Office, Harland and Wolf's shipyard and Rank's mill. The city was badly hurt, so to boost morale His Majesty the King came down to Southampton on 5th December; the result of the visit (as far as we are concerned) was the formation of a Transport Consultative Committee to ensure that railway and bus services were resumed within the city as soon as possible. On 19th January a 2,000lb bomb crashed through the roof of the booking office although the only casualty, was a pet dog which had been the leading porter's faithful companion. A further bomb landed in the booking office that night but it failed to explode, and there it stayed until 6th February when bomb disposal experts were able to take it away. One more serious raid in 1941 was suffered by the railway early on the morning of 22nd June, when three parachute land mines landed close to the station.

Portsmouth was attacked as early as June 1940 and thereafter it became the target for a constant stream of raids, both daylight and night-time. Clarence Pier and the Harbour station were struck with some accuracy, and the harbour terminus suffered what was probably the most severe devastation of any station on the whole Southern system up to that date. On 12th August a bomb explosion set fire to the station building, the offices, gutted access to the landing stage and smashed the water main which, in turn, prevented the firemen from getting supplies to extinguish the blaze.

There was serious damage in the area on 5th December and again on 10-11th January 1941, when high explosive bombs hit the railway at Southsea, Fratton, Gosport and, once again, Portsmouth Harbour. This time the girders supporting the station were actually blown away and a coach from one train crashed down into the mud below. Fires broke out everywhere and saving the station was clearly beyond hope and all that could be done was to save as many moveable vehicles as possible.

The period of 8th to 17th April saw three very bad nights in the Portsmouth area, and then on the 27th no less than 30 land mines fell around Portsmouth and Southsea station. In July there was a five-day long attack on the Portsmouth and Southampton area, but as the effectiveness of the defences improved, many of the planes failed to reach their target and the bombs fell in the rural Sussex countryside; most of these landed well away from vital areas but quite a few came down on railway property and caused serious damage.

Plymouth was a natural target and it suffered to such an extent that the London-based crews who travelled down to the south-west port were often heard to comment that they'd be glad to return to London and the comparative safety of the blitz there. The most significant example of damage here was the tiny little station of Turnchapel that was obliterated in a lake of fire on the night of 27th November 1940 after a German plane dropped four bombs. Two of these fell harmlessly into the Hooe lake, an inlet of the Cattewater, however behind the station lay several Admiralty oil tanks. A bomb hit one of these tanks which instantly burst into flames and the fire raged all around. Firemen working to control the blaze were unable to do so, and on the following night, Friday the 29th, the other oil tanks finally exploded. The superheated oil in them boiled over and sprayed out in all directions; three of the firemen were killed, and the others only saved themselves by jumping into the nearby lake. The blazing oil then poured over a rocky bank and down onto the station; it obliterated it within a moment, and then flowed along the track for a distance of 150 yards. The flames were not put out until the night of Sunday 1st December and when they had been extinguished the station buildings had vanished. All that was left were twisted remains of lamp-stands and automatic vending machines! When the smoke and mist finally cleared, the once tidy little station had almost completely disappeared.

There were many attacks on moving trains and these usually occurred to services running along coastal lines, as for example the Ramsgate - Dover train near Deal, which was attacked by six 'planes killing the driver and wounding the fireman. However these raids also happened far inland as was evidenced in incidents at Halton and between Exeter and Salisbury. The most significant event was 16th December 1942, when a Dornier bomber attacked a Guildford to Horsham train near Bramley, dropping four bombs first of all, and then returning to rake the train with machine gun fire. The fireman, by the name of Fairey, was the solitary person to escape unscathed, the driver, guard and eight passengers were killed and 12 others injured. Fairey dutifully made safe the firebox and boiler of the derailed train, arranged line protection in the absence of anyone else to do this and then attended to the dying and injured; an action in which his training as a member of the SR's Horsham First Aid team played an important role. For this act of devotion to duty and gallantry he was later presented with both the Southern Railway's own medal and also a civilian award.

This incident reveals why many trains would try and head for a tunnel, even if it meant going hard in to reverse gear in order to find shelter from attack, although this was against all the normal safe-working practices. One such tunnel to provide salvation was located on the line to Bere Alston, which was often used by people escaping from Plymouth to get out into the country at night. On one occasion a train filled with 'night-time' evacuees was heading to the station when it was chased by a German 'plane. The driver saw it coming and put on speed to try and reach a nearby tunnel; fortunately a curve in the line came to the rescue of the fully loaded train. The German pilot concentrating on 'lining-up' his bombing attack did not see the curve and so went straight on as the train curved, before dropping its bombs just to the rear of the train and causing no damage whatsoever. Other tunnels were used to keep stock out of harms way, as for example the Kemp Town Tunnel at Brighton which was used for stabling electric stock between October 1941 and May 1944.

Above:
In the midst of the bombing on 16th April 1940 a porter reported that he had just tripped up over a land mine near London Bridge. The signalman did not know that it was close to his box. When warned of it by telephone he replied that he had better stay where he was and continue to warn the station for the fall of incendiaries, of which he had an excellent view from the bridge. Sadly, on that same night a high-explosive bomb or land-mine, no-one knew which, landed at Blackfriars and killed seven railwaymen who were employed on hand-signalling duties

Below:
In May 1943 a 'tip and run' raid saw the 70 feet high London Road Viaduct in Brighton being hit by bombs, with the result that one pier and two arches of Raistrick's monumental construction were completely destroyed. Nevertheless a temporary bridging unit was brought into place and within 5 weeks trains were running across the gap, and by September the whole thing had been fully repaired.

Photos: Both SR Official

Two views of Southern ARP;

Above:
Anti-gas warfare suits pictured as members of an emergency break-down team go on exercises.

Below:
As far as anti-fire precautions went, the ARP teams were provided with some powerful equipment including their own steam powered appliance.
Photos: Both SR Official

A second phase of the German aerial offensive, the V1 'flying bombs', began in 1944 when 8,000 'doodle-bugs' were launched against Britain, most passing over Southern Railway territory en-route to the London area where 2,300 fell. The first landed on the Southern at Cuckfield, Sussex on 13th June, and another 41 landed on or very close to SR property in the period up to 31st August. On 19th June, a doodle-bug managed to accomplish what a landmine had failed to do, blow up Hungerford Bridge. By blind chance this un-guided missile had struck the bridge and blown away 100 feet of the running lines and the footbridge. As may be imagined this was to cause considerable delays to traffic, and as a consequence a Green Line bus service was introduced to convey passengers across the Thames.

Seven days later 17 people were killed and 30 more injured when a V1 struck the General Offices at Victoria. Hither Green was hit twice in June and in the second incident on the 23rd two electric trains were destroyed in a siding. Amongst the other SR stations to be damaged were Ashford, Beckenham, Camberwell, Chiselhurst, Coulsdon & Purley, Croydon, Greenwich, Lambeth, Lewisham, Maidstone West, Mitcham, Orpington, Peckham Rye, Purley, Wandsworth, Wimbledon and Woolwich. As had been evidenced with the conventional bombing raids on Britain (where the Southern had suffered more than any other railway), the South-east of England was to bear the brunt of these rocket attacks. In fact the Southern suffered from more V1's than all the other companies put together as 528 rockets landed on their property. Next highest was the LNER with 226 followed by LPTB 149, LMS 126, and GWR 45.

Before leaving the V1 flying bombs we might mention the Pyrrhic victory which followed the shooting down of a flying bomb near Rainham, by an RAF pilot whose victory turned to tragedy as the damaged bomb landed on a railway bridge some 20 to 25 yards in front of an oncoming passenger train. The engine plunged into the crater that opened up in front of it, overturned and dragged the next two coaches with it, killing eight people and injuring two more as a result. However the devastation might have been far greater had the pilot of the fighter 'plane not managed to signal 'stop' to the driver of a freight train coming in the opposite direction.

When the larger V2s began to fall on Britain, only a small number hit the Southern, but one of these was the infamous New Cross Gate incident on 25th November 1944 when it was reported that 4 people were killed at the station, although rumour had it that there were very many more. The scale of the tragedy was overshadowed by what happened at the nearby Woolworth's store, which was obliterated at a time when it was packed with lunch-time shoppers. As the terror of the V2s became known, there was little point in concealing a report that 51 people were killed by the bomb which landed on the SR's flats at Deptford in March 1945. By comparison the V2 that struck the railway works at Angerstein, near Charlton Junction, (killing three members of staff) was counted as a very slight loss. The last bomb, another V2, struck the Southern Railway near Chiselhurst on 26th March 1945.

Ancillary Services.

In this section we will not concern ourselves with anything other than an account of the Southern's shipping fleet, and start with the fall of Dunkirk. Five Southern Railway ships were lost in that period, two of them before the operation even really began. On 23rd May the *Maid of Kent* was hit by five bombs in the harbour at Dieppe and sank whilst carrying wounded passengers. The steamer *Brighton* was likewise bombed and sunk, even though both ships were clearly marked as hospital vessels and the attacks on these must have been deliberate. Precisely seven days later the Southern suffered a further loss with the transports' *Lorina* and *Normannia*, both being sunk. Finally on 2nd June another hospital ship, the *Paris*, was also attacked by bombs and so severely damaged that she had to be abandoned.

All the railway ships toiled bravely but we might consider one trip of the vessel *Isle of Guernsey* from whose captain's report we now relate:-

'May 29th 1940 at 5:16pm having received orders, we proceed towards Dunkirk following a course that took us well clear of Calais. At 7:12pm we stood off for a while because of an engagement between aircraft and a British destroyer immediately in our track. At 7:30pm an airman was observed descending by parachute close ahead of us and the vessel had stopped to save him. One seaman went down a rope ladder to assist the airman, but before he reached the bottom, ten enemy planes attacked the ship with bombs, cannon and machine gun. By a miracle none of the bombs struck the ship, although considerable damage was done by concussion, shrapnel, cannon shells and machine gun bullets. British fighter 'planes fought off the enemy, and we proceeded towards Dunkirk with a terrific air battle taking place over the top. Arrived off the port at 8:20pm, we found it being bombed and shelled, and we had orders from the shore to keep clear. Returning along the Channel in company with two destroyers we later received orders to wait until darkness had fallen, and then return to Dunkirk. At 11:30pm we entered between the fires of burning oil tanks, etc, and managed to moor up alongside what was left of the quay at 12:30am. Loading commenced at once, by 2:15am we had taken on board as many as we could, numbering four hundred and ninety. All the crew and the Royal Army Medical Corps personnel behaved splendidly throughout, carrying on with their duties and doing their utmost to fill the ship as quickly and as fully as possible, although the ship was shaken every few minutes by the falling of bombs on the quay and in the water. Leaving the quay at 2:15pm we proceeded out of the harbour just outside we found the sea full of men swimming and shouting for help; presumably a transport had just been sunk. As two destroyers were standing by picking these men up we carefully threaded our way through them and proceeded on to Dover. It would have been fatal for us to try and stop and save any of these men, as we made such a wonderful target for the aircraft hovering overhead, with the flames of the port showing [up] all our white paint-work. Everything was comparatively quiet on the way across, except that just before we got to Dover a patrol boat headed us off as we were heading for a recently laid minefield. Arriving at Dover at 7am we received orders to proceed to Newhaven and arrived at that port at 11:15am.' After that amazing eighteen hours the *Isle of Guernsey* had to retire to dry dock for her wounds to be healed and by the time she was repaired and fit to sail again the evacuation was over.

The Southern Railway's steamer fleet also suffered further casualties in 1940 and the *Worthing* was attacked by enemy aircraft that dive-bombed and machine gunned the hospital ship dropping nine heavy bombs in a calculated attack on a vessel bearing the emblems of the Red Cross and protected by the Geneva convention. Early on the morning of 20th September 1941 the Isle of Wight boat *Portsdown* struck a mine and sank, making it another victim in the casualty list of 12 ships that the Southern would lose. By 1944 several boats from the surviving fleet were re-assembled in Southampton harbour, the *Canterbury*, *Biarritz*, *Isle of Guernsey* and *Maid of Orleans* had all been converted for use as 'Landing Ships Infantry', while the *Dinard* became a hospital ship. However the transformation from their pre-war days was great, the *Canterbury* for example had been totally changed from the days when she ran the Golden Arrow service. Her lounges had been stripped out, and filled with hammocks for the troops. Cabins and alcoves along the sides had been torn away to make rooms for the supports holding landing craft, meanwhile the main deck had been strengthened, and covered with some substance that was very similar to concrete.

Above:
As soon as the war had ended, the Southern Railway began to look at ways in which it could improve customer services. Station catering was seen to be one area needing massive improvement and as a consequence a new trolley service was provided as seen above. On offer were sausage rolls 3d, pork pies 5d and bread rolls 2d, along with ice-cream or hot drinks to finish.

Branch Lines Opened
Branch Lines Closed

The last standard gauge railway to be built in Britain, before the onset of war, was in fact the Southern's Chessington branch which opened on 28th May 1939 and it was also the last new line to be built for many years afterwards. Yet 1939 was also a time of closure and on the first day of that year, the Dyke branch which ran from Brighton up into the South Downs was closed for good.

With its closure came the transfer of the Sentinel steam railcar which had been built in 1923 as works number 8740 but became No. 6 in the Southern's list of special miscellaneous passenger vehicles. After the closure of the branch it faced an uncertain future until it was finally withdrawn in 1942 and thereafter used as an air-raid shelter at the Ashford works before being finally scrapped in or around 1946 when its usefulness came to an end.

Concrete At Work

Throughout the war there was an acute shortage of steel, wood, and other natural materials that were widely used for construction purposes on the railway. There was however, a good supply of concrete, a material which had come very much into fashion during the 1930s as the Southern employed it widely in its new construction works. The railway had opened its own concrete works at Exmouth junction which was used to produce a large range of items for use around the Southern system. These varied from lamp standards to notice posts, line-side huts, gradient posts and so on, all of which could be made frugally from ferro-concrete. Designs were even considered with items of rolling stock, and the Southern supplied some technical advice to the LNER in this regard. However, many of the creations suffered terrible condensation problems, and were not all that satisfactory in service although hundreds of lineside huts still remain today (many are now derelict). More common tasks at the Southern's concrete works during the war were connected with military applications, and hundreds of panels for guard huts were produced, along with thousands of items used in defensive emplacements on the south coast. All in all a fascinating part of Southern Railway history, albeit a little mentioned one.

Workshops At War

The Southern Railway had four works involved in war activities, these were Eastleigh, Brighton, Lansing and Ashford. In fact Brighton had almost been closed following the electrification programme of 1928, when much of the steam locomotive work formally done at Brighton was transferred to Eastleigh or Ashford. Thereafter, Brighton was only used for running repairs and of the seven acres on the site, only three and a half were actually fully employed. However, with the outset of war the works were used for special jobs. Machinery which had been in store for many years was transferred from Ashford and Eastleigh to Brighton as a further 66 new machines were installed from outside suppliers, plus 34 from other depots. Brighton began the bulk of its work again in 1943 when 30 large locomotives were built there. At the outbreak of the war 253 men were employed at Brighton, by the end of 1943 there were 755 men and 214 women working full-time, and another 38 working part-time.

Eastleigh works was initially busy with gun barrels for the Ministry of Munitions, but it made such a massive quantity of 'war items' that they are too great to mention here. The machine shop was busy making parts for Matilda tanks, and the boiler shop was at work on parts for landing craft and refuelling barges; landing craft were also built at Eastleigh and provided with bullet proof armour. One of the early contributions to the war effort by the Southern Railway workshops was the construction of a mobile railway workshop that was supplied for service with the BEF. The train of three 4-wheeled vans, each 32 feet long, contained a diesel-electric generator set, lathe, shaping machine, drilling machine, hydraulic press, three 1-ton jib cranes (one per van) and a miscellany of hand tools.

In December 1939 Ashford provided 600, 12-ton open goods wagons for use in France in the form of kits; work commenced on the 4th December and finished on the New Year's Eve. In 1941 they received an order for 1,000, 13-ton open freight wagons for Russia and completed it in less than ten weeks, once again the wagons were built up as kits of parts. Each wagon contained 792 parts; each part was numbered and corresponding photographs were sent out with detailed assembly instructions to the Persian Gulf, where the trucks were to be used on the vital railroad running into the southern part of Russia. On 10th November Colonel Llewellin, Parliamentary Secretary to the Minister of War Transport, came down to Ashford and drove the last nail into the last packing case of the thousandth wagon. When the wagons finally reached their destination the rate at which they were erected worked out at roughly 45 minutes a piece, and yet they were put together by a unit that had absolutely no workshop facilities

Many of the railway workshops were in the direct line of fire, and like the LNER works at Stratford the Southern's were attacked on a regular basis, although very few of the early raids seemed to have had much effect. Nevertheless the works were an important place and 'roof-spotters' were employed to signal the approach of German aircraft at which the railway workers would down tools and head for the nearest shelter. Ashford, the worst affected works on British railways, were initially left alone and the first bombs did not fall there until the afternoon of 17th July 1940 when 12 'screaming bombs' were dropped on the works from a sunlit sky, leaving one person dead and 10 wounded.

Thereafter Ashford seemed to be attacked with every kind of weapon - high explosives, land mines, incendiaries, delayed action devices, machine guns, in fact whatever the Germans could throw at them. Then on, 26th October 1942, the heavy machine shops, brass shop and machine shop were all damaged when ten men and one woman were killed. On 24th March 1943 there was a direct hit on the erecting shop, and this time eight men lost their lives and 41 were injured. The works had a repeatedly hard time, because it was situated next door to an important junction and marshalling yard, and the Germans were only seven minutes flying time away from their bases in occupied France.

At one time the machinists in parts of Ashford were still at work even though they had no roof over their heads. Instead tarpaulins were put up to keep out the elements, but nevertheless they did not cease production. No damage from the air was going to put a stop on the steady flow of railway work that streamed out of Ashford whether this was destined for the Southern railway, the Middle East, Russia or the invasion of France. Amongst the other Southern workshops to be affected were Lansing and Brighton both of which were to experience air raids in one form or another.

Disasters & Difficult Times

Amazingly, despite the Southern's poor overall accident record pre-war, the company progressed through the war in relative comfort, and this in spite of all the heavy enemy attacks that were made on that network. Indeed, after the terrible mix-up at Swanley Junction on 27th June 1936, it only had three bad accidents in the period up to VE-Day. These were collisions at Waddon on 4th November 1942 and Esher two months later, then a locomotive boiler explosion at New Milton on 23rd April 1945. However, one serious problem arose on 28th November 1939 between Abbotscliff and Shakespeare tunnels near Dover, when a fall of chalk blocked the line.

Ironically a similar thing had occurred at the Warren during World War I, when a fall on 19th December 1915 succeeded in closing this vitally important line until the summer of 1919. The cause of the 1939 fall was attributed to three months of abnormally heavy rainfall in the autumn followed by a sharp frost. As a result the waterlogged chalk fissured, and around 50 tons fell on 27th November although this did not land on the railway. A deep crack, which was some 8" wide, was then noted around 20 feet back from the edge of the cliff, and from this it was evident that another fall would follow soon. Watchmen were posted round the clock, but at 6.55pm that evening the signalman at Shakespeare box heard the sound of falling rock and without delay sent the message 'Obstruction - Danger' to the man at Folkestone Junction, in turn he promptly stopped the 5pm from Cannon Street.

In the cold light of the early dawn it could be seen that around 25,000 cubic yards of chalk had detached itself from the cliff face and swept away a considerable section of the track. In view of the heavy traffic using the line, especially that connected with the BEF, speedy action was taken to restore the line by bringing in three mechanical excavators, along with bulldozers and the like. In the meantime East Kent buses ran a shuttle service, and the BEF Christmas Leave trains were sent via Chatham. The line reopened on 7th January, but the hard weather which came in late January was followed by another rapid thaw on 4-5th February, and when more chalk began to fall the line was closed for a further three days. Yet another fall on 24th February closed the line until 10th March, and even then it did not reopen for 24 hours running until Sunday 21st April. It was just one more problem to be endured and overcome as best they could. However, like everything else that happened in these exhausting years, it was yet another difficulty where the long-term solution would have to be deferred until after the war.

In addition to problems on the land, the Southern also had troubles at sea and they were to lose many of their ships during the war years; it is therefore fitting to recount just one of these losses, *The Maid of Orleans*. By just after two o'clock on the morning of the 6th of June 1944 *The Maid of Orleans* reached the Channel, at 5.40am she anchored at the lowering position and waited with her complement of troops for the landing craft that would take them ashore. Within five minutes her 'Landing Craft Assaults' were manned and some 45 minutes later the 'Landing Craft Infantry' arrived alongside, but the 'Landing Craft Motors' were late because the weather had been too bad for them to make the crossing on time. There was also a great difficulty in making the landing crafts fast alongside owing to the heavy swell, and some damage was done both to the landing craft and to *The Maid of Orleans* herself (which was holed in the starboard quarters below the main deck level).

Between 9.50am and 10.30am, five of the Landing Craft Assaults returned and were hoisted aboard, during all of this time the ship had to be manoeuvred to give them leeway and oil was poured onto the water on the windward side to lessen the breaking waves. As the ship was at anchor, the convoy of which she was a part came under heavy gunfire from enemy shore batteries, so all the ships were ordered to make smoke until they were out of the range of the guns. The vessel made several more trips, but on 28th June she made her last. For some reason her usual master, Captain Payne, could not be on board that day and she was commanded by Captain Masters but it was a weary crew that manned the ship as some of them had gone without sleep for three nights.

She had successfully landed 800 troops on the beaches, but as she was coming up the Channel for home she struck a mine. With a violent explosion a massive hole developed on her starboard side, all the lights went out, and the ship was enveloped in a cloud of black smoke and swirling white steam. 'The old girl is going,' said Captain Masters, four life boats and a Landing Craft Assault were got away, and all left the ship with the exception of the Captain and four officers. Then when it was clear that no-one else was left aboard they threw three life rafts into the sea and jumped for it. From the rafts they boarded a Landing Craft Assault, and ultimately a destroyer, but one engineer and three firemen had been killed instantly by the explosion, and the third engineer (who had been awarded the DSO for bravery in Dunkirk) was badly injured and died later that night in hospital.

Above:
Prior to the outbreak of World War II, the Southern Railway had not enjoyed the best of records when it came to safety and accidents. Since its formation the Southern had undergone serious incidents at Fleet, Sevenoaks, Raynes Park, Battersea Park Station and Swanley Junction. Fortunately this catalogue of mayhem and destruction did not continue during the war years, as the Southern had more than enough to contend with due to the enemy action it suffered. One such incident was the destruction of this signal box 'Somewhere in Kent'. No other details have emerged as to the location of this 'box which was burnt out by incendiary devices'.

Far Left:
One of the Southern workshops' ugliest productions during the war years was also one of its most effective locomotives. Bullied's Q1 class 0-6-0 was constructed with various factors in mind, firstly the material shortages, second the high performance to low weight ratio, and third the stringent restrictions on axle-loadings that were imposed by the Chief Civil Engineer. Bulleid's ugly duckling may not have been aesthetically pleasing, but it met all the other criteria. This was particularly important as its route of availability was considerably widened, and it could take even heavy freight trains onto lines which would have otherwise been barred to it With all but the last two digits of the engine number being obscured by a wisp of steam, the Q1 arrives at an unrecorded group of sidings with a train of explosive vans. Note US Army wagon No.44210 to the right of the engine.
Photos: Both SR Official

CHAPTER ELEVEN
Railway Police

One area that we haven't discussed in this book is that of the railway police officers who were employed by the individual companies, but who had powers that were quite compatible with the various City, County and Borough Constabularies around the country. They also wore a uniform that was hard to distinguish from civilian forces, but their job was to protect railway property and ensure that it was kept free from crime, disturbance and general mischief. However at the outset of war large numbers of these servants were called up for duties in the armed forces, and this left the railways with one of its most depleted branches of the service. Yet, it is sad to state that during the war the railway police were needed more than at probably any other time in the history of the railways.

The main problems that emerged in the autumn of 1939 were petty theft and organised crime, and both extremes of law-breaking were directly created because of the black-out. Coupled with this came the hurried packing and transportation of goods, with valuable items often being sent on in unsecured wagons. Even those traffics that were considered as ordinary during peace-time saw a massive increase in their intrinsic value when rationing was introduced, and mundane items were stolen if they could be sold for high prices on the black market. Unfortunately added to this was the loosening of moral standards which are generally to be expected during the time of war.

Probably the saddest cases that were actually handled by the railway police during the war years were those involving railway employees who might have had twenty or thirty years of loyal service behind them, but who succumbed to the opportunities of temptation, overwork and scarcity at home. For example when families did not have sufficient food on the ration, and packing cases broke open in transit, it is not hard to understand how temptation could overcome even usually honest employees. The worst of thieves, on the other hand, were those who deserved to be given the least possible tolerance and the longest possible prison sentences; these were the ones who used the Blitz conditions to loot from unguarded places such as damaged railway goods sheds and railway vehicles.

The numbers of such cases sadly increased during the war, and to illustrate the general decline of honesty we could cite the amount of convictions undertaken by the railway police; by the end of 1944 these convictions had risen by 300% on the figures for 1938, and this was with considerably less constables involved in the actual detection of crime. Indeed, so difficult was it to stem the flow, that the Railway Executive Committee decided that its policemen and women were best employed on crime prevention. Accordingly they were given instructions to concentrate on making effective patrols, securing the perimeter of railway installations, padlocking vans, checking cargo, and so on, rather than actually attempting to catch the villains or get convictions.

The late Lord Inglewood, a member of the wartime Government and a part-time special railway policeman, once told me 'That far more crime went undetected in those dark days, but still the arrest rates were higher than they had been in that last year of peace - in the end the bad lads got too cocky, and they were frequently surprised and arrested, often by a pair of patrolling female officers, some of whom were railways clerks and typists during the day and 'specials' at night'.

There are a number of interesting cases that history has recorded, and lest we should forget them it is worthwhile mentioning them here. One incident in Cheshire came about when a maintenance gang found the doors on a railway van had been tampered with. When the constable they fetched shone a torch into the van, he came across a group of thieves with eleven sides of stolen bacon, and one of the men that was hovering in the darkness behind an ominous looking shotgun kept shouting 'Shoot the B*****d.'

Another incident involved a thief who had managed to steal fourteen cases of cigarettes from a 'bonded store', and hide them in a luxury Rolls Royce car which was being moved by the railways to another goods yard. He had an accomplice waiting in the other goods yard, who he'd had the audacity to contact on the railway telephone to ask him to unload the cigarettes on their arrival. A less luxurious case was brought to the attention of a Buckinghamshire magistrate's court concerning a sneak thief who was at the time reported to be earning £5,000 a year. He'd begun after listening to gossip in a railway carriage about the carelessness with which some people treated their luggage, and he decided he could make quite a good practice of stealing luggage, suitcases, and earning quite a living from that. However the police became suspicious of what was happening and left a decoy suitcase on Bletchley platform, and caught the man. When he appeared before the Magistrate he asked for eighty other previous offences to be taken into consideration.

Actually this type of theft, that against the person, was still the exception rather than the rule, but the railways and their business customers (especially the Government) were considered fair game and thus many of the thefts were of a far larger nature. More general fraud was found in the cheating on tickets, with many a serviceman attempting to get home on a weekend leave over-riding his ticket. Most would simply take the chance of receiving a fine for doing this rather than pay for the additional cost of travelling back to his home town. The police encountered more novel ways of fare-dodging, as for example the rather interesting way of getting round the problem of paying that was discovered by people who used the Southern Railway in Kent.

Now as it happened there was actually a station named Charing two stations north-west of Ashford, and men who were stationed in the Kent coast area could get a six pence or a shilling ride and by adding the word Cross, after the name Charing, thereby travel to Charing Cross in London. The problem in trying to stop this kind of thing was increased by the procedures at most small stations where booking clerks wrote out tickets, rather than used printed ones. In most of these stations the destination was filled in on blank tickets by a clerk using pen and ink, and the way to override these tickets was to buy a cheap ticket and take it into the gentleman's toilet as soon as possible after purchase, then let a dripping tap run on top of the ink until it was obliterated. When this was done they would dry out the ticket (that had been bought for a few pence) and then write in the name of a more distant station.

Another more chemically minded fraudster maintained (when he appeared in court) that a pint of beer made his saliva so potent that two licks with the tongue would obliterate the ink and produced a blank onto which he could write what he wanted. The police undoubtedly attributed this feature to the strength of British beer rather than the weakness of war time ink!

Holiday Camps

The popularity of holiday camps, already beginning to make their mark before war broke out in 1939, increased greatly once it ended in 1945. It was soon realised that adequate transport facilities were vital for these ventures, so to serve the holidaymakers, three new rail links were established in 1946 and 1947. The LNER put in a new line to serve the holiday camp run by Butlin's at Filey, on the Yorkshire coast. Connected to the line from Hull to Scarborough, the mile-long branch opened on 10th May 1946, and went on to carry 100,000 passengers in its first summer season. It joined the main line at a new double junction, halfway between Filey and Hunmanby. Also in May 1946, the GWR unveiled their new station at Penychain, between Afon Wen and Abererch in Wales, which served Pwllheli Holiday Camp. After the war a decision was made to develop the site as originally planned and the new holiday camp was completed as two self-contained sections either side of the railway. When it opened it could accommodate 5,000 guests but was soon set to expand, and the GWR made plans for the likely expansion, including doubling a mile of line and re-laying the engine yard.

Sites for another holiday camp in south-west Scotland were being considered before 1939 but no building schemes were begun. However, looking to their long term use, both Butlin's and the LMS were allowed to have a say in the construction of a naval training centre at the Heads of Ayr, about three miles from Ayr. The base, named HMS Scotia, opened in 1941, and then re-opened as a holiday camp on 4th June 1947. The Ayr-Turnberry-Girvan line passed through the upper part of the camp but was not used for passengers in the war as the section from Turnberry to Girvan had closed to passengers on 29th November 1930. Furthermore passengers were barred from the rest of the route on 28th February 1942 but, in order to serve the holiday camp, new facilities were provided; accordingly the new single platform Heads of Ayr station opened on 17th May 1947.

CHAPTER TWELVE
Defeat In Victory

At the end of the war the railways had proved their worth in sustaining the nation in the difficult days when invasion seemed imminent, and then carried on through the hail of bombs that fell in the blitz. Furthermore, they then went on to carry a prodigious level of traffic as the fortunes of war changed and Britain and her allies went on to the offensive. To recount all that followed would take many more pages than we can even fit into a book of this size, so to conclude the social account of the railways it is essential to present an overview of the situation that faced the Big Four between the end of hostilities in 1945 and the birth of British Railways on 1st January 1948.

We logically begin on 8th May 1945 when German military leaders surrendered to the Allies and Victory in Europe (VE-Day) was celebrated near and far. Sir Ronald Matthews of the LNER commented that now 'the public would enjoy a restoration of railway services, but that they must accept the inevitability of a certain amount of gradualness in connection with the return of passenger and freight traffics to their pre-war levels.' However, even though the railways said they were working towards 'business as normal', it was clearly evident that things would never be normal again.

Throughout the war, there had been a gradual move closer to nationalisation of the railways, and the close co-operation between the State and the various transport undertakings was already attracting many politicians towards the permanency of the arrangement. For example just because war ended, it did not mean that the control of the Railway Executive Committee was in anyway diminished. Indeed, the war in the Far-East would continue until the Americans demonstrated the horrendous power of nuclear weapons against Japan in August. Even after Emperor Hirohito surrendered to the Allies, the war traffic would continue for many months ahead. After all it had taken several years to get men and equipment sent overseas, and the repatriation of the survivors or the equipment that was considered reusable was to involve the railways in massive flows of return traffic. What is more, and surprising as it may seem, military equipment that was sent to France and the Low Countries was being brought back into Britain well into the 1950s. Similarly the flow of personnel was not as swift as it might be considered to be. It came as a considerable surprise to me, when researching an article for the magazine *Steam World*, to note that German Prisoners of War were used in clearing up a railway accident that occurred on 20th July 1952 near Shawford station on the main line from Southampton to Winchester. Closer examination revealed that this was not an isolated case, and in a subsequent book we will look at the levels of 'war-time derived traffic' that was carried by the newly formed British Railways.

So, bearing in mind the fact that the railways had to carry high levels of military traffic right up to the end of the Big Four, we must accept the involvement of the Railway Executive Committee as being essential in meeting the overall needs of the nation. Yet, in other ways some normality returned bit by bit, as the Big Four tried to get back to 'Business As Usual'.

As early as 22nd October 1941 Colonel Llewellin, Parliamentary Secretary told the House of Commons 'The Government has always given the railways a square deal and the taxpayers a fair deal.' Whilst there were many who doubted the accuracy of this statement, the railways who had had to cope with the special considerations of operating under wartime conditions were desperately in need of a fair deal if they were indeed to get back to business as usual. Yet, in reality the Big Four companies were already sowing the seeds of their own demise.

History shows that by passively allowing themselves to be affected by the restrictions of capital expenditure and serious labour shortages, the railways were not facing the serious issues that would come from repeatedly deferred maintenance. It might be wrong to blame passive acceptance of the situation by the railways, as all industry was affected by the same post-war problems. However, the railways were (in more ways than one) the prime movers of the nation's economy at that time, and with a moribund and worn-out system they were failing to provide the services that were needed to effect a good recovery. Obviously there was thus an impelling reason for the railway lobby to strenuously fight for their own corner. Fight they did, but history suggests that the fight was not hard enough and what is more it is obvious that many in the industry felt that nationalisation was already a foregone conclusion - others openly welcomed the idea.

Now before someone writes in and says we are being unfair in our summary, or that we have got it all wrong, we should say that this is no reflection on the men doing the jobs, as there is irrefutable evidence that those employed on the railways did their utmost to make them work whatever the prevailing situation. However, these efforts were in spite of the many existing problems and it can never be said that things worked because the path was an easy one. Indeed the problems which bedevilled the railways would become even more manifest in 1945-6, and also increasingly apparent to the public when wartime reporting restrictions were finally lifted.

The fact remains that although the companies made the best of the situation, and they made the usual noises about lack of funding, need for development and so on, there was just too much subservience to the national need for their own good. The railways were an exception to the need for general austerity, and this fact should have been seized upon by the companies if they were to take advantage of their unique right to funding and thus be able to rebuild a good national transport system upon which the nation's recovery could be based. As it was they did not do this, and so they staggered from one set of problems to the other and, like the national housing crisis of the immediate post-war years the Government did little to address the situation. Again these 'powers that be' did make some placatory moves to help the railways, but it was too little, too late and nothing near what was wanted.

When the true state of affairs is known, we can confidently state that the railways were in a dangerous state with track, locomotives, rolling stock, infrastructure and personnel that were clearly worn-out. Labour shortages were affecting recruitment and this was every bit as serious as the material shortages, even more so when one considers that as early as December 1940 some 80,000 railwaymen had enlisted (or been 'called-up') for military service, with some 38,000 women being enrolled to replace them. Yet, numbers employed showed a deficit of 42,000 from a railway service workforce which had been pared down to the bare minimum in the financially difficult years of the 1920s and 30s. Not unnaturally, comment was passed that 'this was a tremendous number to be taken from so important an industry.'

Yet despite this, the railways had been asked to handle ever-increasing levels of traffic, for example during 1940, an extra 17 million tons of coal were carried over the previous year's figure. In the first six months of 1941 alone, military traffic saw an extra 11,218 passenger trains and 11,739 special freight trains. Furthermore, by the time that Colonel Llewellin made his speech in 1941, 281 railwaymen and women had been killed and 1,500 more injured by enemy action whilst they were on duty. These losses, and those that followed would ultimately affect post-war railway recovery to such an extent that it would prejudice both good operation and safety.

As an indirect result of the clearly serious situation that was already developing, on 6th January 1942 the four companies set up a Commission to consider post-war planning and reconstruction of the railways. In the months and years that followed, much work would have to be done!

Above:
Another sight to emerge at London's termini after the war were the long lines of black cabs which had been considerably less in number between 1939 and 1945. No longer in short supply a group of Austin and Morris taxis are seen in 1947.

Below:
Remaining at Euston station our final picture in this selection of LMS official views shows platform 13 thronged with passengers, their luggage and pets. In the sunshine and shadows this picture portrays a moment in time on our railways in that brief interlude between war and nationalisation. Sadly this was also a time when confidence in rail travel was at an all time low as the LMS had suffered a series of disasters at places like Ecclefechan, Bourne End, Lichfield and Grendon. Just three days after the picture was taken the Southern also suffered a catastrophe at South Croydon and two days later still it was the turn of the LNER at Goswick.

Speaking of this Commission, the *Railway Magazine* for March 1942 said; 'The new body has the distinction of being established by the railways themselves, instead of being imposed upon them by an outside authority and also of having as its members essentially practical railwaymen. It will be necessary to some extent for the railways to plan for their re-establishment in the minds of the public as the primary transport agency of the country, in order to offset the disabilities arising from a long period of wartime Governmental control, and in respect of passenger and freight facilities they will have to give attention to such matters as the acceleration of services, not only to the pre-war standard which has suffered during the war, but in excess of that level in order to cope with the developments which no doubt have been made in other forms of transport.'

The commission was made up of Sir E. Lemon (LMS), K. W. C. Grand (GWR), C. K. Bird (LNER), Major F. A. Pope (LMS Northern Counties), F. J. Wymer (Southern) and T. E Thomas (LPTB). On 17th June 1942 Lord Reith (a former Transport Minister) initiated a debate in the House of Lords by asking 'whether the Government was giving immediate attention to the future constitution, control and management of the essential public services.' After commenting that the civil service should not be concerned with the management of these services, the peer suggested 'the formation of a corporation which would embrace the whole of the transport services including the railways, which would then be brought under unified management and control.' Another former Minister of Transport, Lord Brabazon, suggested that there should be separate corporations for running each of the various types of transport undertakings, roads, canals and coastwise shipping.

In an editorial in July/August issue of the *Railway Magazine* that same year, the comment was made 'The State already owns the permanent way of the road hauliers - the roads - and it would, of course, be possible for the State to acquire the permanent way and the terminals owned by the railways, leaving them to carry on the operation and maintenance work without the necessity of earning sufficient interest to remunerate the capital expended on providing the lines. This would go a long way to equalise the future position of the railways in relation to road transport, and it has been pointed out that in round figures £800,000,000 is represented in the permanent way, etc., and the interest on 4 per cent of this sum comes to £32,000,000, or within £12,000,000 of the fixed rental paid by the Government.' So the Railtrack concept of the 1990s was nothing new, and it could have been conceived as a farsighted solution to the worn down railway infrastructure half a century before it actually was. Who can say how different the story would have been, had the proposal been developed; as it was the Big Four had to seek other solutions. So, early in 1944 the railway companies once again outlined proposals for post-war reconstruction, which was based on a five year programme for the construction of all classes of locomotives and rolling stock.

The immediate priority was, however, to clean all the existing facilities, both fixed and rolling, and repaint as much of these as possible within the first year. Priority was also to be given towards the restoration of newspaper trains, travelling post offices, long-distance business services, holiday resort workings, commuter trains, and restaurant, buffet-car and sleeper coaches. A steady increase in average speeds was planned, but this would necessitate great improvements in the permanent way being undertaken if the planned 80 mph schedules were to be implemented. In many instances this would involve complete relaying or even the construction of new lines, bridges and so on to take heavier locomotives and faster traffic. Hundreds of stations were to be rebuilt on modern designs, and electrification would be introduced on densely worked lines.

This would of course be more readily achieved in areas that had been badly bombed, and thus needed rebuilding anyway. Standardisation of locomotives would also be aimed for, and much more use made of diesel or diesel-electric vehicles, such as railcars for local branch services and powerful locomotives for shunting duties. It was also envisaged that a substantial rebuilding of London would take place, and in view of the Greater London Plan and the County of London Plan (published 1944 and 1943 respectively), it was thought that there would also be substantial rebuilding of London's termini. For example, it was proposed that all the Southern Railway's electrified services would be taken underground, and many of the other railway's commuter services entering the city would also be electrified. Yet, without Government funding, it was an impossible dream albeit one which would have been such a great benefit in the years that followed. In the economic climate of the day it was not to be, but as the current Government now announce plans to get people out of their cars and back on to a modern public transport system, isn't it a pity that we are finally considering it all fifty years too late?

From Peace To Eternity?

As the war finally reached a climax, the slow process of rebuilding our railways began. But this began not with a bang, but with a whimper. The opportunity had been presented, and then dismissed so the railways had to make do and mend. To their normal business was added repatriation as prisoners of war, injured personnel and servicemen from many nations all of whom had to be carried the length and breadth of Britain. Thousands moved to and from transit camps, de-mob centres, repatriation, ports and the like. This extensive traffic all placed an additional burden on the railways, at a time when they were still heavily involved in moving military freight, leave trains and so on. All of this was over and above the essential freight and passenger traffic, which was vital to the country's economy as it made the transition back to peace. A notable step towards 'the Business as Usual' process became evident on 1st October 1945 when restaurant cars were reintroduced on the LMS, LNER and SR, although the GWR decided to opt for train service improvements instead.

Travelling post office service reinstatements were also proposed but the Minister of War Transport deferred the request and only those between Euston and Aberdeen and Paddington and Penzance were restored on 1st October, though several more were to be resumed on 6th May 1946. In the same winter timetable the reintroduction of pre-war 'named' train services such as the Yorkshire Pullman, Bournemouth Belle, and East Anglian once again reappeared. Both the LMS and the LNER announced new schemes to brighten up their buildings and furthermore many locomotives reverted to bright pre-war colours as opposed to the uniform wartime black. The LNER for example, announced that it was to repaint its entire fleet of 6,400 engines in either garter blue (streamlined Pacifics) or green.

The LMS announced a new series of liveries for its locomotives, whilst its coaches were to be painted in a maroon shade as opposed to the Midland red that had previously been in vogue. They also decided on a new colour scheme of maroon and cream for station buildings, the GWR on the other hand began the refurbishment of its stations by making a study of the visual appearance of their buildings. To this end the station at Ealing Broadway was used to carry out a number of experiments involving railway engineers, architects and design artists. One of the new innovations was a series of new station name-boards painted on a red and white background, and placed at eye-level about a carriage length apart. On the LMS a series of substantial improvements were proposed, and when we set these out alongside some of the aforementioned plans from the biggest member of the Big Four, it will suffice to show the general direction that the railways were going in the days of post-war recovery.

Home Again James

Between D-Day and VE-Day, there were exceptionally heavy levels of traffic running between supply depots, military camps and factories to the embarkation ports. New troops were flowing down to the same destination, along with all their supplies, armour and heavy equipment. In the return direction, a regular flow of servicemen were coming back home on leave and it was eventually found necessary to implement a special leave train.

Under the title British Liberation Army Leave Train, five sets were each made up from 11 corridor coaches and two Pullman buffet cars. Three King Arthur class 4-6-0s were transferred from the Western section of the SR to handle these trains, these being Nos. 767, 768 and 771. Through trains were also arranged to the LNER and LMS.

Below:
Reconstruction work was also an important feature of the post-war period and many bomb damaged or life-expired facilities had to be replaced during this period. For example the LNER's slipway at Immingham was rebuilt by Cowans, Sheldon Ltd. as our picture shows. Note the building in the background which can be clearly identified as the LNER's fish quay warehouse.

Above:
Post war normality returns to the Scottish coast as the Duchess of Hamilton *is seen thronged with passengers awaiting a cruise from Ayr harbour in 1946.*
Photo: LMS Official

LMSR FLEET'S WAR SERVICE

Thirty-five members of the fleet of ships operated by the LMS were pressed into service at one time or another during World War II, to serve as Military Transports, "Flak" ships, minelayers or sweepers, assault ships, Commando ships, hospital carriers, Boom defence vessels, ammunition carriers, as well as just ordinary transports. Eight of these ships were destined never to return to normal railway duties. One of them, the *Scotia*, was destroyed while taking part in the epic Dunkirk evacuation in May 1940. She sank when a bomb fell down the aft funnel. Several LMS ships had served in the First World War as well as the second. These included the Clyde steamers *Duchess of Rothesay*, *Queen Empress*, *Kylemore*, *Eagle III* and *Duchess of Fife*. Six LMS steamers also took part in the "D-Day" Normandy invasion of 1944.

With the first peaceful New Year for seven years, the LMS were beginning to plan again for the future. For them 1946 began with bold plans for a new fleet of locomotives and rolling stock. Although the company accepted that post-war austerity would mean it would take several years to get back to normal, they went ahead with their plans to upgrade their trains and services. The magazine *Railways* enthusiastically reported that 'there were going to be 135 new locomotives on the LMS including: five classes of high-powered 4-6-0 passenger express engines; two new classes of 2-6-0 freight engines; and 2-6-2 passenger tank engines were also planned, with ten engines of each class.' It also said that ten of what it described as the "popular Royal Scot" engines were to be upgraded, given improved boilers, and ten other passenger locomotives were to be given the same treatment.

The same magazine also advised its readers that a total of 716 third-class passenger carriages were also planned, with a total capacity of 38,000 seats. They planned to have them rolling off the production lines as fast as possible, but to do this they would have to be to immediate pre-war designs as the company needed a short-term plan just to get things moving. A *Times* editorial commented at the end of 1945 'So long as a decent, clean service is offered to passengers by the LMS, there will not be too many problems from its patient customers whilst the company sets out its long-term ideas for improved designs for carriages and comfort for passengers.'

The *Railway Magazine* reported that between VE Day on 8th May 1945 and March of 1946 over 250 of the "stop-gap" carriages entered service. Eight of them were leaving the works each week. As passenger ferries and "steamers", were also an important part of Britain's railway network which had been badly affected by the war, new vessels were urgently required. The Heysham-Belfast steamer was refitted in the first months after the war, and was set to enter service in time for the 1946 tourist season. Three out of the 11 Clyde steamers were also being refitted after being "called up" for war service. Six more were waiting their turns to be refitted in early-1946, and the other two were still on Government service. The new LMS Stranraer-Larne ship was under construction at the time, and plans were already made to replace the old vessel which served this route, along with six others sunk during the war.

Unfortunately, despite these plans and some restorations and improvements to services, all was far from well with the railways when the Ministry of War Transport was finally abolished on 1st April 1946. Civilian control of the railways resumed under the new Transport Minister, Alfred Barnes, who had been appointed on 7th March following the Labour victory in the General Election. A new broom might have come into power with the intention of making a clean sweep, but as the first week of January 1946 had shown the only broom that was needed was the one to sweep up the debris of a series of railway disasters that shook the nation's confidence in 'British Railways.' This sad state of affairs continued throughout 1946 and into 1947, but it had begun under the previous Government with a pair of nasty accidents on the West Coast Main Line in the summer of 1945.

Accidents & Disasters

It has to be said that one of the most significant legacies of the war years, as far as British railways is concerned, was the atrocious state to which the lines, locomotives, and rolling stock had been allowed to deteriorate. The heavy trains, poor maintenance, inferior materials, poor coal and poorly trained recruits in all the grades of the railway service each had their own cumulative effects. Combined, these effects were likely to lead to disaster if immediate steps were not taken to address the arrears of maintenance etc. As Crump says in his official book on the LNER, 'the engines were flogged to death.'

Funding was therefore urgently required to get the railways back on their feet, new equipment and materials were manifestly necessary for every branch of railway engineering. Fresh labour was also required to supplement those coming back from the services or those who had 'given their all' during the war years, and above all good quality coal and lubricants were needed by the locomotive departments. These were the things that were desperately needed but, when neither they nor adequate compensation payments were received by the railways, disaster was inevitably bound to follow. This sad fact is particularly revealed by events in the years following the war, when the aforementioned conditions led to a large number of serious rail accidents.

I do not propose to highlight each disaster in detail, but a brief summary of those which occurred on the worn-out Big Four during the latter part of the 1940s will set the scene. We begin with a collision at Grays on 14th June 1945, but twelve days later the LMS handed over the mantle of disaster to the Southern who suffered a collision at Caterham. Then, on a misty, drizzling day in the Scottish borders an inexplicable collision took place on the WCML at Ecclefechan on 27th July.

September was another bad month with a collision on the LMS at Haywards Heath (on the 2nd), a landslide near Llangollen (GWR) on the 27th, and an even more mysterious derailment when an experienced and most conscientious LMS driver took a diversion from the fast lines to a slow loop at Bourne End on the 29th. A derailment on 10th October at Carcroft (LNER) was followed by a collision at Woking (SR) exactly one month later. The year was rounded out by a terrible collision (followed by fire) between two London Transport locomotives at Northwood Hills on the joint Metropolitan and Great Central line on the morning of New Year's Eve.

The accident of 31st December 1946 was the start of what the press called 'British Railways' Black Week', which is interesting as it shows that the term B.R. was already being applied, even though nationalisation was still two years away. This 'Black Week' is also of interest, because more than any other sequence of events, it shows how badly the railways had deteriorated in the war, as every accident can clearly be identified as having its contributory cause rooted in either the abuse handed out during the war years or the post-war staffing shortages.

The second accident took place on New Year's Day at Lichfield Trent Valley Station, when an LMS fish train ran in to the back of a stationary local passenger whilst it was standing at the platform. Four days later, it was the failure of a drawbar hook and the division of an LNER freight which caused wreckage to spill in front of a down express at Browney Signal Box, near Ferryhill, Co. Durham, (which is pictured below). In total BR's Black Week claimed no less than 33 lives and injured the same amount. The following month a multiple train collision took place on the LNER at Potters Bar, but it is a real wonder that only two fatalities were sustained after the three trains piled into each other at speed.

British Railways Black Week

The New Year Week of 1945/46 began on Monday December 31, but in those days there was no public holiday on that day except in Scotland. Accordingly, that Monday morning was the first day of a new week, and for many the first day back at work after the Christmas Holiday. As the public began making their way home after the celebrations and commuters recommenced their daily travel to work, a series of disasters were waiting to strike at the railways. These were of such shocking severity that questions would be asked in both Houses of Parliament. Although severe pressure was placed on the Transport Minister, he in turn could rest behind the statement that 'Official Boards of Inquiry have been opened into the accidents and it would be a matter of *sub-judice* for him to make any statement at this time'. He did, however, offer his sincere condolences to the relatives of those killed in the crashes and added 'claims from relatives and survivors will be met with promptitude by the railway companies... The first urgent need to be considered would be the issue of funeral expenses, and at each inquest the senior claims officer of the railway company involved was in attendance to make arrangements for all burial costs. The respective Coroners all thanked these claims officers for their kindness.'

With this side-step / cover up the issue of railway safety began to lapse back into obscurity, the papers taking up a story as to whether or not the photograph of a 13 year old boy found in the late Adolf Hitler's papers was a picture of his son. With this debate and other more pressing issues, such as the national coal shortage, the issue quietly disappeared - however, less than six weeks later the whole debate was reopened as an extraordinary series of collisions occurred at Potters Bar. Although this only claimed two lives, the fatalities could have been extremely high, for the events were such as to bear a striking similarity to the awful disaster which would take place on the former LMS main line at Harrow & Wealdstone Station just six years later.

143

Disaster At Croydon

The accident at Croydon was a series of failures most of which came about because of inadequate training for the signalman who made the fatal mistake, but there were other issues as well. For example, the accident report said that treadle failures had deluded the signalman to a great extent, observing: 'this means all in authority should be kept aware of the extent of such failures, and of the efficiency of maintenance.' It also concluded that the accident would never have occurred had the prewar proposal to re-signal this section with colour-light signals and continuous track-circuits gone ahead. This new scheme would have certainly prevented an accident of this type resulting from the misuse of the Sykes re-set key. He also passed comment about the over-crowding of the two trains which undoubtedly led to the high number of fatalities and injuries. Obviously the traditional problems which affected the Southern Railway stemmed from exceptionally high commuter use in the peak periods morning and night, and limited mid-day and evening demand. Shortages of rolling stock and this high-concentration of passengers at peak times were further exacerbated by the poor training, poor maintenance and other staffing problems. That grim day in October 1947 at South Croydon tragically showed that lives really did depend upon the railways quickly sorting out the postwar difficulties, but were the lessons quickly learned?
It would seem not!

On 19th March it was the turn of the Southern to suffer a collision at Mottingham, then it was back to the LNER, this time with a derailment at Hatfield on 15th July (pictured below). On the 25th a collision took place between a train and a motor vehicle at Balmuckety Level Crossing in Scotland, and two days later another collision took place at Edgware on the London Passenger Transport Board system. At the same time the LMS were experiencing problems with its trans-Pennine line (see page 150) when an inadequately maintained canal aqueduct broke its banks and washed away the track below, seriously disrupting services between Lancashire and Yorkshire. We must then return to London, where a derailment took place on 29th September at Catford (SR), before recounting another incident of the same type at Marshmoor on the LNER six weeks later. On 7th December the LMS suffered a collision at Stafford, and the Southern rounded out the year with a derailment at Byfleet two days after Christmas.

We now move to the last year of the Big Four, and it is sad to say it is one littered with serious incidents, many of which were of such severity that they have been covered in *Trains In Trouble*. We must begin by recalling the awful collision which took place within the fog-bound confines of the LNER's Gidea Park station and claimed seven lives, after the failure of a fog signalman to turn up for his duties. This was followed by the high-speed derailment of a Duchess class 4-6-2 at Polesworth due to worn track which claimed five victims from a train that was crammed with over 800 passengers, of whom 130 were standing at the time of the accident. A fatal collision caused by a signalman's error and the failure of the LNER to fully re-signal the main line at Doncaster led to a rear-end smash between two trains on 21st July in which 18 folk were killed.

On the 17th September another collision rocked the LNER at Burton Agnes, but worse was to come on the SR at Croydon on 24th October (pictured above). Here an inadequately trained signalman panicked when faced with heavy train movements in dense fog, and he used a master key to reopen his Sykes Lock & Block equipment. In the confusion which followed an EMU was to run through Croydon South Junction into the rear of a heavily loaded train which was moving slowly through the fog. Of the 1,800 passengers on the two crowded commuter trains, 31 were killed and 183 injured. Stupidity by the crew of a Scottish express allowed an unauthorised passenger aboard the footplate of the A3 Class *Merrie Hampton*, which was derailed in suspicious circumstances at Goswick south of Berwick-on-Tweed killing 28 people in the process. The Southern suffered a spate of collisions as the year drew to a close, two came on 6th November at Herne Hill and Motspur Park Junction, but the worst of all was at Farnborough on the 26th in which two people died after yet another signalling error. It was left, however, to the LMS to carry on its reputation for wrecking trains and gain the distinction of being the last serious accident on the Big Four, as a runaway was followed by a collision at Manchester Victoria on 10th December.

Unfortunately, a study of these various accidents clearly reveals that the valiant war-time effort of the railways had not been accomplished without the payment of a heavy price. The abuse and over-use of the railway network, along with repeatedly deferred maintenance work had left the Big Four companies in a terrible position. Of immediate national concern was their financial state, a position which could only be addressed by huge investment, but safety was fast becoming of paramount significance. The vast majority of locomotives in service were almost worn out, and many should have been scrapped a decade earlier. In addition, track conditions were often right up to, and frequently beyond, the limits of safety. The difficulties of operating defective engines with life-expired rolling stock on suspect track was, in reality, far more dangerous for travellers than any hazard encountered in the war years. Yet to add to these problems, came the terrible winter of 1946/7 which sent the already staggering railways reeling and led to the establishment of the Winter Transport Executive Committee.

Ex-GNR Ivatt engines in Hitchin in 1937:
Class D2 4-4-0 No.4337 and large boilered Class C1 4-4-2 No.3272.

Folkestone in 1938, three East Kent buses await duty beneath the arches of Foord viaduct,
while a Wainwright Class C 0-6-0 No.1723 crosses with a non-corridor local.

Trans-Pennine Traffic Disrupted

Between the sharply curved running lines approaching Standedge Tunnel, stood the overflow channel for the Reservoir which fed the Huddersfield Narrow Canal that the LMS abandoned in November 1943. This overflow dates from the construction of the third tunnel, and replaces an earlier by-wash though the existing channel into the River Colne was retained. With the lack of maintenance during the war years, problems soon arose. On 20th September 1946, after a period of torrential rain, this by-wash gave way under the weight of a sudden rush of water. It smashed down the side-wall, and as a result thousands of gallons of water flooded across the tracks. The deluge caused so much subsidence that the rails were left twisted and suspended in mid air, causing disruption to train services for several days.

The railways once again got through the winter of 1947 somehow, in fact they had weathered another serious situation, just as they had done with crashes, labour shortages, deferred maintenance issues and material shortages. But, 'despite the fact that we [they had] got through by the skin of their teeth' (to quote A. H. Peppercorn) the problems caused at the start of 1947 were just another series of nails in the proverbial coffin. Nationalisation was, by now, probably the only answer, but the lack of action by Government and the many contradictory views that were being expressed by some new ministers undoubtedly gave rise to bitter resentment amongst the Big Four as evidenced by a statement by Sir Ronald Matthews, Chairman of the LNER.

'It is a matter requiring immediate attention when a Minister of the Crown uses inaccurate statistics which have the effect of disparaging the value of a business which the Government is proposing to acquire compulsorily at a price which many people consider grossly inaccurate. In his opening speech in the Transport Bill Debate, Mr Barnes, referring to the London & North Eastern Railway, said: "Its locomotives, on an average, are 32 years old. That also applies to wagons and all other elements in the rolling stock, and at a time when it is vital that transport should render an efficient service to British industry we are having to impose widespread restrictions on commercial traffic ..." Now, while it is true that on 31st December 1945, the average age of LNER steam locomotives was 32.41 years, it is emphatically not the case that this applies to "wagons and all other elements in the rolling stock". Wagons averaged only 17.73 years old, passenger carriages averaged 23.70 years old, and non-passenger-carrying coaching vehicles (brake vans, horse-boxes, etc.) 17.82 years.* As regards the old-fashioned carriages on the Liverpool Street suburban services, which the Lord President of the Council criticised in his speech towards the conclusion of the Debate, it should be remembered that but for the war a substantial proportion of the routes served would have been electrified and orders had in fact been placed in 1939 with the manufacturers for the construction of new electric trains. It is no fault of the LNER that the old steam stock still has to be used six years after it was due to be scrapped. The average age of LNER steam locomotives at the end of 1939 was only 27.70 years. The rise over the war period to 32.41 years was mainly due to the necessary diversion of our locomotive shops to war work, such as manufacturing tank, aircraft and artillery components, rocket guns, and many other items, including no less than 1½ million shell cases. Incidentally, during the past year the LNER locomotive stock has benefited from the purchase of 75 shunting locomotives and 200 "Austerity" heavy freight locomotives from the Ministry of Supply, by the delivery of about 70 mixed-traffic locomotives from outside builders, and by new construction in our own locomotive shops. In his speech, Mr Barnes, referring to the effects of industrial depression and the competition from road transport

Actually, the LNER fleets of both wagons and non-passenger-carrying coaching vehicles were the youngest of those owned by the three major freight-carrying railways

between the wars, added that "the LNER suffered probably more than the others, with the result that necessary capital was not expended, as it should have been, on keeping their capital equipment up-to-date". Even an elementary acquaintance with business practice or accountancy will demonstrate that it would be very wrong indeed to raise and spend capital merely on keeping equipment up-to-date. This is a charge on revenue and, in the case of the railways, it is met through Renewal or Depreciation Funds. Any business that raises large amounts of capital merely to effect renewals or depreciation will soon find itself in "Queer Street"; and if Mr Barnes' new Transport Commission is going to follow this method of finance the outlook is indeed an alarming one!'

However, despite all the rhetoric the ultimate price which had to be paid was nationalisation! Just as the Grouping of most private railways was a result of World War One, the formation of British Railways in January 1948 was a direct consequence of this second major conflict. Under the terms by which the Railway Executive Committee took control of the 'Big Four' companies in 1939, the Government were eventually obliged to spend several millions of pounds to bring the railways back up to an acceptable standard. Yet despite the role played by our railway system in the period from 1939 to 1945, most of the major post-war transport funding went on road improvements. Respective politicians continued to withhold the cash until another period of conflict, the Suez Crisis of 1956 (with its attendant petrol rationing that showed that roads could not readily replace the railways), finally forced the Macmillan Government to provide the cash required to institute the British Railways Modernisation Plan - But Once Again It Was Just Too Little and Far, Far, Too Late!

151

Trans-Pennine Improvements

Following the wartime break, the upgrading of the Manchester-Sheffield trans-Pennine route for electric trains was to be re-started by the LNER in a scheme set to last four years and cost £6,000,000. In addition to the main line, in which some 75 route-miles, (a total of 300 miles of track and sidings) were to be electrified, the lines from Barnsley Junction to Wath and from Fairfield to Trafford Park and Manchester Central were also to be converted. It was reckoned the scheme would save 100,000 tons of coal a year, and that the introduction of electric trains would allow accelerated services to begin on the route.

The three-mile-long Woodhead Tunnel, was the fourth-longest on the British railway network and was always a headache for ventilation, maintenance and snow. Earlier in 1947 the tunnel was having repairs for damaged roof-linings, and the LNER had already been given the go-ahead for a new tunnel to accommodate the electric wires and posts. The old tunnel's linings had been damaged by years of punishment by smoke from steam engines, and the smoke was hanging around the tunnel long enough to damage the health of anyone working in it. The coal industry was a main customer of the M&S railway, with around sixty per-cent of trains on the busy route carrying coal. Almost 100 trains passed through the lengthy tunnel each way every day. With electrification, that traffic would be increased even more, possibly by around 25%. The electrification scheme had actually begun before the war, and the earliest experiments had commenced as early as 1934. In the autumn of 1941 a new, 1,870-horsepower electric locomotive successfully completed trials on an electric line between Manchester and Altrincham. Although it had then been stored (then loaned to the Dutch), it was modified and underwent further tests before the scheme for the route to from Manchester to Sheffield was re-started. Power would be supplied - at 1,500 volts - from overhead wires, a system like the one for Altrincham.

No.6832 Brockton Grange *at Birmingham Snow Hill,*
seen in the wintery sun in February 1939.

An ex-MR 4-4-0, No.1014,
waiting for its next job at Shrewsbury in 1938.

*The ultimate Gresley three-cylinder pacific, streamlined A4 No.4484 Falcon
at Edinburgh Haymarket in August 1938.*

*Also seen at Shrewsbury in 1938 on a running in turn,
is nearly new LMS non-streamlined Coronation Class 7P 4-6-2 No.6232* Duchess of Montrose.

Above:

Fashionable streamlining treatment was given to a few unlikely locomotive types in the 1930s. Above is one of two LNER Class B17 4-6-0s (No.2859 East Anglian) to be given A4 style casings for use on the 'East Anglian' express, the route being, at that time, incapable of accepting any heavier type of locomotive. Larger tenders were provided but this then created problems at the terminal stations because the turntables were not big enough to accommodate the lengthened engines. To resolve the problem new turntables were ordered from the firm of Cowans, Sheldon Ltd.

Photo: LNER Official

Below:

By contrast with the LNER, the GWR seemed to have been poking fun at contemporary trends when it applied this very curious treatment to 4-6-0 No.5005 Manorbier Castle.

Photo: Brad Leigh Collection

Below these 'flagship' engines, all four companies could offer a more than adequate range of secondary express power in the 25,000 - 30,000lb tractive effort field. These were generally somewhat older designs which, in their time, had been at the top of their own respective trees until outfaced by heavier trains and by 1938, their construction had effectively ceased, though they were too important to be ignored and much development work took place on them. To these should also be added the many much older designs (mostly dating from the pre-group period) which could still be found much useful work to do on the less demanding tasks; it should never be forgotten that the typical lifespan of a steam locomotive was rarely less than 30-40 years until more modern times and our private railways were commercial animals who would want a good return from any form of investment, regardless of age!

By 1938, the traditional idea of 'horses for courses' in terms of specific locomotive designs for each and every form of operation had started to undergo a massive conceptual re-appraisal in most parts of the country. Instead, there had begun to develop the notion that a general all-purpose 'mixed traffic' locomotive was capable of performing a great deal of main line work which did not fall at the extreme ends of the operating spectrum (i.e. the heaviest express passenger and freight operations). In consequence, many examples of this new type of locomotive, neither full blown high speed thoroughbred nor ponderously slow and powerful, started to be seen on our railways. Some companies took this idea further than others but all were aware of the advantages, if only in terms of the long term benefit of having fewer types to service and for which to keep spare parts: in a word, the value of standardisation (in concept if not always in reality) was beginning to take on ever increasing importance.

That said, however, the concept of standardisation was no new notion and it should certainly not be supposed that it was a distinctively unique feature of the late company period. The economic advantage of fewer types of locomotive which, in an ideal situation, would also utilise a maximum number of common parts even within different classes, had been well appreciated by more than a few of our bigger companies even in pre-group days. Several of them had, indeed, gone well down this road before 1923 so it can be no surprise that the Big Four continued the process. However, as stated, the steam locomotive was a long-lived machine - and still expected to be so in strictly commercial terms - so it was too much to hope that these new ideas would immediately result in wholesale re-stocking on a nationwide basis. That it never happened either in steam days or in the post-steam corporate BR period probably sums it up nicely!

The fact is that at no time have our railways ever achieved a total unity of approach - and probably never will; but this should not stop us looking at their achievements in the light of what they all knew to be a theoretical ideal. Thus it was that outwith the locomotive areas so far discussed, the Big Four still had to provide for a considerable number of other operational categories, especially when we consider that they were operating in an age when the motor vehicle had not assumed the dominance which it now holds. Many were common to all but others were unique to but some of them, so there were both similarities and differences to be observed.

Dealing first with the similarities, it can safely be said that in the field of local railway activity - be it urban or rural in nature - there was much in common, be it pick-up freight from individual goods yards or relatively light weight (and sadly, increasingly less-patronised) passenger working.

Here, at the start of the period in question, a fairly universal solution was to use elderly and almost life-expired engines (often of pre-group origin) with almost equally elderly rolling stock. This sort of traffic, in the absence of real competition, was not perceived to justify much if anything by way of new investment in by far the majority of cases. Indeed, in the realm of freight traffic, the situation was little short of disgraceful by global standards; but this was not confined to local operations for reasons we shall soon see.

Another area of similarity was the ubiquitous inside cylinder 0-6-0. This was the archetypal British goods engine from mid-Victorian days onwards and all four companies could still offer hundreds of examples in 1938. Cosmetically, they differed considerably, many having been built in the pre-group era, but all were of broadly similar concept and usage. More surprisingly, in spite of what has been said above regarding the development of mixed traffic types, all four main line companies added considerably to their totals after 1923, the Southern actually introducing two brand new designs in 1938 and 1942. Even the LMS under William Stanier found scope for building a few more (to what was basically a 1911 design from the pre-1923 Midland Railway) as late as 1941!

The value of the 0-6-0 lay in its incredible versatility. At the basic level (i.e.: in its simplest cheap-to-run form which went back well into pre-group days) it was the ideal choice for short and medium distance goods working. Give it automatic continuous train braking facility* and it was equally at home on a similar form of passenger working if high speed was not important; while beefing it up a bit in absolute size allowed it full reign on much main line freight until well into the period covered by this account. Small wonder that all four railways found plenty of use for them - as indeed did BR until almost the very end of the steam era. Where the ubiquitous 0-6-0 fell down was in its uncertain performance at the sort of higher speeds which were being increasingly demanded as years went by and which had reached what might be termed a critical point by the start of our period of study. Essentially, it all boiled down to the matter of stability in terms of the engine chassis; haulage power was not a factor.

The 0-6-0 was a remarkably effective machine, having little by way of superfluous trimmings no matter who had designed it. In consequence it undoubtedly endeared itself to a management structure which was geared to making a dividend at minimum capital cost - so it lasted long. But when customers began to demand quicker transits for certain types of consignment, the inherent mechanical disadvantage of an engine with (relatively) large leading wheels soon became apparent. Now in the passenger field, it had long been appreciated that if leading non-driven wheels of smaller diameter (whether in the form of a single pair or a four wheel bogie) were provided, these bestowed much greater stability and speed potential to the locomotive and this proved to be a turning point. It took time for the same considerations to be apparent in the freight field (indeed, it was still in process of development during the last years of the Big Four, hence continued building of 0-6-0s); but the logical outcome where no great increase in haulage power was needed, was to add two leading wheels to the faithful old 0-6-0, thus producing a 2-6-0 type. This too had happened in several areas prior to the grouping but it was the Big Four which took it to its apogee in the British context. All four of them developed the type and the story of this line of evolution was by no means completed as 1938 dawned, thus offering yet another area of conceptual similarity, regardless of actual end product.

Heavy main line freight was not terribly different, viewed in retrospect. Here the needs of industry led to ever increasing consignments of heavy goods being shipped by rail over quite considerable distances. The Big Four responded from an early stage, a common interim solution (which actually pre-dated the 1923 grouping) being to enlarge the traditional 0-6-0 to the 0-8-0 arrangement. But this solution was neither wholly satisfactory nor, in the event, a permanent answer. Only the LMS had assayed new 0-8-0s in the post-group era (along with a massive re-building of over 500 of its inherited examples of the genre - see later); but by 1938, the preferred heavy freight locomotive in a national sense was the outside-cylindered 2-8-0 type which was beginning to be appreciated as an ideal goods engine for long distance work, its leading pair of small wheels being seen to offer the same sort of speed advantage in the heavy haulage role as had the 2-6-0 over the 0-6-0 (above). Apart from the Southern, which had less of this sort of traffic, the eight coupled freight engine, be it 0-8-0 or 2-8-0, was therefore a sort of accepted 'norm' by the start of our period and all three other railways had them. On the Southern, however, the need was less critical and apart from modern 2-6-0s, of which it had more than a few, its solution took on the rather different form of enlarging the 0-6-0 type and regarding not a few of its more powerful overtly passenger engines as 'mixed traffic - a fact which will be considered later. At this point, the mention of outside cylinders in connection with freight locomotives, leads to the consideration of yet another area of 'coming together' which the grouping period was to exemplify in locomotive terms.

For readers who are not wholly familiar with the utterly primitive nature of goods train working during the steam era, it may be worth making the point that during this time, only passenger trains had to carry fully automatic brakes and many goods engines were not equipped with the necessary apparatus to operate such trains.

The 0-6-0 was a veritable maid of all work and here are three examples of the variety which could be seen. Other than the GWR example, the rest were built during the Big Four period. Details as follows, top to bottom:

a) LNER Gresley Class J39 No.2788 seen between Bridge of Orchy and Tyndrum with a typical goods train, carrying 'Through Freight' headlamp code.
Photo: NRM Collection

b) GWR (ex-Cambrian Railways) No.894 on local passenger duty in 1939 at Barmouth Junction. By now, this pre-group engine had acquired many standard GWR fittings.
Photo: Pendragon Collection

c) LMS Class 4F No.4511, one of hundreds built to a former Midland design after the grouping and seen here in charge of a largely non-automatic brake fitted 'Through Freight'.
Photo: R.J.Essery Collection

This fine LMS 2-6-2T design dated from 1927 was often used for outer suburban work,
here No.2328 is on the Midland main line from St. Pancras and at St. Albans in May 1939.

A former GER Class J67 0-6-0T No.7169 in a particularly charming duty on the Kelvedon and Tollesbury branch in 1938.
Working a mixed train of passenger and goods stock, not a particularly unusual sight in the late 1930s.

One of the more interesting facets of the final company years was the final severance with the long held British 'inside cylinder' tradition of locomotive design. Many writers have put this down to a wish to keep the working parts hidden (a manifestation of Victorian prudery if you like), but this writer tends to the view that this is mostly romantic nonsense.

The real virtue of the inside cylindered engine lay in the fact that the drive to the wheels was nearer to the centre line of the locomotive than for the outside cylindered alternative. In days when the art of metallurgy was such that structural strains were a key factor in the design of moving machinery, it made sense to minimise such forms of stress by reducing lateral leverage - thus the preference for inside cylinders - this factor generally tending to outweigh the undoubted complications of fabricating (or casting) the consequential crank axle.* But once this problem was solved - which was undoubtedly true by the grouping years - it made much more sense to put as many of the moving parts as possible where they were more readily accessible: i.e. outside the frames. Indeed, the wonder is that it took so long for folk to realise this simple fact; but such was the case as far as Britain's railways were concerned. Whatever, it was not until the late 1930s that this view had become well nigh universal and even though there were still a few inside cylindered engines to be built, the general move was towards outside cylindered simplicity (usually allied with Walschaerts valve gear), a change which was rarely associated with more than two cylinders - the exceptions will be noted later.

Nowhere was this better exemplified than in the suburban passenger field wherein the railways were increasingly faced with competition from other forms of transport in the shape of electric tramways and (later) trolley and motor buses. In this field (and with the benefit of hindsight) railway electrification was to be the ultimate answer (we can give the Southern Railway full credit for grasping this nettle well ahead of the rest); but this was not to be universally manifest until well into the post-steam BR era. Meantime, the other parts of the Big Four system (and let us not forget that this notion was copied by BR for the best part of the next generation) tried to find a solution with steam power - and it is a matter of record that they mostly succeeded.

Accepting the limitations of broad generalisation, the main instrument of this fight back was the 'modern' passenger tank engine. The suburban passenger tank locomotive had a long and honourable ancestry, whether it be in the form of the dainty little Stroudley engines on the Brighton line, the rather larger 0-4-4Ts of the Caledonian, LSWR and Midland, the more 'puissant' 0-6-2Ts of LNWR, GNR or GER origin, the 2-4-2Ts of the LYR or the 4-4-2Ts of the London Tilbury and Southend line - to mention but some of the many types which might be cited. All had in common the undoubted virtue of versatility - they need not be turned at the end of the journey and were not burdened by excess weight as a consequence of having to carry fuel and water for excessively long distances.

These prime operational considerations did not really change during the grouping period, but trains got heavier (in consequence of more folk entering the 'commuter' category) and carriages likewise got larger. In consequence, the logical outcome was a larger and more powerful form of the same sort of engine. In general this took upon itself one of but two basic wheel arrangements: the 2-6-2T or 2-6-4T, the latter mostly being favoured where additional fuel/water supplies needed to be provided for longer distances. Perhaps the most surprising thing was that those railways which needed to address the problem came up with broadly the same sort of solutions, cosmetic variations apart, and yet again we can witness this 'coming together' in conceptual terms as far as individual companies were concerned by the end of the grouping period. One must, of course, beware of extending any generalisation too far - the Southern was a little different in this as in some other aspects previously considered and we shall have need to come back to this later; while the GWR never assayed a 2-6-4T. But what is perhaps more relevant is how close they had come (in 1947) to a reasonable degree of unanimity in terms of what was actually needed in purely locomotive terms.

Much the same was true in the carriage and wagon field: "No man is an island" was certainly true as far as Britain's railways were concerned when it came to the business of the people and goods they were carrying and it is to this we must now turn attention. By the late 1930s, the railway was regarded as *the* sophisticated method of moving across the face of the earth as far as land travel was concerned. It is true that a few folk had private cars, but in general, whether you be a film star travelling from New York to Los Angeles or a politician visiting a Scottish constituency from Westminster, the first choice was almost always the train. Over the years, this widespread acceptance of the railway travel mode had led to a degree of unanimity concerning what, exactly, should be provided on a 'good' train. In the long-distance field there was little real debate; no matter whether you travelled first class or third: comfortable seats, well-equipped dining cars and well-founded sleeping cars were expected to be available - and, for the most part, were.

* The writer is aware that this is something of an over-simplification and is not unmindful of the fact that the immortal 'Crewe' type (with outside cylinders) was evolved to cope with the problems of broken crank axles in the 1840s. But taken overall, the predominant 19th Century British locomotive form displayed inside cylinders and this style of construction remained popular well into the grouping period - hence the nature of the offered generalisation

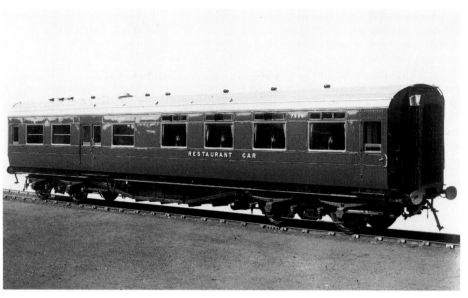

Curiously, in the British context, third class really meant 'second' by 1938, the real second class having mostly been abolished in Edwardian days - its residual survivors (a few commuter trains in North London and a handful of three-class Continental Boat trains) did not really count! It is a curious fact of life that this typically British nonsense was not resolved in the formal sense until 1956, long after our period of interest, when third class finally became second. Over its subsequent transmogrification to standard class in later BR days, along with the general confining of decent dining facilities in most cases to first class only, it is perhaps best to draw a veil.....

No matter, the Big Four knew exactly where they were in 1938 and in the long distance field, could stand comparison with almost anything the rest of the world could offer when it came to passenger comfort and amenity. In fact, there was little to choose between any of them at the best level of provision, most of the differences being either cosmetic (in design terms) or conceptual (as a consequence of the type of service which they were providing). Thus it was that the LMS and LNER tended to dominate the field in both dining and sleeping car terms, having the longest routes and most of the overnight business, not to mention the bulk of the business traffic between the major industrial regions and London. By contrast, the SR had no sleeping car trade at all; but it and the GWR (which also had a fair bit of mid-distance business and overnight travel to Wales and the South West) were both highly experienced in that rather crucial business of getting holiday-makers to their destinations in a reasonable degree of comfort and style - or else they would not come back next year, of course!

Above:

This stylish Maunsell design first class dining car No.7998 for the Southern Railway in 1934 was typical of the well built stock which all railways were using at the time, though rather more old fashioned in appearance than some of its contemporaries. It would normally have been found on West of England services in company with an open non-kitchen third class dining carriage.
Photo: SR Official

Below & Right:

Contrasting carriage interiors from the 1930s. On the left is a GWR first class compartment from the 1936 'Sunshine' stock, while on the right is a third class interior from the somewhat earlier 1933 LMS Stanier stock. If truth be told, there is little of significant difference between the two.
Photo: GWR and LMS Official

Although each company had its own particular emphasis, every one of them had every good reason to provide their patrons with decent carriages - and this they did in no small measure. The upshot was that during the period under study, there began to evolve a remarkable level of consistency between the best carriages of all four companies. It typically took the form of a 57-60ft bogie coach wherein could be found either a traditional compartment configuration with associated side corridor, or a fully open saloon type with either 2 + 1 seating (first class) or 2 + 2 (third class). Toilets (usually better than anything to be found elsewhere in either Europe or the rest of the world) were always present, while big observation windows were very common in the 'open saloon' category. During company days, the fully open carriage never achieved the position of universal dominance which it was to assume during the BR period. The British rather liked their individual compartments, so all four companies tended to favour this type although there was some degree of of disunity between them regarding whether or not passengers should have individual outside doors to the compartments, or precisely how many seats each compartment should contain. Sleeping and dining cars likewise tended to be somewhat similar in concept wherever they were to be found, though each company had its favoured approach in terms of cosmetic and design trimmings.

Likewise in the short distance field, by far the most dominant carriage style was the non-corridor vehicle with its vast number of individual compartments, each with its own side door. Their main virtues lay in their huge carrying capacity and speed of loading and unloading rather than in matters of comfort: many of them were pretty dire and some few were utterly disgraceful! But even the otherwise enterprising Southern Railway reckoned that its new electric trains would best serve their purpose if they continued to follow the traditional compartment form. However in that somewhat amorphous area of passenger travel which rested between the long distance express and genuine commuter services (and the railways had a lot of this sort of traffic in the pre-motor age), there was less degree of consistency - probably because such services could range from not much more than long distance outer suburban via extended cross-country services to the requirements of the bucolic rural branch line. A common solution was to provide a few intermediate lavatories in an otherwise basically suburban type train but this area of operations was probably to see rather more regional and company variations than many parts of the travelling scene; and we shall return to them in due course.

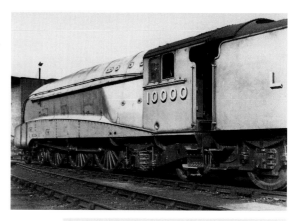

The LNER Class W1 4-6-4 No.10000, rebuilt in 1937 from Nigel Gresley's experimental 'Hush-Hush' design of 1929 and mentioned in the story below.
Photo: Ransome-Wallis Collection, NRM

It was in the field of freight vehicles where the British companies fell most short of the ideal. Throughout the company period - and, indeed, during the greater part of the subsequent BR steam period - a typical British goods wagon was that most astonishing legacy from the early Victorian railway: the four wheel 'truck' with primitive suspension, relatively low load capacity (both in absolute terms and related to its own empty weight) and, in by far the majority of examples, no form of automatic brake at all. There were, of course, many sound historical reasons for this state of affairs (small goods yards, limited space around the sidings etc) but given that the Big Four taken as a whole obtained the majority of their revenue from freight (roughly two thirds of LMS and LNER receipts came from goods trains and only on the Southern was passenger revenue to dominate), it is no great credit to any of them that they did so little to improve the breed, either in vehicle size or operational sophistication. In fact, one can argue cogently that the neglect of the freight infrastructure was the most adverse legacy which they bequeathed to their BR successor. Mark you, there was no great rush to improve matters during the next twenty years either, so the old four-wheelers trundled on as before, losing ever more traffic to the increasingly sophisticated road vehicle competitor until, in many cases, the battle was finally lost. That said, however, even these primitive vehicles were not without some interest and this will be addressed in due course.

However, when dealing with freight traffic in the company era, one is faced with a slight dilemma. There is no shortage of published information about the actual vehicles which the companies built, but information is less easy to find as far as their operation is concerned - and it is, of course, the latter which tends to reveal most in terms of explaining what was actually built and why. Add to this the fact that much freight traffic was of an inter-company nature and it will be appreciated that it is not quite so easy to isolate the practices of the individual companies as it is with locomotives or coaching stock. Indeed, by the time the Big Four entered their last decade, the bulk of company owned goods vehicles were regarded as 'common user'; in other words, unless specifically marked 'non common-user', or similar, any company could use any other company's empty wagons for re-loading if they were available, rather than send them back empty to their 'home' area. For this reason, before looking at the individual company offerings, it is probably helpful to see how they stood both relative to each other and against the broader British picture, starting with a few statistics - see summary table (overleaf). The table itself is based on data published in 'British Goods Wagons' (Essery, Rowland and Steel; David & Charles, 1970), to which acknowledgement is duly given, and relates to the position ten years after the grouping. The totals quoted were slightly less than in 1923 and fell a little more by the late 1930s, but the overall picture in terms of relative proportions and so forth, changed but little during the final company period.

The first thing which stands out clearly is the huge number of vehicles in absolute terms and to these should be added a near identical total of wagons in private ownership, more than half a million of which were in the 'coal and other mineral' category. These wagons were almost wholly put into a single operating pool during the war (i.e. effectively 'nationalised'). As such, they came to BR along with all the former company wagons in 1947 at which time the wagon fleet was quoted as containing 1,223,634 units of all kinds! More than anything else, this incredible total of Victorian-inspired ironmongery reveals the magnitude of the task which faced the railways in terms of freight vehicle modernisation. When the totals are broken down by category, a further vital factor can be seen to emerge: the relatively small number of more specialised vehicles. These would normally be non common user types (above), containing a fair proportion of such wagons as did exist which had automatic brakes. Of the other types, only the covered merchandise vehicles would be expected to contain anything like a significant number of fully braked vehicles and all told, given that almost all private owner wagons were also hand brake only, it is unlikely that much more than 5% of the total British wagon fleet was automatically braked and capable of higher speed running even in 1947. In many ways it is remarkable that the system worked at all, much less as well as it did!

Above:
These wagons were just about as sophisticated as it was possible to get in the 1930s as far as general merchandise vehicles were concerned. The GWR open wagon (wood body on a steel chassis) has a longitudinal bar to allow a tarpaulin cover to be kept clear of the, often quite vulnerable, contents of the wagon. Below is real 'hi-tech' (sic!) in the form of a covered LNER goods van fitted with automatic vacuum brake. Both are essentially Victorian in concept.
Photos: GWR and LNER Official

Right:
Coal wagons as far as the eye can see at Toton Yard in LMS days, all of them highly unlikely to have any form of automatic brake. Covered vans (of which a mere handful can just be discerned in the far distance) are most noteworthy by their absence, much of the general merchandise which was handled being conveyed in sheeted down open vehicles. The miracle is that the system worked at all, much less as well as it did!
Photo: LMS Official

Far Right:
This delightful, if not entirely typical view at Stapleton Road near Bristol, in the late 1930s, shows Castle class 4-6-0 No.4082 Windsor Castle *on local passanger duty with a two coach 'B' set*
Photo: Soole Collection NRM

SUMMARY TABLE: COMPARATIVE WAGON STATISTICS BY COMPANY IN 1933

a) Numbers of Vehicles by category

Wagon Type	LMS	LNER	GWR	SR	TOTAL
Open Merchandise	152705	114202	51025	25325	343257
Covered Merchandise	42693	34979	21483	5053	104208
Mineral	65212	85584	1611	741	153148
Others*	21961	28641	9474	3627	63703
Total	282571	263406	83593	34746	664316

b) Percentage by category within company

Wagon Type	LMS	LNER	GWR	SR	TOTAL
Open Merchandise	54.0%	43.3%	61.0%	72.9%	51.7%
Covered Merchandise	15.1%	13.3%	25.7%	14.6%	15.7%
Mineral	23.1%	32.5%	2.0%	2.1%	23.0%
Others*	7.8%	10.9%	11.3%	10.4%	9.6%
Total	100%	100%	100%	100%	100%

c) Percentage by company within category

Wagon Type	LMS	LNER	GWR	SR	TOTAL
Open Merchandise	44.5%	33.3%	14.8%	7.4%	100%
Covered Merchandise	41.0%	33.5%	20.6%	4.9%	100%
Mineral	42.5%	56.0%	1.0%	0.5%	100%
Others*	34.4%	44.5%	14.9%	5.7%	100%
Total	42.5%	39.7%	12.6%	5.2%	100%

* Includes cattle wagons, special wagons, 'twin wagons' and brake vans - i.e. the bulk of 'non common user' vehicles - see text.

A few further general points might be made before dealing with specifics. Firstly, the bulk of the company owned mineral wagons (98.5%) were in the hands of the LMS and LNER; virtually all the GWR and Southern Railway mineral traffic was carried either in private owner vehicles or those of the other two systems. Secondly, although by far the biggest of the four railways, the LMS wagon fleet was not appreciably greater than that of the LNER in spite of their relatively disparate sizes. Thirdly, even excepting mineral wagons, the actual number of company vehicles owned by both the GWR and SR was proportionally smaller than their overall sizes might have led to be expected. One must, of course, beware of the dangers of generalisation and also of reading too much into broad statistical data, but the figures offered do suggest that there were probably more differences to note between the Big Four in terms of goods handling than in most other areas of their activity. It will thus be appreciated that only against the background of this more general appraisal of the problem can the individual solutions can be assessed and to this we now turn on a company-by-company basis.

CHAPTER FOURTEEN
GWR Locomotives & Stock

Before discussing the complexities of the two biggest companies in the Big Four, it is something of a pleasure to start with the one railway that began its post-group life in a totally self-confident mood; for the Great Western was undoubtedly a different sort of railway in strictly philosophical terms. The pre-1923 GWR was so dominant in the proposed 'Western' group that the adding to it of several smaller companies (mostly in Wales) was more 'absorption by' than 'amalgamation with', a fact which the post-1922 retention of the old name made clear beyond doubt. This allowed the company to take full publicity advantage of the fact that its corporate identity dated back to 1835, thus allowing it to celebrate its centenary during the grouping period. This pre-1923 dominance also meant that in practical terms, there was very little coming together of ideas; instead, the old GWR policies continued much as before and one could hardly see the join. In the locomotive sphere this not only made for considerable continuity but was actually of huge potential benefit to the newly enlarged company: by 1922 the GWR had taken locomotive development to a point which, viewed 'across the board' so to speak, had put it well ahead of the rest. The fact that in the event, the GWR did not take as full advantage from this lead as it could (and perhaps should) have done is another matter, and was to be one of the more fascinating consequences of the grouping.

As the Big Four entered their last decade, it will be shown that LMS and LNER locomotive policy was very much a consequence of earlier events, a fact even more applicable to the GWR. Throughout its whole 20th Century life, the GWR was very much a product of events which began in the Edwardian period (earlier in some respects) and whose end product was already more than obvious by 1922. This was just as true (if not more so) by 1938 and the key to it all was standardisation. We have seen in the previous chapter how there was much 'coming together' in locomotive terms during the Big Four period (in terms of concept if not in the more cosmetic sense of appearance) and it is almost entirely to the credit of the GWR that this harmonisation of ideas was to take place broadly along the Churchward principles which had already taken practical form on the GWR by the time of grouping. Where the GWR had led, the others (mostly) followed.

Starting, as usual, with express passenger locomotives, the GWR of the late 1930s was dominated by two very fine 4-6-0 designs, both of which had emerged during the 1920s under the supervision of C.B.Collett, Churchward's immediate successor from 1921. First to appear (in 1923) was the 'Castle' Class, a four-cylinder type which, in all essentials, was an enlarged version of Churchward's 'Star' Class of 1906-7, many of which remained in service throughout the GWR period. Some Stars were converted to Castles and eventually some 167 of the latter engines came into service (some not actually built until BR days). In spite of the later Kings, the Castles were the principal express engines to be seen on the lines out of Paddington until the end of steam itself.

The Castles were also influential in a wider sense, having been examined in some detail by both the LNER and LMS soon after grouping. Comparisons with a Gresley Class A1 4-6-2 revealed that the Castle was the more efficient design (and marginally more powerful), thus resulting in a redesign of the LNER valve gear and, indirectly, leading to the development of the A3 type. Meantime, the Castle design was used as part of internal LMS politics when one of them was borrowed in 1926 mainly, or so it seems in retrospect, to demonstrate that a modern 4-6-0 could do the job for which some LMS men (including Henry Fowler) were advocating a 4-6-2. The engine was wholly successful and the LMS is said to have asked the GWR either to lend them the drawings or build 50 Castles for use on the West Coast line! When this request was refused, the outcome was the Royal Scot 4-6-0 type - not really a Castle at all, but very much a big 4-6-0 none the less, with a bit of the Southern's 'Lord Nelson' for good measure.

The Castles were followed in 1927 by the even bigger 'King' Class wherein the Churchward four-cylinder approach was increased to about the maximum size that could be fitted onto a 4-6-0 chassis. Thirty were built for the heaviest express duties and they were severely route restricted because of their high axle weight. But they could easily claim to be Britain's most powerful express locomotives in pure tractive effort terms at a time when these things seemed to matter. In 1926, the Southern had made a bit of a song and dance about the fact that its new Lord Nelson type was Britain's most powerful express type, being marginally larger in tractive effort terms than a Castle; but the GWR put the matter beyond all doubt with the Kings; there is even evidence that dimensions, including a reduced driving wheel size of 6ft 6in, were carefully calculated to get it above the magic 40,000lb figure (see also footnote, page 155). Be that as it may, the Castles and Kings were in effect Churchward Stars 'writ larger' and, as we shall soon see, the story was not to end there. It is often said that where the parents lead, the children follow but they sometimes go further too; and it was left to Collett's assistant, William Stanier, when he joined the LMS (page 177), to take the essentially Churchward four-cylinder style to its logical conclusion in the form of the Princess and Duchess 4-6-2s.

Staying in the express passenger arena, Churchward's second contribution (which actually preceded the Stars by a few years) was also to be seen in front line work in the 1930s in the form of the two-cylinder 'Saint' Class of 1902. This design was one of the first fruits of Churchward's move to modernity and, apart from employing inside Stephenson valve gear (which the GWR always tended to favour) rather than the outside Walschaerts type, was also to display most of the essential elements of what we have already identified as the most common 'modern' steam type - a robustly built machine with two outside cylinders. In the context of developments by the 1930s and later, the Saints (which were express engines with 6ft 9in driving wheels) were to be of rather more significance in terms of where they led in this two-cylinder field and before coming onto the secondary express workings, it will be as well to complete their part in the story. Though not as 'public' as his association with Castles and Kings, Charles Collett's main objective claim to distinction in the locomotive design field probably lay in the more radical development which he authorised to take place based on the Saint design.

Above:
The last locomotive type in a famous line of two-cylinder GWR 4-6-0 designs was the County Class of 1945, the last example of which is featured here: No.1029 County of Worcester. *Apart from the continuous wheel splasher, its lineaments were firmly in the best GWR tradition.*
Photo: Pendragon Collection

In 1924, Collett arranged for the rebuilding of the very first Saint (*Saint Martin*) with 6ft driving wheels but otherwise little altered. The idea was to produce a sort of 'go everywhere, do anything' type of locomotive embodying what were now well-established GWR standard components and the first rebuild was to become the prototype of the well known 'Hall' Class 4-6-0, adopted in 1928 as a new standard type when the first of an eventual 328 additional engines came in service. They were Britain's first modern mixed traffic 4-6-0s to be built in quantity and of long lasting significance. It is pretty well certain that Stanier had a large hand in their design (he was also Swindon Works Manager) and they were undoubtedly the operational inspiration for his own Class 5 4-6-0 type for the LMS which, in turn, set similar parameters for Thompson's LNER B1 4-6-0. The Class 5s and B1s were not 'LMS and LNER Halls' in the pure technical sense, of course, but they were built to do much the same sort of job which the GWR had first identified (but see also the chapter seventeen regarding the place in this story of the Southern 'King Arthur' type and its relations). The remaining Saints were allowed to carry on, mainly in a secondary role until life-expired, rather than be rebuilt, but such was the quality of the Halls that Hawksworth, who succeeded Collett in 1941, decided to develop a modified version in 1944 (with larger superheater amongst other things) which was built continuously into BR days. Here, interesting parallels with Ivatt's post-Stanier work on the LMS Class 5s come immediately to mind.

Meanwhile on the GWR itself, and long before Hawksworth's 'modified' Halls appeared, a further 100 essentially similar 4-6-0s had come on stream in the late 1930s (80 'Granges' from 1936; 20 'Manors' from 1938), differing mainly from the Halls in having 5ft 8in driving wheels. These engines had arisen partly out of the success of the Halls, partly from a need to have a similar sort of type for secondary lines and partly because some of Churchward's earlier '43XX' 2-6-0s (see overleaf) were life-expired. The upshot was that opportunity was taken to use the wheels and some other parts of 100 withdrawn 43XX locomotives in the new 4-6-0s which were otherwise very similar both to the Halls and to each other; even the thematic names followed on in the Hall tradition. Manors were some five tons lighter than Granges and with slightly smaller cylinders, thus allowing them to be used on lines where axle weight was restricted.

The last GWR development of an idea which had started with the Saints in 1902, took place in 1945, still in the mainstream of Churchward-type evolution, when Hawksworth introduced the first of 30 brand new engines which were to be the biggest-ever two-cylinder 4-6-0s to be assayed. Known as the 'Counties' and classified mixed traffic because of their 6ft 3in wheel diameter (a new size for the GWR), they have almost become the most forgotten GWR engines. Of comparable power to a Castle, they were particularly useful on the steep banks of the far South West, especially beyond Plymouth where the Kings could not penetrate. An interesting feature of the Counties was their higher boiler pressure (280lb) and the fact that their new boilers were made using flanging plates which Swindon had available as a result of building Stanier Class 8F 2-8-0s during the war - full circle indeed. There have been several reasons advanced for the somewhat surprising fact of their introduction (apart from the obvious human one that all CMEs liked to have a new design to their name), but one of the more convincing explanations is that Hawksworth would have liked to design a 4-6-2 (he is known to have been working on one) and the Counties were either a sort of first step along that road or a substitute for them.

The Kings Of Wales

The July 1938 issue of the *Railway Magazine* reported that 'experiments recently conducted with the "Kings" in South Wales.... prove to have been of a very unusual description, and were made in view of the heavy iron ore traffic which is anticipated up to Ebbw Vale in connection with the large new steelworks there. One "King," successfully hauled 32 loaded 20-ton wagons up the Western Valley line from Newport to Aberbeeg, with several stops and restarts on difficult gradients; with brake van, this was a load of over 950 tons. The load was then increased to 44 wagons, about 1,350 tons, and with the second "King" as banker the journey up to Ebbw Vale was completed. Presumably a new locomotive design is in contemplation for this service, based on "King" dimensions.' The steel works were opened after the firm of Richard Thomas Ltd. decided to revive the industry in this locality in 1935.

Above:

A Churchward 43xx 2-6-0 No.8327 at Patchway in the late 1930s in charge of a through working of Southern Railway stock. These punchy little engines, whose tractive power was almost equal to that of the much newer and later Hall Class, were highly suited to this kind of work and their introduction in 1911 was to pave the way for the widespread adoption of the 2-6-0 mixed traffic type throughout Britain.
Photo: Soole Collection, NRM

Below:

The by now venerable GWR Bulldog Class 4-4-0s (see also picture on page 155) served out their time at a variety of locations but their small 5ft 8in driving wheels and modest axle load made them particularly suited to many secondary routes in Wales. Here is No.3342 Bonaventura at Ruabon in June 1938, just a few months before it was withdrawn; note the old style combined name and numberplate. The still serviceable frames from many of the withdrawn Bulldogs were re-used for 32xx (later 9xxx) Class 4-4-0s - see text.
Photo: Pendragon Collection

Having introduced the mixed traffic concept by way of this fine series of related 4-6-0s, this side of the story was largely completed by the hundreds of examples of an almost equally versatile design, the above-mentioned Churchward 43XX Class 2-6-0. Dating from 1911, only a year before Gresley's original 2-6-0 design for the GNR, the pioneering 43XX was not only part of Churchward's move to standardisation but was the sole GWR contribution to the growing realisation (see chapter thirteen) that the 2-6-0 conveyed significant operational advantages over the traditional 0-6-0. The GWR never needed another version: the 43XX as it stood was in every way comparable with its later LMS and LNER equivalents and by the time the last was built (1932), the class total had reached 342, by some margin the most numerous British 2-6-0 type ever. Some subtle detail changes were made down the years (including a rather more luxurious side window cab by Collett in the twenty new engines of 1932 - GWR cab design was not always kind to footplatemen!) but nothing significant was to change the basic design. The first 100 to be withdrawn were used as a source of parts for the Granges and Manors (above) and it was intended that all the 2-6-0s should eventually be replaced in this way but the war intervened to put an end to that idea. In consequence, all the rest went through to BR in their original form and further withdrawals did not start until 1948. For the record, however, a further ten Granges did appear in BR days but these were brand new locomotives.

The availability of over 400 modern mixed traffic 4-6-0s, not to mention the surviving Saints and Stars and the continued availability of hundreds of 43XX 2-6-0s, meant that the GWR had less need for secondary passenger tender engines than the rest of the country and, in fact, never built any new examples of the type after the grouping (passenger tanks were rather different as we shall see). Such jobs as could not be tackled by either the 4-6-0s or passenger tanks were, by the late 1930s, mostly in the hands of two, by now very archaic looking 4-4-0 types with outside frames in the William Dean tradition, though one of the classes was not quite what it seemed.

Oldest (and numerically well in the ascendant) were the surviving 'Bulldog' Class 4-4-0s, a 40 year old design by 1938 but still finding plenty of useful work to do. Originally some 156 engines strong (and part of the principal GWR main line fleet until Churchward's 4-6-0 revolution), withdrawals had begun in the late 1920s, but well over 50 survived the war and some ran through into early BR days. Their taper boilers (acquired in consequence of Churchward's GWR standardisation) kept them 'in the family' as far as appearances went, in spite of their outside frames, and they were one of Britain's outstanding designs.

More astonishing however and, moreover, still being 'built', were the other 4-4-0s, which really did look like ancient relics of Victorian times. These were the 32XX Class (9XXX from 1946), dating from 1936 and sometimes regarded as a 'new' Collett design. Intended mainly for use on those lines with very restricted axle weight limits (some of those in the ex-Cambrian Railways area for example), they were in effect rebuilds using still-serviceable main frames from withdrawn Bulldogs and small parallel boilers to a Dean design which had first been seen on his 'Duke' Class 4-4-0s of 1895. In some cases, new boilers were actually built for these 40 planned conversions, the implementation of which stopped at 29 units on the outbreak of war. Instantly nicknamed 'Dukedogs', these appealing little engines put in much useful work for a generation and their undoubtedly economical first cost was living proof that the GWR could be just as frugally minded as the LMS when it so chose!

Passenger tanks were another area where the GWR achieved a great degree of standardisation and consistency of approach and by the start of our period of study, the 2-6-2T reigned supreme, albeit by way of a number of variants and supplemented by two important alternatives, of which more later. The 2-6-2T was yet another type which could trace its origins back to the pioneering work of Churchward and again very much in the two-cylinder tradition already discussed for the Saints and their descendants. By late GWR days, they had developed into quite a number of subtly different varieties of the fairly trivial and arcane nature beloved by enthusiasts, but in essence there were but two fundamental types, each of which could be further refined into two basic sub-groups, defined by driving wheel size. In practical terms, all could trace their origins back to the great man himself, and again the GWR never thereafter found much need to depart from his ideas in most respects.

The earliest to appear were what might be called the 'large wheeled' type with 5ft 8in driving wheels that first came out in 1903 in the shape of the 31XX (later 51XX) Class. This was the tank engine equivalent of the 43XX 2-6-0 which it preceded into service by several years and 40 were originally built, followed by a further 41 a few years later with larger boilers, sometimes seen as a sub-group (3150 Class). Thereafter, no more were built until 1929 when the first of a further 210 examples came into service (51XX Class - 140; 61XX Class - 70), the only significant difference between the two series of newer engines being the higher boiler pressure of the 61XX series, built 1931-5 and intended for use in the London area. These engines formed the GWR equivalent (though 'precursor' might be the more appropriate word) of the many similar LMS and LNER 2-6-2Ts and 2-6-4Ts mentioned later, their power output (in tractive effort terms) being much the same as that of the large fleet of LMS 2-6-4Ts, though not quite as beefy as the last Thompson L1 class 2-6-4Ts. Since the GWR did not need quite the same coal and water capacity as did the LMS for this sort of locomotive, the absence of a GWR 2-6-4T design is probably understandable.

In 1938, two small and, in the event, insignificant sub-groups came into existence, a 'new' 31XX Class (five rebuilds of the original 31XX engines with 5ft 3in driving wheels for banking purposes) and ten 81XX rebuilds of withdrawn 51XX engines given new 5ft 6in wheels for greater acceleration. In this form, given also their new higher pressure boilers, they were comparable with the 61XX type, but in all conscience neither of these two alternatives were of any great improvement, though more 81XX rebuilds may have appeared but for the war.

Mention of variable wheel diameters in respect of large wheeled 2-6-2Ts serves as a useful reminder that Churchward himself could see no real need for the sort of small wheel diameter differences which seem to have been seen as so significantly important elsewhere. It is an interesting fact that the bulk of his standard locomotive types made use of but three basic wheel sizes, each of them no less than one foot away from its immediate neighbour (6ft 8in, 5ft 8in and 4ft 8in, give or take half an inch or so - an insignificant refinement). It was left to others to fill in the spaces, not that this subtlety generally made much difference, though it kept enthusiasts happy!

Interestingly, at the lowest end of the diameter scale, Churchward did once find it necessary to move away from his ideal and this was in the very first of his 'small wheeled' 2-6-2T designs, the 44XX Class of 1904. This design appeared immediately after his initial 5ft 8in 2-6-2T (above) and was only the second GWR 2-6-2T actually to come out - in effect a scaled down version of the bigger tank and produced before the latter was multiplied. Designed purely for improving branch line services, they were given but 4ft 1½in driving wheels and their consequential frantic acceleration and *'joi de vivre'* immediately endeared them to all who encountered them and although only ten were built, all were still in full song until well into BR days. Their main but not exclusive area of operation was in the far West Country (Exeter and beyond).

However, enchanting though these pioneer engines undoubtedly were, their main significance lay in what followed, the essentially similar 45XX type with 4ft 7½" wheels, a type which was to become synonymous with almost every GWR rural branch line and similar operation until steam vanished. Eventually 175 in number (built between 1906 and 1929), they had no real equivalent on any of the other Big Four systems, though they were in every respect part of the broader GWR standardisation picture and a somewhat rare occasion of 'horses for courses' in Churchward's otherwise unsentimental approach to the subject. Alone of the Big Four (and even prior to that time), the GWR had a near monopoly in the sort of rural branch line type of operation beloved of so many. In fact, this sort of thing was almost a GWR cliché, to which the 45XX tanks were ideally suited; and they could also operate local freight as well. That they all survived to reach BR (and most of them did not vanish until the start of major dieselisation or line closure), probably says it all. Their nearest equivalents (and a generation or more later to appear) were probably the Ivatt LMS 2-6-2Ts of 1946, but these were designed to meet rather broader operational criteria than the 45XX type.

Above:
A 51xx 2-6-2T on typical outer suburban passenger duty. This is No.5168 and it was photographed near Solihull in March 1938. The train itself, not fully in focus, is a typical seven coach formation of fairly modern but uninspiring non-corridor stock, much the same as was to be seen on all companies.
Photo: Pendragon Collection

Below:
Like the 51xx tanks, the 45xx 2-6-2Ts were also multiplied in some quantity after the grouping. This is No.5540, dating from 1928 and it is seen in charge of that unique GWR formation, the two coach non-corridor 'B' set consisting of a pair of brake ended carriages. These sets were popular for branch line and other less busy services and varied a little in terms of their exact compartment configuration. Photo: Soole Collection

Apart from the 2-6-2T, there were only two other passenger tank varieties which could in any way be regarded as a 'standard' solution - and one of these was just about the only instance where the pre-1923 GWR did not have its own 'Churchward' answer. Down in the South Wales valleys, the various independent small Welsh railways which had come into the larger GWR (e.g. the Barry, Rhymney and Taff Vale) had always favoured the 0-6-2T for passenger use, often because they were also suited to freight (mostly coal) haulage on the usually short distance routes to the ports. In consequence, Collett decided to perpetuate this long-established tradition. In many cases this took the form of simply grafting standard GWR boilers and fittings onto pre-group designs but as early as 1924, a decision was made (presumably based on the overall quantity of engines which were needed) that a new standard GWR 0-6-2T would offer a far more economic solution than expensive alterations to the many existing types. This led to the creation of the 56XX Class 0-6-2T which was soon to become as familiar in South Wales as the 2-6-2T on other parts of the GWR.

There was no strict equivalent to the 56XX class on the other railways (the ex-GER Class N7 probably came closest) but the fact that 200 of the new GWR type were in service by the end of 1928 is significant. As an aside, it is interesting to note that William Stanier had been involved with this wholesale replacement of a variety of older types by one single design (and its beneficial financial effects), which knowledge he no doubt took with him to the LMS in 1932. Suffice to say that the 56XX type was to serve its purpose throughout the whole of the GWR period and all of them went to BR.

A somewhat similar story lay behind the fairly late introduction (1932) of what was soon to become the familiar 48XX (14XX after 1946) and 58XX series of 0-4-2Ts for branch line passenger service where even the neat little 45XX type was deemed too big. In fact, the GWR was displaying sensible economy where the nature of the operation did not demand the ultra-sophistication (or added first cost) of Churchward-type designs: the engines in question were little more than an updated version of a 19th Century 0-4-2T which had proved satisfactory. All 95 engines were identical save for the auto-train (push-pull) gear fitted to the more numerous 48XX variant which represented 75 of the total. These engines were most familiarly seen in charge of another GWR institution, the auto-trailer, whose significant place in the passenger train hierarchy will be discussed in due course.

Meantime, in the freight field, the GWR was once again highly standardised throughout the grouping period, but although most of its goods engines could be seen to have equivalents elsewhere in the country, it did reveal one distinctive difference because of its absolute dominance in the South Wales coalfield. As ever, there was the mandatory (and large) quota of 0-6-0s which, even at the grouping, had not been rationalised to quite the same extent as had many other areas of the fleet, not least because of the variety of such types which came both from the GWR itself and from the smaller constituents. However, by the late 1930s, the GWR had effectively reduced the fleet to but two varieties, the older of which was already on its way out - a state of affairs which other companies must have envied.

This older type was the ever-celebrated 'Dean Goods' of 1883 which had been multiplied to a total of 260 when construction ceased in 1899. Apart from twenty conversions to 2-6-2T form in 1907-10 and a few more early withdrawals, the main group remained intact until as late as 1929.

Even then, scrapping was by no means rapid, over 70 still existed in 1944 (additional to the many others which had actually been 'called up' by the WD for overseas service) and some 50 of them lasted to BR days - no bad record.

A fundamental reason for the reduction of 0-6-0s was the ever-increasing emphasis placed by the GWR on the 2-6-0 and 2-8-0 types. The 43XX class 2-6-0s have already been considered but for heavier work, again as part of his standardised approach, Churchward had adopted the 2-8-0 from the outset in the form of the 28XX Class of 1903, by a long way Britain's first 2-8-0 and the direct lineal ancestor, inter alia, of the Stanier class 8F some thirty or more years later.

Once again, the GWR found no need to change the design after the first example and eventually 167 were to be in service. Interestingly, however, almost exactly half of these (83 to be precise) did not appear until 1938-42 (the rest were all in use by 1919) and this was partly because, like the LNER, the GWR also chose to acquire a fleet of ex-ROD

Robinson 2-8-0s when they became available in 1919 - see page 193. Fifty were selected, thus letting the GWR defer further 2-8-0s until much later, which economical solution also allowed the company to get the last mileages out of some of its older heavier freight engines. The 'Collett' 28XX engines (sometimes known as the 2284 Class) were an updated version with later modifications, notably the rather better cab which he preferred; but nothing significant was changed.

The fact that the GWR did not build any new locomotives for heavy freight working for almost 20 years between 1919 and 1938 is additionally explained by the peculiar circumstances of the South Wales coalfield and is not dissimilar in rationale to that which underlay the above-mentioned 0-6-2Ts. The narrow and largely north-south trending valley routes tended to serve as feeders for the mainly east-west alignment of the South Wales main line and in heavy freight terms, this created a need for a powerful locomotive which did not have the range of a tender type but which could handle much the same sort of load. The big eight-coupled tank engine (i.e. the equivalent of the 2-8-0 tender type) was the obvious solution and thus it turned out to be: needless to say, Churchward again had the sort of answer that was still relevant in the 1930s.

The first outcome of this thinking was the 42XX 2-8-0T of 1910 which, in due course totalled 195 units built from then until 1930. It was, of course, the tank engine equivalent of the 28XX Class and originally (1905) intended to be a 2-8-2T. The elimination of the trailing wheels is generally reckoned to have been a consequence of fears about excess wheelbase and the engines went into service much as planned. But things were to change during the early grouping years and a somewhat more complex state of affairs existed by the later 1930s. By then, the years of depression had caused a downturn in the South Wales coal trade and there were too many 2-8-0Ts. It was thus decided to rebuild some of them as 2-8-2Ts to allow them to be used on the main line where their range would be nearer to that of a tender engine and their wheelbase less critical. This would also save the need for further 2-8-0s (above) and between 1934 and 1939, 54 examples were so treated, becoming the 72XX Class 2-8-2Ts. There was an interesting side effect: in 1940, as a result of increased wartime demands for coal, the conversion of the 54 2-8-0Ts had actually produced a shortage of that type, so they built 20 replacement 42XX engines, which took the running numbers of those which had been converted to 2-8-2T form.

As for its other freight tanks, the GWR was very much the domain of that familiar yet 'unique to company' type, the 0-6-0 pannier tank. It had a long pedigree and its many and various sub-species could be seen just about everywhere from humble local shunting to branch line working in the mixed traffic role. Many of them were fitted retrospectively with pannier tanks, but the most familiar of the purpose-built series were undoubtedly the 57XX Class of 1929, which alone totalled an astonishing 857 examples as late as 1957. The company was to be for ever updating and improving the type and it is maybe sufficient testimony to the basic soundness of the idea to mention that the last variants of the genre did not appear until 1947 (94XX Class) and during BR days in 1949 (16XX Class) - no small tribute to a basic concept which dated from 1898, albeit not in the 0-6-0 form as far as that far-off pioneer was concerned.

Unlike other companies, the GWR, confident in its own approach to problems, was not really accustomed to taking a look over its shoulder to see what others were doing. It was aware of such obvious matters as streamlined trains and many other fashionable flights of fancy and, to its eternal credit, does not seem to have been too fooled by such nonsenses; but one does wonder whether it was as aware as it should have been of those forward strides in locomotive development that the other companies (notably the LMS) were beginning to take which were to be of such importance later.

Churchward had been so far ahead of the field in his own time that it may have been difficult for his successors to appreciate that others might move the process further. But events were to show that while the others may not have been able to achieve quite the same system-wide standardisation that the GWR had demonstrated in the 1930s and 1940s (time was against them given their late start date of 1923), they had focussed attention on areas where more than normal economies might be expected and started to produce rolling hardware in support. For example, the smaller LMS rebuilt Royal Scot could outperform the far larger GWR King in terms of thermodynamic performance on a strict power to weight basis (the 1948 exchanges proved that); and it was not a lone example. The upshot was that in the context of what followed after 1948, the GWR input was not (on the surface) as significant as its track record would suggest should have been the case, However, GWR enthusiasts could undoubtedly take much consolation in the fact that what became a dominant LMS influence on subsequent BR steam locomotive affairs was, via Stanier at second remove, so to speak, a natural evolution of what had happened far earlier on the GWR; but one cannot help wonder what might have happened had these long-term lessons been learned properly by the company which started it all.

Passenger stock

When it comes to the matter of GWR passenger stock, interesting parallels with the locomotive situation suggest themselves. Once again, most of the pioneering work had been carried out before 1923, in consequence of which a fair degree of design stagnation tended to follow as far as most new carriages were concerned. By the late 1930s, many of the newer GWR main line carriages had fallen rather behind by comparison with the rest, not excluding those of the Southern which, as we shall see, had little experience in this field in 1923. As ever, we need to start by looking at the events that led to this state of affairs.

Immediately after the grouping, GWR main line carriages were as good as you could find. The majority stemmed from the Churchward era which had seen a similar sort of forward progress in carriage design as in locomotives. During the Edwardian period, the GWR took advantage of its generous structure gauge (afforded to it in consequence of old broad gauge clearances) by building its carriages to the largest possible dimensions (up to 70ft long and often over 9ft wide) and the first fruits of this were truly magnificent - e.g. the well known 'Dreadnought' stock, most of which was still to be seen in the 1930s, including some memorable dining cars. Unfortunately, these fine carriages were often too large to be acceptable to other companies and since through running between systems was always important, the GWR had to 'down-size' to use a modern term and eventually settled on a smaller size 'envelope' for most stock (57-60ft x 9ft) which was much the same as most of the others.

In this field, its most significant carriages were the various 'Toplight' designs which had actually started to appear in the 70ft era but whose later batches conformed to the smaller structural parameters. The 'Toplight' name derived from the characteristic small windows which appeared above the main ones and during their currency, Churchward moved from wood to steel panelling well before the grouping and the later examples were as good if not better than could be found anywhere in Britain. Technically quite advanced for their time, they formed the mainstay of the principal GWR expresses for many a long year and lasted well into the final decade and some to BR as well.

At the grouping, it seemed at first that the GWR was not content to rest on its laurels when it reintroduced its famous chocolate and cream livery, it being often forgotten that 'Churchward's GWR' was a 'dark red railway' when it came to passenger trains, the colour scheme being dignified but economical to apply. But it soon became clear that the revival of the older scheme (last used before the first world war) was more of a publicity move than anything else and in terms of actual carriage design, the time of the grouping in fact marked the start of a period of conceptual stagnation which, sadly, dominated thereafter for the best part of a generation. Even the fully panelled lining gave way to a simpler form at a very early stage. This was (officially) justified as being to give the more modern look to the trains which their new flush-sided panelling (below) represented, but truth was that the new simplified lining was cheaper to apply and this was what really mattered!

'Bow ended' was the name given to this uninspiring period of design and most objective commentators have remarked on its lacklustre character. It was, as always, substantially built and was also to see the start of the move to a modern flush-sided style of panelling by the simple

expedient of eliminating the traditional outside window frames and fitting the fixed glazing from inside the carriage. Unfortunately, this did not at first go hand in hand with any form of re-styling to match the structure. Compartment dimensions were rather cramped, individual outside doors to compartments still reigned supreme and the waist level remained high, relative to the seats. All told, they were not as good in many ways as the older Toplights, neither did they harmonise with them too well externally.

In the general service long-distance field, matters continued thus during most of the pre-war period, with the usual variety of types emerging, the GWR having much the same sort of carriage needs (albeit smaller in absolute terms) as the LMS and LNER. The problem seemed to be that unlike other companies, and in marked contrast to its approach to locomotives, the GWR never really settled down to one identifiable set of design criteria as far as main line carriages were concerned, This lack of uniformity generally tended to impart an uneven and untidy look to the majority of GWR expresses at the time, compounded as it was by a lack of consistency in either width or length: carriages were built to both the larger GWR limits and to more nationally acceptable dimensions. This situation was all the more remarkable when one considers that in the more specialised field, the GWR was perfectly capable of matching the rest both in style and quality as witness the magnificent Super Saloons of 1931 (built to rival those of Pullman) and famous Centenary stock of 1935 in which, for the first time, the GWR suppressed outside compartment doors on side-corridor stock.

The upper of these two views shows a somewhat unimaginative bow ended corridor third No.4840 of 1926, a type seen widely throughout the system from then onwards; even on the corridor side, there is a full set of outside doors. By contrast, the lower image shows what the GWR could do when it was really trying: one of the quite superb 'Super Saloons', No.9112 Queen Mary, built in 1931 as the GWR did not enjoy the best relations with Pullman . The carriages were an unashamed copy of Pullman cars and arguably even better finished.

Left:
Redolent of the 1930s, this clearly posed view shows the not unattractive interior styling of a 1938 GWR buffet car; one suspects the view through the windows to be phoney! The table itself seems to be laid for full meal service and the badge on the waiter's lapel reads 'GWR Restaurant Car'.
Photos: All GWR Official

Railcars Rule

Although the number of diesel or petrol engined railcars working in Britain was a comparatively small number prior to the war, they were demonstrating remarkable efficiencies in both terms of operation and maintenance. The GWR's fleet of AEC railcars were arguably the most technological advancement of this form of traction, and by 1939 18 cars were in service. They were stationed at 10 different depots, from where they worked a regular schedule of 747 route miles and served no less than 247 stations, from Birmingham in the north to Weymouth in the south, and from London in the east to Swansea in the west. They limited availability of the cars meant that the sheds had to keep the units in daily service, despite the fact they suffered hard usage on services which could vary from stop and start branch line workings which were operated at an average 30 mph, to fast express services of 55 mph. The first car entered service in February 1934, with its AEC London bus-type engine and a David Brown designed gearbox, seating for 70 passengers and a small luggage compartment. By July the same year the Cardiff - Birmingham railcar service had commenced, but with its introduction the twin-engined sets showed they could achieve speeds of over 70 mph. In 1935 three more cars, all twin-engined, began working in the Worcester and Oxford areas. Ten more came in 1936, although one of these was designed solely for parcels and is seen in the adjacent view. By 1939 there were 18 cars in service, some of which had the luxury of toilets which had been considered essential for the Weymouth - Bristol and Hereford - Oxford cross-country services. They were then operating some 22,530 miles each week, around 3% of the GWR total. One problem was reported from permanent way crews who could not distinguish the railcar horn from those of motor vehicles on nearby roads, so a new Desilux 8-horn system was employed. Parcels railcar No.17 is seen right when newly introduced to service in 1936. The car first went into service in the London area, being later transferred to the West Midlands.

Photo: Pendragon Collection

There were also some spacious (if internally unimaginative) new sleeping cars during the late 1920s/early 1930s and, later, some imaginative refurbishment of older dining cars with new interiors and modernised exterior panelling (which latter policy extended into the post-war era).

But it was not to last, nor was it consistent; the many excellent examples of the carriage builders' craft which could be seen at the individual level were never numerous enough to set broader and better standards system-wide. In this respect, the nearest the GWR came to a change of emphasis was in 1936-7 when the so-called 'Sunshine' stock began to appear, so named because of their new and larger windows. These carriages were certainly in the more modern idiom with their large windows and low waists; indeed, some of them were visually very reminiscent of the contemporary Stanier stock for the LMS, than which no higher praise can be given. But they were followed in the late 1930s by another phase wherein lack of consistency and harmony both in terms of dimension and precise styling was to re-appear, almost as if the company could not quite make up its mind - a very strange thing to say about the GWR.

Some of the later 1936-40 carriages were, however, to establish some of the broad parameters, principally in terms of interior layout, which governed the final GWR main line carriage stock of the post-war Hawksworth period. These carriages, most of which were not in fact delivered until BR days, would have imparted a more uniform and modern look to the GWR had things been different. As it was, they were visually attractive with low waists and domed end roofs (the latter rather in the Gresley style) and very much in the fashionable flush-sided idiom. But the GWR never totally eliminated the outside compartment door: one or two compartments in every vehicle usually had one (as had some of the later 1936-40 stock after the short 'doorless' period of the Sunshine style), reinstated to improve the speed of loading - or so it is said. Neither did the GWR ever adopt three per side third class in side corridor stock as had the LNER and LMS; the need to cater for heavy holiday loadings plus complications in seat reservations were the usual reasons advanced for this policy, as indeed was also the case on the Southern.

In its non-corridor stock, the GWR was just as uninspired as the rest if not even more so in some of its high capacity suburban carriages. Change the outside colour and it could just as easily have been LMS and once inside, it was scarcely differentiated at all. The only slight innovation was the ubiquitous two coach close-coupled 'B' set, a standard but spartan offering on many short distance and/or branch line services. As for lavatories in new non-corridor stock - no way...... That said, however and like all the other railways, the GWR did have one or two areas where it offered its own unique solutions and in its case, they took the form of two different but equally interesting solutions to the short distance problem.

Chronologically, the first of these was the familiar auto-trailer with an open saloon interior configuration. These dated from Edwardian days when the GWR had been the British leader in the first generation of steam railcars. That idea was destined to be short-lived but most of the vehicles concerned took on a new and much longer lease of life when converted to locomotive-hauled trailer form. This was the typical GWR solution when even a 'B' set would be too large for the traffic on offer and it remained a feature of former GWR lines through the whole of its final years and until the end of steam. Indeed, new examples of the genre were built in BR days to GWR design.

The second distinctive solution was the first truly successful introduction of diesel railcars in Britain from 1933 onwards for both short and medium range duty where loads were not excessive. As recorded elsewhere they were almost an instant success and although never very many in number (less than 40 units all told), they undoubtedly pioneered a form of travel which was to become, and still remains, a very widespread feature of the British railway scene.

Freight stock

Much of the operational nature of GWR freight traffic is implicit from the kinds of locomotive it built - and which have been considered already. But what this disguises is the rather unusual nature of wagon ownership as far as the GWR was concerned. As we have shown, it scarcely owned any mineral wagons at all, because virtually all the mineral traffic which originated within its bailiwick (mostly; but not exclusively, coal) was carried in private owner wagons. Additionally, of course, most of the mineral traffic which came from outside the GWR system (be it coal or not) originated in LMS and LNER operating areas, so even if carried in company wagons, these would still be non-GWR. In consequence, in its heyday, a 'full load' mineral train on the GWR main line could be a very colourful and varied sight indeed.

At the company-owned level, things took on a more normal pattern (see summary page 164) and the only reason why the GWR had a higher proportion of merchandise wagons than the rest was because of its lack of mineral vehicles. When this factor is removed, its total merchandise wagon fleet (covered and open) was almost exactly in proportion to the size of the GWR relative to the total national picture - and it built and used them in much the same way. Thus it was that the humble hand brake only merchandise wagon dominated the scene as it did elsewhere and the GWR proportion of 'other' wagons was not wildly out of line with the rest. That said, however, there were a few areas where the GWR wagon was perhaps a little more distinctive than most. For one thing, there was more consistency and continuity in design terms, this being, as ever, a natural consequence of the pre-1923 situation. Thus, although usually built to much the same size and shape as anyone else's freight stock, that of the GWR was always that little bit simpler to recognise even after the large 'GW' had vanished from its sides.

Secondly, and arguably yet another consequence of pre-1923 events, the GWR wagon was normally better built than most of the rest. Like most things which could trace their origins back to Churchward's time, the GWR wagon was usually well built and of lasting quality. To some extent this was due to the early use of steel underframes - as with carriage panelling, so in wagon building, the GWR was an early convert to the more widespread use of steel in rolling stock - and this could allow heavier than average loads to be carried in what were, broadly speaking, 'normal' sized wagons, and also facilitated the making of larger, more substantial vehicles wherever relevant. It can therefore be no great surprise that GWR wagon design influenced that of BR to a considerable extent, including the continuation of some of its own types, mostly unchanged save in detail, as BR standard designs - cattle wagons, for example.

Unfortunately, however, this superiority in basic wagon technology did not go with a parallel improvement in operation. Here, the GWR was in much the same sort of 'cleft stick' situation as the rest, a victim of the conceptual inertia which has already been mentioned more than once. The real problem was that in the freight context, there was no advantage in one company moving upwards in a technological sense as long as the rest stayed put - through running of goods wagons between systems would work against that sort of approach.

What is perhaps worthy of brief, albeit slightly whimsical, comment in the GWR context is that it had been this way before: the abolition of the Broad Gauge in 1892 was as much to avoid the problems of freight transhipment (by using wagons to a common gauge) as to anything else, given that the passengers could, of course, walk between trains! Had the GWR taken a similar lead in terms of better freight vehicles (we are not criticising it for not so doing), evidence strongly suggests that it would have been the best equipped to do so.

Above:
Perhaps the most characteristic looking of all goods vehicles was the guard's brake van with a long verandah at one end only. Code named 'Toad' in GWR 'telegraphese', they were often marked for allocation to specific locations.
Photo: Pendragon Collection

Below:
This typical mixed freight could stand duty for almost any railway in Britain during the 1930s and 1940s. The cargo could be anything from individual coal wagons for local merchants to major consignments of materials for industry. Such trains when running on the main lines were the ideal work for the ever increasing numbers of genuine mixed traffic locomotives, an appropriate example in the shape of 43xx 2-6-0 No.4377 being employed here.
Photo: Soole Collection, NRM

CHAPTER FIFTEEN
LMS Locomotives & Rolling Stock

On its formation, the LMS had received over 10,000 steam locomotives from its pre-group constituents, but by 31st December 1947, this total had been reduced to less than 8000. When to this statistic is added the fact that of the final total, some 5000 locomotives were to LMS standard designs (i.e. including those which appeared during the BR period), it will be seen that some 60% of the fleet was 'standardised' by the time that BR designs took over. This one observation admirably sums up the LMS approach to motive power and this sets it apart from the other three companies, none of whom had taken this re-equipping process quite so far in such a short time, though the GWR had less need to do so as we have seen. Most of the essential components were in place before 1938 and the LMS fleet which was inherited by BR was very much a consequence of pre-war thinking. Therefore, before looking at the types which were to be seen, it will be helpful to review the rationale behind latter day locomotive policy.

In its time, the LMS was the largest Joint Stock Corporation anywhere in the world in terms of transport and its management structure was, from a very early stage (the later 1920s), somewhat different from that of the rest. The instrument of change, having been brought in by the LMS Board in effect to sort out the incipient management chaos which was threatening to engulf the company soon after the grouping, was Sir Josiah Stamp (later Lord Stamp of Shortlands) who was, in very truth 'Mr LMS' during its most important years. He introduced a management structure which was run very much on American corporate lines with a President of the Executive in charge (Stamp himself, who was also in effect the General Manager), below which were four executive Vice Presidents, each in full charge of a specific operational area. On the LMS, therefore, the Chief Mechanical Engineer (the top man in the locomotive department) did not report direct to the General Manager but to the appropriate executive Vice President. To some extent this gave him less independent freedom of action than other CMEs but this was in accordance with Stamp's wishes and in the end, it worked well.

A fine but unsentimental businessman, Josiah Stamp could see little point in trying to run a modern transport system on essentially Victorian lines and he it was who was finally to come to grips with the internal factions which had so bedevilled the company during its early years, in particular the lack of any decisive forward movement in locomotive matters. This could trace its origins to the pre-group constituents of the LMS (and their respective rivalries), coupled with the accepted custom of appointing the top men, not least those in charge of locomotive matters, on a seniority (i.e. 'pecking order') basis rather than on merit. The story has been well recorded elsewhere so need not be repeated here, but as far as the 1938 situation is concerned, we need to extract two themes which were to be of influence throughout the whole of the remaining LMS period, regardless of the personalities involved. The fact that Lord Stamp lost his life during an air raid in April 1941, tragic though it was, had little or no effect on corporate LMS policy; he built his management structure on rocks not sand.

Stanier's design masterpiece, but it was the Class 5s which transformed the railway 'across the board' so to speak. They were an instant success, everybody liked them and by 1938, a total of 452 had already gone into service. They continued to be constructed throughout the rest of the LMS period to a final total of 742 units, BR adding 100 more after 1947.

Stanier was, it would seem, extremely fond of his Class 5s - and with good reason. When added to the almost equally effective 2-6-0s, it meant that the LMS had a fleet of over 1,000 modern mixed traffic engines by the end of 1947 and all broadly in the same power class - well down the road to what Stamp had always wanted. They were seen at work all over the system on almost any sort of duty (fitted freight and the less demanding express passenger duties were their main, though not exclusive forte) and the two types made up some 13% of the total LMS fleet at the end. Because of their slightly larger wheels and leading bogies, the 4-6-0s tended to be used for the quicker trains but there was considerable interchangeability.

Much the same sort of revolution was also taking place in the passenger tank lists when the LMS entered its last decade. Here again, Stanier was able to build on ideas that had started before his arrival, though not with universal success as it was to turn out. In 1927, for reasons which, even now, are not fully explicable, some of the more enterprising brains in the LMS locomotive department had managed to sneak a design past the 'Midland Mafia' for a much needed large 2-6-4T which embodied all the best features of the Crabs and Royal Scots. Henry Fowler took the credit for it, 125 were built (30 of them during Stanier's first years) and a fine machine it turned out to be.

Needless to say, Stanier eventually produced a taper boilered version, the first of which were given three rather than two cylinders. There was a view that this gave them better acceleration (useful in the suburban context) and they were successful machines; later on most found their way to the Tilbury line where they put up prodigious haulage performance with anything up to thirteen fully laded suburban bogie coaches. But further investigation revealed that there was no great advantage over the original two-cylinder version so the bulk of the Stanier 2-6-4Ts emerged in that more economical to build form. Over 300 of the three types were in service by 1938 and the Stanier two-cylinder version continued in production until superseded by a shorter wheelbase type which, although introduced in 1943 under the name of Stanier's immediate successor, C.E.Fairburn, was in all significant respects a Stanier design.

The success of these big tanks (something over half of the eventual 277 examples of the Fairburn variant were actually built by BR) meant that the LMS could slaughter many older classes with impunity - and it did so without much remorse, even in the war years. But the same was not true in the 'smaller tank engine' field. Here, emboldened by the success of the 2-6-4T, the LMS (in 1930) had introduced a scaled down 2-6-2T version. Sadly, however, this time the ex-Midland men did get a shout, back came all the inefficient and outdated ideas and the result was one of the most feeble locomotive designs of the modern era. It was again attributed to Fowler and, in due time, the Stanier taper boilered version appeared. But even the great man himself could not produce a 'silk purse out of a sow's ear' and although the combined group totalled 209 engines (70 of the Fowler type, the rest by Stanier and all in service by the end of 1938), the results were disappointing. Their newness gave them maintenance advantages but they were not 'Josiah Stamp' engines in the strictest sense! An interesting consequence of this state of affairs was that while the LMS could and did get rid of a lot of its bigger pre-group tank engines as 2-6-4Ts came on stream, the 2-6-2Ts did not have quite the same effect and many older (and smaller) pre-group passenger tanks survived as a result right through the last company decade - no doubt to the great delight of the enthusiast; the LMS was not normally sentimental! But a solution was at hand as we shall soon see.

Meantime, the purely freight side of things (two thirds of the revenue, remember!) was not left out. The success of the mixed traffic locomotive meant that much fast freight (and certainly most of that which had even some form of continuous automatic brake) could safely be handed over to these engines. But this was only a fraction of the total traffic and in the heavy 'drag' freight department, which also included pretty well any goods train which had no form of automatic brakes (i.e. most of them!), the LMS took longer to sort itself out. By 1938, however, the picture was beginning to clarify.

Above:
The legendary Class 5 4-6-0 was built over a period of 17 years from 1934 onwards. No.5029 was one of the first examples to appear in 1934 and is later seen when working from Inverness, where many of the early examples were sent. It has a taller chimney than later became standard and does not (as yet), display the 'platform' between the front frames - added later to make the smokebox door easier to open. This was also one of the original 'domeless' series, later examples having domed boilers, some of the earlier examples being also altered to match.

Below:
A Stanier 2-6-4T on duty in 1946. No.2573 is climbing Shap with an interesting trio of carriages forming a local train: open third, corridor composite and brake third. They also display three types of body construction which from the front are wood body, steel panel sheeting over timber frame and all steel respectively.

Photo: Ransome-Wallis Collection, NRM

For most of its first 15 years, the LMS relied upon older 0-6-0 and 0-8-0 types for this work - indeed it had enlarged the ex-MR Class 4F 0-6-0 total by some 530 units by the end of 1928, giving a 1938 class total of 727 (including the pre-group examples). To these should be added well over 500 ex-LNWR 0-8-0s (progressively rebuilt and improved right down to 1937 and later), plus a batch of 175 0-8-0s to LMS design between 1929 and 1932 (evolved from the old LNWR type but bedevilled by MR detail design weaknesses where it mattered) and a small fleet of 33 Beyer Garratt 2-6-0 + 0-6-2Ts which were an almost totally ineffective and expensive-to-maintain alternative to the pigeon pairs of 0-6-0s on the heavy coal trains to London on the Midland main line. Had Derby left Beyer-Peacock alone to develop these engines, a very different tale might have emerged, but all told, it was not the happiest inheritance for William Stanier when he arrived. Trouble was that when to this already mixed bag of assets one added the hundreds of other older but still serviceable pre-group goods engines (mostly 0-6-0s but with some exceptions) which 1930s economics decreed should still be found work, there was simply too much antiquated and obsolescent machinery trundling round to enable a simple solution to be found.

The eventual answer, though not fully developed in LMS days, was a typical Stamp-cum-Stanier solution. As early as 1935, more or less in parallel with the Class 5 4-6-0, with which it shared many detail features, Stanier had introduced a thoroughly modern and equally outstanding heavy freight engine of the 2-8-0 type (Class 8F, originally 7F, 'F' signifying freight in the LMS power system). In due course, the Class 8F turned out to be the most numerous Stanier design (852 units being built compared with the 842 Class 5s) and had the LMS survived as a corporate entity, it was intended that it should replace virtually all the older heavy freight engines. By 1938, only 95 were in service (other operational criteria had taken priority) but the next decade saw a partial implementation of this policy as 8Fs took over on an ever-increasing basis, somewhat slowed down on LMS lines proper by the exigencies of war. The 8F was selected as a wartime standard goods engine, many being taken immediately into War Department service. They were constructed all over the place (including the workshops of the other three big four companies) but it was not until 1947 and later that the whole class, save for those which had been lost during the war (or left overseas), were put to work in Britain.

Meantime, the LMS finally came to grips with the few problems which had not been totally solved by Stanier's designs. He left the company for other vital war work at the end of 1942 and we have already seen how his first lineal successor, Fairburn, had modified his 2-6-4T. But Fairburn died before his time and Stanier's LMS mantle fell upon George Ivatt, son of the famous Henry Ivatt of the Great Northern Railway, the immediate predecessor of Nigel Gresley - GNR, later LNER at Doncaster. Ivatt had started on the North Staffordshire Railway and by the time he took over, most of the major problems had either been solved or were well on the way to solution.

Yet there were a few places where the LMS still had scope for major improvement. These tended to focus on two particular areas of activity: local freight and passenger working and the matter of intermediate freight power. Ivatt's solutions were typical of the Stamp/Stanier philosophy, though both these men were no longer there. By the end of the war, the LMS was beginning to question the accepted philosophy of running its lesser services with 'hand-me-down' older locomotives of questionable suitability or efficiency, not least in terms of higher than acceptable operational and maintenance costs. It was felt that a purpose-built new design might well solve this problem just as it had on the main lines and the outcome was a pair of radically new lightweight designs in 1946: a Class 2 2-6-0 and, for shorter distances, its 2-6-2T equivalent. Only 20 of the former and ten of the latter had emerged by the end of 1947 but they were to prove to be of seminal importance after nationalisation.

The intermediate freight role turned out to be a harder nut to crack. The LMS had conducted endless studies to see if a modern replacement could be found for that old warhorse, the Class 4F 0-6-0. Indeed, it actually built another 45 examples between 1937 and 1941 to tide things over, its replacement having been accorded less priority than other more pressing needs. But the 4F was never the best of engines, and the LMS had arguably far too many of them even before this final build. Eventually, Ivatt came up with the answer in 1947 by way of another overtly modern design, this time a Class 4 2-6-0. Its lineaments were to shock contemporary opinion and its ugly double chimney turned out, in the event, to be neither efficient nor necessary and was soon changed. The LMS built but three of them itself, but again, its legacy was to be more than significant.

Above:
During the war, the Stanier Class 8F was selected as the War Department's heavy freight type and examples were built by all four main line companies. Most were marked with LMS or WD insignia but some of the engines were built for the LNER and carried its markings. One such was No.7675 built by the SR at Brighton in 1944 for the LNER (renumbered 3124 in 1946 and 3524 in 1947). In late 1947 it was lent to the LMS and became their No.8729, later BR 48729; but it was by no means the only 8F to have a very complicated history....
Photo: SR Official

Below:
LMS No.6415 was one of only twenty Ivatt Class 2F 2-6-0s to enter service in company markings, the rest being built by BR. The engine is seen here at Bank Hall in 1947 and fully epitomises latter day LMS locomotive thinking. The equivalent 2-6-2T was mechanically identical to the tender version but was classified 2P.
Photo: Ransomme Wallis Collection   NRM

The rest of the LMS locomotive story was mostly one of refinement rather than revolution. In the steam field, Ivatt continued to develop the product in line with LMS thinking - particular attention being given to greater efficiency and maintenance - but much of this took place after BR was formed so is more properly considered there. Suffice to say that with the introduction of the new Ivatt designs, the LMS had achieved its goal of a standardised fleet in terms of modern locomotive types by the end of 1947, albeit with some way still to go in terms of eliminating all their predecessors.

So far, that most humble and vital of engines, the shunting tank locomotive, has received no mention, largely because in the steam field, the LMS had said all that could be said on the subject before the end of 1931, when it built the last of its numerous fleet of Class 3F 0-6-0Ts.

The extensive freight marshalling yards, so characteristic of the steam railway age, employed prodigious numbers of shunting engines, mostly 0-6-0Ts. But even the simple shunting tank, though it could remain on duty for hours on end, had to return to its shed for servicing and maintenance at some point and this reduced its availability. It can hardly be surprising, therefore, that the prospect of a shunting engine which could offer 23 out of 24 hour availability, with but one hour for re-fuelling and attention, had great appeal to the cost-conscious LMS. After all, marshalling yards generated no revenue as such; they were merely tiresome necessities in the business of getting freight traffic to its destination and cost savings were very worthwhile. The 1930s were to see much experiment in pursuit of this ideal and eventually the LMS arrived at the solution in 1944 in the form of a diesel-electric shunter with English Electric equipment which was to become the direct lineal ancestor of the familiar BR Class 08 shunter, still in widespread use at the end of the 20th Century.

The arguments in favour of greater availability applied equally well to main line activity, but this was slower to emerge and even the Americans, who rather pioneered this sort of thing, mostly developed their ideas after 1945. But the LMS was in the vanguard at the time and just managed to get Britain's first main line diesel electric into service in company colours at the end of 1947. Its 'twin' followed in 1948, at which point it was left to BR to continue the story - as indeed was the case with the steam locomotive.

Passenger Stock

As in the locomotive field, so too in the carriage department, the LMS had by far the largest fleet of all the Big Four and could lay claim to a fair degree of superiority over the rest in its last ten years in terms of carriage quality taken overall. However, its general superiority was by no means universal, some of its vehicles were definitely uninspired and the most innovative ideas were usually found in the context of long distance operations. Here, the LMS pursued a policy of general upgrading 'across the board' rather than concentrating its efforts on a handful of more publicised services - thus the already mentioned emphasis on increasing the overall total of 'mile a minute' trains.

The LMS had inherited some fine long-distance carriage traditions from its pre-group constituents, principally the LNWR and Midland but with significant contributions from the Caledonian and Lancashire and Yorkshire Railways; and for once in the company's history, there appear to have been far fewer conflicts to resolve. By 1938, LMS main line carriage practice had been well and truly established and is considered under the two facets of concept and style.

Conceptually, the LMS drew most of its long distance philosophies from the former LNWR which had, after all, been the principal long distance constituent of the LMS both in terms of the number of trains operated and carriage fleet size. This position was consolidated by the dominant LNWR role in the operation and construction of the West Coast Joint Stock (used for most services north of Carlisle), responsibility for which was shared on a somewhat unequal basis with the Caledonian - the LNWR built all of it! By contrast, the Midland influence, though it too had some fine carriages, was of less significance, though this did not stop Derby (for a while) trying to impose the Midland principle of frequent and lightly loaded trains throughout the new LMS. That it did not work in most non-Midland areas was a part cause of the locomotive crisis already mentioned: LMS expresses tended to continue the pre-group tradition where big formations were more normal in most areas.

Above:
The Ivatt Class 4 2-6-0, although very much an LMS product, was to arrive on the scene almost too late to qualify for company insignia. But the first three to appear did so as LMS engines late in 1947 and this is the second example, No.3001 at Bletchley in 1948 on passenger duty, in spite of its 4F classification. The double chimney was neither successful nor sightly and in due course it was replaced by a single blastpipe on all those engines so fitted.
Photo: Ransome-Wallis Collection, NRM

Below:
During the 1930s and 1940s, the LMS conducted wide ranging trials with a variety of diesel shunters and the various designs culminated in a quite excellent English electric concept in 1944 which the LMS began to put into series production. No.7120 was the first of them to carry LMS markings (in 1945) after 14 had gone to the WD. Well over 100 examples were to come into service between 1944 and 1952 until superseded by the familiar BR Class 08 diesel shunter.
Photo: LMS Official

Most important expresses carried dining cars of which the LMS had a large number, both inherited and of its own build. By the later 1930s, the older cars that remained were mostly relegated to occasional use (weekends, holidays &c), the mid-1930s having seen their massive replacement by a considerable fleet of magnificent 12-wheelers. But on many of the bigger trains, such was the demand, it was necessary to employ a full kitchen car between at least a pair of fully open vehicles and serving up to 80 or more meals at a sitting was no problem. Two complete sittings were quite regular and three not unheard of. Likewise, it was by no means uncommon for two completely independent sets of catering cars to be found in the same train, either one for each of the two classes (as, for example, the 'Merseyside Express') or one for each principal destination where a train served two places of equivalent status (eg the independent Edinburgh and Glasgow portions of the 'Royal Scot').

The LMS had most of the longest distance trains in Britain and it must be remembered that in those days, transit times, though good, were still quite long by current standards. London to Lancashire would be a three to four hour journey, London to Holyhead an hour or two longer, Glasgow would be some seven or eight hours distant from Euston while Inverness and the far north of Scotland could take the best part of a day, regularly involving overnight travel. The dining car was therefore no sinecure and it was easily possible to find it in continuous use throughout the journey. Thus, for example, the dining cars of the main Anglo-Scottish train on the Midland Division, the 'Thames-Clyde Express' would serve breakfast on leaving London, lunch somewhere in Yorkshire and afternoon tea and/or early dinner before arriving at Glasgow. At one point in time, this particular set of dining cars got themselves in the 'Good Food Guide'! A consequence of this was that the LMS operated relatively few Buffet Cars, though it had some. This type of car was better suited to shorter distance services such as were more often found on the other railways.

Likewise in the overnight sphere, the LMS was fairly dominant, again using a large fleet of well-appointed first class 12-wheel sleeping cars supplemented by an almost equally large number of the somewhat lighter in weight third class equivalents. It was nothing unusual for bigger overnight trains from Euston to contain anything up to eight or more sleeping cars which, together with the mandatory dining and luggage (and sometimes mail van) provision, not to mention ordinary carriages for passengers not using the sleeping cars, could easily put 600 tons or more of train behind the engine: the real task for which most of the Duchess 4-6-2s were designed.

Lighter weight expresses broadly followed these general principles (eg: a full blown dining car set in the normally six-coach only 'Thames-Forth' express), while through carriages to destinations which did not merit a full train could be found attached to almost any suitable working. The LMS was not unique in this respect, of course, but it probably had more such examples than the others.

In stylistic terms, the LMS carriage fleet of the late 1930s reflected a somewhat similar policy of 'Scrap and Build' as for locomotives. Inevitably, the newest carriages went to the best trains and by 1938, all new construction had been following Stanier styling since 1933: modern looking flush sided carriages with large picture windows and, except for the dining areas, dominantly side corridor with no separate outside doors to the compartments on most expresses. Third class passengers had armrests and courtesy lights and the proportion of first class carriages was normally quite low, save for some of the overnight services and those with a high proportion of business travellers. But first or third, the LMS offered a very high standard on its principal express routes.

The LMS also had a large fleet of general service gangwayed open stock in which it was the UK pioneer. This was most often used for 'strengthening' (i.e.: adding a few extra coaches to a service train) or for extra and/or excursion purposes. Indeed, the whole business of augmenting trains or running duplicated (relief) services was a common practice in those days. Usually, a standard 'set' of coaches would suffice for normal purposes and be kept assigned to one specific service. But on some days, extra carriages would be added to meet the higher demand while on Summer Saturdays, a particular 'train' might well run in several 'parts'. Locomotives had to be big enough in size and plentiful enough in numbers to cope with this fluctuation and there was an elaborate system of loading categories (and time schedules to suit them) to try and ensure that as far as possible, the motive power provided could operate the service (no matter how many or few its carriages) to time - not that it always worked by the way!

There were still, of course, a lot of older carriages around - and this was to remain the case throughout, though gradually diluted in variety over time. In the case of the LMS, dominant amongst the older carriages were first and second generation post-group standard vehicles (1923-32) which were mostly rather more traditional in appearance than the Stanier breed. Until 1929, these mostly copied Midland practice in terms of exterior styling (wood panelling with full external panel 'beading') but their interior layouts strongly reflected LNWR practice - a happy compromise as it turned out. By 1929-30, individual compartment doors had been eliminated from

Above:

When it entered its last decade, the LMS had already placed in service some thousands of new main line carriages to Stanier's familiar flush-sided designs dating back to 1933. All generic types were to be seen and this is a 60ft corridor composite No.4298, built in 1939. The LMS had been a pioneer in suppressing the draughty outside compartment doors as early as 1928-9 and in so-doing, set the style for most of the rest of the country.
Photo: LMS Official

Below:

If truth be told, Stanier's carriages were little more than cleaned up versions (in terms of their exterior lineaments) of those which had been built from 1930/31 before he arrived. Both embodied steel panels over a timber frame and the main difference was in the adoption of fully flush windows after 1932. This is a non-corridor composite of immediate pre-Stanier vintage, as unmemorable as most non-corridor stock of the time, though the LMS usually gave you a bit more leg room!!
Photo: LMS Official

corridor stock and larger 'picture' widows began to appear; while by 1930-31, lower waist levels and steel-sheet side panelling had replaced the older-fashioned style. Stanier's new carriages merely continued this well established tradition with their more modern external outlines.

Likewise, the best of the pre-group long distance carriages were still well evident in 1938, though not often seen in the very best trains. Many were still quite new, especially the better examples from the immediate pre-1923 period which, in terms of size, style and seating accommodation, were near-identical to their LMS successors. This allowed the LMS to start a process of what is now called 'cascading' - i.e.: moving older corridor coaches onto less and less long distance work as newer types emerged. A consequence of this was that over the years (a process well established by the late 1930s) the LMS was increasingly operating many semi-fast services with short formations of cascaded corridor stock rather than non-corridor vehicles. They were known as 'Inter-District Corridor Sets' and typically consisted of three or four carriages whose stylistic (and company) origins were many and various.

This process may well explain the relatively uninspired LMS approach to the non-corridor carriage. At best, its offerings in this field could only be said to be 'adequate'. In the pure suburban/high density mode, nothing much changed for some 25 years save for outward styling, which ran the usual gamut from fully panelled via steel panels to flush sided 'Stanier' depending on when, exactly, it was made. It was largely a matter of chance what you would get at any one place and time, new carriage provisioning usually being determined by the number of 'seats' which any district may have needed.

Nor was it much better in the intermediate distance field as far as brand new carriages were concerned. In its early days, the LMS introduced a few non-corridor coaches with an intermediate lavatory or two (you had to be alert to find the compartments so-served!), but it always seemed very half-hearted and even this modest concession to amenity had been more or less abandoned by 1930. Even at its best, LMS lavatory non-corridor stock was not quite as well served with toilets' as the best of the pre-group equivalents and one senses that the possibility of cascading (above) had much to do with it. A nice ex-LNWR corridor carriage with lavatories at both ends was a more than agreeable way to travel cross-country for an hour or two - not that this stopped the LMS from adding a few spartan non-corridors to any train at times of real need!

After the Southern, the LMS was probably the largest user of multiple unit stock in Britain, not that it had too much: the London-Watford service, some ex-LYR lines and a joint share with the LNER in the Manchester, South Junction and Altrincham line being the principal areas of interest. In 1938, such stock as it possessed was either pre-group in origin or early LMS standard non-corridor in outline. But in 1938, the LMS could at least make one small claim to fame when it introduced Britain's first sliding door stock onto our main line railways (i.e.: London Transport excepted). This took the form of some rather nice lightweight trains for the Mersey/Wirral electrified lines and, a few years later, a more or less total re-equipment of the Liverpool-Southport (ex-LYR) route with somewhat larger but conceptually similar stock. The latter was of technical interest in that it was of integral 'all-steel' construction (a harbinger of BR practice as it turned out) as was the very last design of LMS 'ordinary' stock which did not actually appear until early BR days and is therefore outwith our immediate concern.

Meantime in the more specialised coaching stock field, the LMS was little different from the rest. It held a dominant (but never monopolistic) role in the carriage of mail via Travelling Post Office carriages with 'en-route' sorting and trackside pick up apartatus. Here, of course, it ran the celebrated 'Night Mail' train, immortalised in film form and the only all-mail train in Britain at that time. It had the usual range of what were called 'non-passenger coaching stock' vehicles for the conveyance of high value and/or perishable cargo (prize cattle, horses, milk &c) but in the specialised passenger-carrying field it was never quite as dominant as some of its rivals. Even the 1937 'Coronation Scot' (much though it was milked for publicity purposes) was mostly formed from re-worked older carriages - conceivably a mute testimony as to how good the latter were anyway - while the 1939 train, the only real LMS attempt to make something a bit out of the ordinary, never ran as intended in Britain, being deemed too luxurious and extravagant to be reinstated when something approaching normality returned in 1946.

In terms of passenger traffic and trains, the war had little effect save for the elimination of most dining cars, the vast increase in military passenger traffic which more than offset the reduction in ordinary travel (which decline mostly resulted from Government propaganda: "Is your journey really necessary?") and a general run down in the condition and maintenance of carriage stock, not to mention cleanliness. Train speeds became less as conditions became more difficult while carriage building all but ceased until 1945, at which time the LMS re-launched itself in a big way, putting in service a vast number of new main line carriages in an attempt to catch up. Fortunately for the LMS, the pre-war Stanier designs were such that they could be left essentially unaltered without seeming dated and by the end of 1947, although the end-to-end speeds had not reached pre-war levels, most 'on train' amenities which passengers had come to expect in pre-war LMS express trains were back 'on stream' again. As with the locomotive situation, so too with passenger traffic, the LMS of 1947 was largely a product of its mostly excellent pre-war foundations.

Above:
LMS main line carriages were almost always well finished and furnished, though there were exceptions. These interior views are not untypical of their period. A light and airy first class sleeping compartment interior in 1939 when fashion moved away from more sombre finishes. Third class sleeping compartments became almost equally as good after the war, differing principally in terms of having a twin berth arrangement.

Bottom:
In two dining cars in 1946, the LMS experimented rather half-heartedly with a form of loose seating which seemed to anticipate the worst aspects of Festival of Britain styling five years later. Unhappily for posterity, BR chose to copy this not very good idea (the LMS never repeated it!) and many BR MkI dining cars came out with frightfully uncomfortable chairs rather than properly upholstered seats!
Photos: Both LMS Official

Above:
These views show a few fairly typical LMS approaches to the carriage of freight and livestock:

Top:
Covered goods van No.501086 - a typical mid-1930s product for the merchandise trade which, although it carried both roof and end ventilation, was not given automatic brakes.

Middle:
Furniture container mounted on a pre-group wagon. The modest growth of container traffic was a useful step forward but in an attempt to get it going quickly, the use of older wagons was common.

Bottom:
High value livestock (especially racehorses) was well worth conveying and usually went in passenger-rated vehicles. This new LMS horsebox dated from 1935 and, like most of its kind, included a small compartment for the travelling groom.
Photos: All LMS Official

Freight stock

Within the wagon field, the LMS again had the largest fleet of all the Big Four, and a closer examination of the summary table on page 164 reveals that, not surprisingly, it was nearest to the national average of all of them in terms of wagon category. This was almost certainly because its hinterland embraced the most typical cross-section of the whole country (again a function of its absolute size rather than for any other reason) whereas the others were more affected by distinctive regional factors, all of which were different. A simple example will suffice to explain.

The summary table given earlier reveals that the LMS was not quite as numerically ascendant over the LNER in terms of wagon totals as the relative company sizes would suggest. However, there is little doubt that if one excludes mineral wagons, the LMS fleet would then display a very similar proportional relationship (size for size) to that of the LNER as it did in the locomotive and carriage field. And mineral traffic was the key. Here, the LNER wagon fleet reflected the particular circumstances of its NER inheritance, for reasons which will be considered in the next section. Meantime, back to the LMS wagon itself....

Although in carriage terms the LMS could perhaps lay claim to a degree of superiority over the rest in its last ten years, the same could not really be said of its wagon stock. Here it displayed much the same sort of humdrum and, it must be stated, rather primitive quality as the rest. By far the bulk of its own vehicles (more than 90% of the total) were common or garden mineral and/or merchandise types and none of them had any particular claim to distinction. Goods trains being what they were, the LMS, like all the others, tended to get the last mile of useful traffic out of anything it inherited and its wagon building policy was largely to replace like with like when new stock was called for. As years went by there was a gradual increase in the payload weight which any one wagon could carry but it was hardly earth-shattering in technical terms. In consequence, as in many other things, the LMS standard wagon was mostly, in essentials, a developed version of the Midland types.

Compared with locomotives and rolling stock this was not of mammoth significance, nor of any overwhelming technical disadvantage either. Midland wagons were neat and serviceable and no whit worse than any of the others inherited by the LMS; but in this case they also had the overwhelming advantage of numbers compared with the other wagon fleets of 1923, so it actually made commercial sense to keep them going: the LNWR, for example (the only other conceivable contender in corporate LMS terms), had nothing appreciably better.

There were gradual cosmetic changes, of course, and the company did offer a few new designs which did not look quite so overtly 'Midland' as, for example, the standard LMS goods brake van; but one had only to take a look at a typical goods train of the late 1930s to appreciate how little things had changed at the fundamental level and 1938 dawned in a very 'pre-group' philosophical state as far as goods trains were concerned. By then, steel underframes had largely taken over from the favoured pre-1923 wooden form of construction (a form of progress mostly dating from the later 1920s), but handbrakes still ruled over more sophisticated alternatives and innovatory ideas were pathetically few in number. But the motor lorry had not yet been perceived as a real threat, world war was looming and one cannot escape the conclusion that 'complacency ruled'!

All of which is, no doubt, a very harsh judgement on what was our biggest private railway company; but it was little different from the rest and in many ways had no choice. This is not the place to go into the political ramifications which so adversely affected the private railways in the 1930s, save to say that they were not free agents by virtue of the Government-imposed 'common carrier' status which obliged them both to declare their rates in public (road operators were free to keep such things confidential) and to accept any load which would clear the structure gauge even if uneconomical to convey at the declared rate. Small wonder that they all got together in the celebrated 'Give the Railways a Square Deal' campaign of the later 1930s.

In these circumstances, it is no surprise that the LMS tended to focus its innovative ideas in areas where it could see prospect of genuine fiscal reward: cheaper to operate modern locomotives and better than average passenger trains. Meantime, while the playing field was to remain so manifestly 'unlevel' in the freight side of business, there was little incentive to improve vehicles, so who can blame the LMS if, like all the others, it chose to maximise freight revenue (of which there was still plenty on offer) at minimum capital cost?

What is surprising is that the company did still make some efforts. It had a slightly larger proportion of 'high value' merchandise vehicles in percentage terms (again see summary table) relative to overall company totals, the latter figure being distorted by the fact that neither the GWR nor SR had significant quantities of mineral wagons, thus making their merchandise vehicles assume a greater numerical significance; and it tried to run an ever-increasing number of freight trains at higher speed by the simple expedient of running many of them with a few 'fully brake fitted' wagons at the head of the formation thus putting extra 'automatic' brake power at the driver's disposal. Such trains were noted in working timetables by a Maltese Cross symbol and working 'Maltese' freights was to afford the crews involved almost as high status as top link passenger duties. Needless to say, Stanier's Class 5 4-6-0s made much of this possible.

Apart from special wagons designed specifically to carry 'awkward' loads (heavy machinery and the like), which sort of vehicles had long been part of the railway scene and whose provision the LMS, like the other companies, continued to ensure, perhaps the two new areas where the LMS was to make a significant contribution were in the field of container traffic and shock absorbing wagons, both of which (and their use was not confined to the LMS) had some influence in future developments, both road and rail.

The first of them was very much a child of the 1930s, though anticipated to some extent in the pre-group era, and in essence took the form of conveying containers (which could be loaded well off-site and conveyed to the rail head by road) on suitably adapted (or purpose-built) flat wagons. Called 'inter-modal' in our modern day, this was a valuable add-on to the conventional form of wagon loading and it is a pity that wartime constraints did not allow the idea to be developed as quickly as might otherwise have been the case.

One only needs to observe the commercial traffic on a modern motorway to see where it might have led had circumstances been different, though at least the modern railway still has some of this form of traffic. Likewise, the shock-absorbing wagon, in which cargo was loaded in a quasi-container which had in-built movement independent of the wagon chassis, and thus less likely to suffer from external disturbance, was an attempt to minimise damage to fragile cargo which conventional British wagons made all too likely in consequence of their own mechanical deficiencies!

Unhappily, these were but straws in the wind and the LMS, like all the others, was to see too few of them too late. In consequence, the company was to hand over what should have been potentially profitable freight business to BR in the sort of 'technical response condition' which was all too vulnerable to alternative competition; it was all very sad.

Above:
Those (relatively few) freight trains which had at least some wagons with automatic brakes, carried their own headlamp code, could run more quickly and were often referred to as 'fitted' or 'semi-fitted'. They would often get passenger engine power too - albeit of an older generation in many cases. This is one such, running under 'Express Freight' headcode at Shap c.1938. This code was for a partially fitted train and judging from the vehicles, the automatic brake was probably confined to the first three vans only. The engine is ex-LNWR Claughton Class 4-6-0 No.6017 Breadalbane, rebuilt with larger boiler by the LMS in 1928 and re-classified 5XP.
Photo: The late Eric Treacy, courtesy Pendragon Collection

Above:
The more common side of the LNER coin is seen in this view at Penrith, in 1938, with a former GER 'Intermediate' 2-4-0 No.7416 setting off for Darlington (via the Stainmore route) with a local train of elderly ex-North Eastern clerestory non-corridors - no lavatories either for this rather extended working.

Below:
The classic LNER image of the 1930s - streamliners leaving King's Cross. This picture shows the celebrated 'twin' 4.00pm departure. On the left, Class A4 pacific No.4466 Herring Gull, is well into its stride with the down 'Coronation' streamliner and is already well ahead of the much heavier Leeds train of normal stock on the right. On this occasion, the Leeds train was in charge of Class W1 4-6-4 No.10000.

Photo: Herbert Collection, NRM

CHAPTER SIXTEEN
LNER Locomotives & Rolling Stock

The LNER was arguably the most fascinating and frustrating of all the Big Four companies to analyse. It ought, in terms of sheer size, to have been somewhat akin to the larger LMS (with which it shared much in common in both operational terms and sphere of influence), yet it was wholly different in actuality and, though not hampered with the sort of locomotive controversy which had severely affected the LMS system during the first ten years after 1923, had not 'got its act together' (to use a modern form of expression) as well as had its larger rival by the time the Big Four were absorbed into BR. Nowhere was this more apparent than in the locomotive field; and this is where we start.

Unlike the LMS, the LNER was managed along traditional railway principles with a Chief General Manager in overall charge. Below him came the three main operating areas (broadly reflecting old pre-group boundaries) which were allowed a much greater degree of autonomy. They were virtually independent of each other in almost all respects save that of motive power wherein policy was set centrally for the whole railway. This meant that the CME enjoyed more individual power and answered direct to the Chief General Manager and not to the separate area managers. Fortunately for the LNER, this did not lead to the same degree of overt rivalry as on the LMS, but it also meant that locomotive policy was more strongly influenced by the CME in person.

The LNER was also the poorest of the Big Four in strictly financial terms, having relative more 'depressed' areas in its territory, relative to its size, than the others - the North East springs readily to mind in this regard but it was not the only area. In consequence, the company did not feel itself able to invest so heavily in new equipment as did its rivals and never adopted a 'Scrap and Build' policy to quite the same extent as its principal competitor. However, the writer is inclined to think that the long-accepted reasoning behind this state of affairs (i.e. no money) may be an over-simplification. The LMS was little better off than the LNER (neither of them paid as good a dividend as the GWR), but managed to find the capital for locomotive replacement largely because its detailed investigation of locomotive costings was able to demonstrate the near-certainty of the long term financial benefits of standardisation. The LNER never conducted any investigations on quite the same scale but one cannot escape the feeling that had it done so, a different situation might have developed. However, this was not quite the LNER style and brings us back to the more independent role of the CME.

For most of its first twenty years, this position was filled by the former Great Northern chief, the famous Nigel (later Sir Nigel) Gresley whose right to hold the position had been unquestioned since the grouping. The only other possible contender for office (J.G.Robinson of the old Great

Central Railway, 'senior' to Gresley but near to retirement), had graciously offered to stand down in favour of Gresley (a younger man) and the LNER was to benefit enormously from the continuity which was likely to and did result from this decision. Gresley was a fine engineer in any case, but a consequence of this early post-group decision was to enhance the prestige and power of a CME who never had to look over his shoulder to quite the same extent as did his LMS counterpart; even Stanier was occasionally summoned to the presence to answer for his actions and one can hardly imagine that happening with Sir Nigel! When combined with the far greater regional autonomy of the LNER management system and Gresley's innovative character, the continued locomotive variety which was to be seen on the LNER can be seen to be a little more complex than a simple consequence of lack of money for new engines. One senses that Gresley may well have preferred to work on a variety of older types and try to improve them, rather than scrap things out of hand - and he had the power and authority to do so.

Thus it was that by the late 1930s, the LNER could still offer a veritable kaleidoscope of motive power and it was not until after Gresley died (in 1941 before his due time) that the LNER began to contemplate the sort of locomotive standardisation 'across the board' which was already beginning to show benefits on the LMS. This was initiated by his successor, Edward Thompson, but was accompanied by considerable controversy. Gresley was in many ways 'an impossible act to follow', being regarded as almost a demi-god by many of his team, so any changes which Thompson instituted were almost bound to be viewed with a degree of questioning.

Even so, changes were needed on the LNER, largely in consequence of the altered operating conditions of the war. Gresley's main line engines were thoroughbreds and though capable of prodigious haulage feats when in good order (there are too many examples on record to deny that statement), their sophisticated nature often needed more careful maintenance than could be guaranteed in wartime. The new imperative, therefore, had to be towards the greater simplicity which the LMS had adopted during the 1930s and this Thompson attempted to provide, with some success as we shall see. The trouble really began when Thompson started to pay attention to the big Gresley engines, where he appears to have gone about matters with the same degree of tact and diplomacy as a bull in a china shop! We shall come back to this as well but the last years of the LNER cannot be understood without a consideration of the effect of this much misunderstood man, who was succeeded after only five years in office by A.H Peppercorn in 1946.

Thus it was that whereas on the LMS, locomotive matters had gone from a state of near-chaos to one of broad agreement by the end of the company period, the LNER was to see something of a reversal of this situation. The confidence of the Gresley years had given way in part to an element of doubt and confusion with which Peppercorn was only beginning to come to grips when the BR period dawned. In consequence, LNER influence on subsequent BR steam locomotive affairs was probably less than its quality deserved.

At the grouping, some 7,400 locomotives came into LNER ownership. Apart from the modest Great North of Scotland contribution (122), the rest came from five major companies whose fleets were broadly comparable in size. The North Eastern had the most (2,156) and the North British the fewest (1,074) with the Great Northern, Great Eastern and Great Central contributions broadly identical at around 1,350 each. Twenty years later, the total stock had been reduced to some 6,550 including 1,571 new locomotives built after 1922. The last five years were to see a further 389 added. There was thus a gradual changeover, but only 30% of the pre-group stock had been replaced in the same time as it had taken the LMS to get rid of some 70% of its (larger) 1923 fleet. Partially offsetting this was a determined effort by the LNER to standardise such things as boiler and engine fittings on a system-wide basis, thus affecting some economies.

This relatively slow rate of replacement combined with the even size of fleets within the five major constituents meant that by 1938, much of the LNER still largely reflected its pre-group ancestry, made even more apparent by the relative rarity with which individual pre-group classes departed from their home area, this being a reflection of the above-mentioned area management policy. Moreover, although Gresley was a Great Northern man whose LNER standard types naturally tended to reveal their GNR ancestry, a large number of new engines during his time (over 350 in fact) had been built to pre-group designs. It will therefore be seen that trying to make broad and valid generalisations from this situation is well nigh impossible but some trends had emerged.

At the principal express passenger level, Gresley's famous 4-6-2s reigned supreme in 1938 and also reached their crowning moment of glory in July of that year when the streamlined A4 *Mallard* captured the world speed record for steam on a special run down Stoke Bank between Grantham and Peterborough. This year was also to see the completion of the final Gresley pacific when the last of the A4s came into service. There were 35 of them all told (reduced to 34 during the war when one of them was destroyed by bombs at York). Though the A4s were undoubtedly Gresley's most famous design, they were well outnumbered by his earlier 4-6-2 type whose origins went back (just!) to Great Northern days.

Above:
The LNER was a carriage enthusiasts delight, largely because of its generally poor financial state which ensured that many old-timers survived for a long time. It kept more six-wheelers in service that anywhere else in Britain and here are just a few of them forming an excursion train near Woodhouse (ex-GCR). The exact date is unknown (probably c.1930 and before the period of our survey) but the scene is typical of the whole period. The locomotive is former great Central 4-6-0 No.5052 (LNER Class B6) and note that it is carrying express' headlamps!
Photo: Pendragon Collection

Below:
The old NER area was also a happy hunting ground for any who sought to find older stock in the 1930s and 1940s. This is Ripon viaduct in 1938 with a Leeds to Newcastle semi-fast headed by ex-NER 4-4-2 (LNER Class C7) No.735. The train is wholly composed of ex-NER non-corridor and mostly non-lavatory stock in a variety of forms and the writer has vivid memories of travelling to places like Scarborough and Bridlington in the mid-1940s in just such a train.
Photo: C.A.Davies Collection

The LNER period was to see the totals of these earlier 4-6-2's gradually increase to 79 examples when the last of them appeared in 1935. Development of the design had take place progressively over the years and by the late 1930s, two principal variants were to be seen: the original A1 type and the developed A3 version with higher boiler pressure and other refinements that dated from 1928 following a successful rebuild of one of the A1s in 1927; and thereafter all the A1s were gradually rebuilt to A3, a process which was completed in the first year of nationalisation.*

Contemporarily with the final A3s and early A4s, Gresley also introduced a fine 2-8-2 design (Class P2) for use on the Edinburgh-Aberdeen route, two in 1934 and four more in 1936. These very powerful engines, rarely seen in England save for their routine visits to Doncaster for heavy servicing, marked the start of Gresley's final design phase but were not to last too long in their original form, being converted to 4-6-2s in 1943 by Thompson, not without controversy (see later). There was also a unique 4-6-4, dating from 1937 and a conventional rebuild of what had started life as an experimental four-cylinder compound with water tube boiler in 1929. In rebuilt form (Class W1) it was virtually a larger A4 with a pair of extra wheels at the rear and slightly bigger cylinders. Unlike the P2 class, it remained in this form until withdrawn and tended to work turn and turn about with the main 4-6-2 fleet.

Meantime, from 1936 onwards, the already large fleet of 4-6-2s had been augmented by the first of what many would aver was Gresley's finest design in purely thermodynamic terms, the Class V2 2-6-2 of which 184 were eventually to be built. Developed from the A3s - their boilers were virtually identical - but with cylinders equivalent to and valves even more effective than those of the speedy A4s, it is a moot point whether they should be considered at this stage at all. They were regarded as mixed traffic and designed (originally) for high speed goods trains, including a famous working from King's Cross known as the 'Green Arrow' service, from which the first of the V2s actually took its name. The V2 design was, of course, a tangible manifestation of Gresley's well known 'big engine' philosophy and with this, at least, Edward Thompson could not argue when he took over, accepting the need for large locomotives and adding a modest quota to the total. But it was the manner of his so-doing which upset folk; it seemed like an overt attack on the memory of the famous man. Thompson was not convinced of the total reliability of the celebrated Gresley 'derived' valve gear for the inside cylinder (all LNER 4-6-2s and V2s had three cylinders) which did, indeed need careful attention if it was to be kept in good order. In many ways Thompson was to be proved correct in later BR days, but his initial moves were perhaps tactless to say the least.

In 1943, he offered his first 4-6-2 by way of rebuilding Gresley's Class P2 type. These eight coupled engines had (or so it is said) caused trouble north of Edinburgh by way of 'spreading' the track as a consequence of their long fixed wheelbase, so Thompson removed the leading pair of driving wheels, took away the Gresley valve gear in favour of three independent sets of Walschaert motion and substituted a leading bogie. Quite apart from this complete departure from Gresley's precepts, the finished result was somewhat ungainly looking (the outside cylinders were set well back with a large gap between bogie and leading coupled axle) whereas the original Gresley design was typically elegant. This change did not please everybody, nor was Thompson much more popular when, in 1944, he cancelled the order for the last of the popular V2 type and used their boilers and wheels on another quartet of new 4-6-2s, displaying much the same outlines as the rebuilt P2s. All ten engines had the 6ft 2in wheels of the P2s and V2s and were classified A2, ostensibly 'mixed traffic'.

But what really set a tiger by the tail was when Edward Thompson turned attention in 1945 to the genuine express 4-6-2 with 6ft 8in wheels. As with the A2, he decided to start with a rebuild and chose one of the older A1 type as an alternative to rebuilding it to A3 form (above). But what a choice: the original Gresley pacific of all, *Great Northern*. It is said, in Thompson's defence, that this engine was simply the next A1 due into shops, but few believed that; there is evidence to indicate that Thompson had previously disagreed with Gresley and this writer is unqualified to comment further. Whatever, when *Great Northern* re-emerged, it again displayed the clumsy lines of the rebuilt P2s (with far less cause) and retained the A1 classification, thus causing the original un-rebuilt A1s to become A10 until converted to the A3 form. It was all most unfortunate; but no more Gresley 4-6-2s were to be similarly treated.

Thompson's final 4-6-2s came out in 1946, a batch of 15 new locomotives of the smaller wheeled A2 type, based rather more on the rebuilt P2s than the modified V2s (above) and these

Above:

Doyen of the class and giving its name to the whole type, Gresley Class V2 No.4771 Green Arrow gets into its stride from King's Cross goods yard with just the sort of fast freight train for which it was designed. It also became clear that their performance was fully up to 4-6-2 standards when on passenger duty and the LNER treated them as express motive power whenever it suited; in effect, therefore, by 1944 the company had at its disposal approximately 300 modern Gresley locomotives of broadly comparable power.

Below:

The Thompson pacifics were somewhat ungainly looking when compared with the 2-8-2s from which the first were rebuilt. The upper view shows the original No.2001 Cock o' the North as built and the lower view is of Class A2/1 No.3696 when new in 1944 (later No.507 Highland Chieftain), one of four engines built instead of the last four Class V2s - see text - but otherwise similar to the 2-8-2 rebuilds.

* The missing A2 designation (the LNER locomotive classification allotted a letter to each wheel arrangement, 'A' being the 4-6-2 type) originally applied to six former NER 4-6-2s, all of which were scrapped before 1938. It was later re-used for new Thompson engines.

turned out to be good and powerful machines and formed the basis of the final LNER 4-6-2 designs by Peppercorn. In striving to be fair to the controversial Thompson as far as the 4-6-2 type is concerned, it is worth concluding this review of LNER express power by making the point that when Peppercorn, who was very much a Gresley man, took over in 1946, he did not reinstate Gresley's valve gear but preferred Thompson's three sets of independent motion. However, by shortening the wheelbase and thus closing up the ugly gap, he produced a much more stylish looking ensemble and this was, apparently, acceptable to the more vociferous critics. Fifteen of the Peppercorn A2s were eventually built and the first of them was rushed out late in 1947 in company colours, carrying the designer's name.

Moving down the scale to secondary express working, the LNER was never to witness the degree of universality which Gresley's big engines had afforded to most of the East Coast route expresses. Here, much of the work continued to be in the hands of pre-group types (including those built/rebuilt by Gresley after the grouping). Noteworthy amongst these were the former GC 'Director' 4-4-0s (LNER Class D11, new examples of which were built by the LNER for Scottish use) and the Gresley rebuilds of ex-Great Eastern 4-4-0s (LNER Class D16) and 4-6-0s (LNER Class B12). All three types were outstanding of their kind and ran through well into BR days.

The nearest approach to a standard 'intermediate' LNER express type took the form of two Gresley three-cylinder designs of 1927-8, the Class B17 4-6-0 (often known as 'Sandringhams') and the Class D49 4-4-0 in two variants with conventional and poppet valves respectively, usually known as 'Shires' or 'Hunts', the latter name identifying the poppet valve version. There were 70 4-6-0s and 76 4-4-0s (42 with poppet valves), all broadly equivalent in power but slightly smaller in absolute terms than their equivalents on the other three main lines. As with many LNER types, they tended to be more regional in distribution than the 4-6-2s and were built to meet specific area needs. Thus the 4-6-0s were originally built for use in East Anglia and named after country houses of that region - hence *Sandringham* itself, the first of the line. When more were needed for the former Great Central line they usually received Football Club names, whose geographical spread was, nevertheless, rather wider than their sphere of operation. Two of them were fashionably streamlined in 1937 to work the 'East Anglian' service but reverted to normal in 1951. From 1943, many B17s received Thompson's larger B1 type boiler (below) while in 1945 the first of an eventual ten examples was completely rebuilt with the same B1 boiler type but with two (larger) cylinders, becoming Class B2 in the process. These two variations both had greater power than the original B17 and were broadly equivalent in power to the LMS 5XP type. This manifestation of Thompson's standardisation policy was not as controversial as his work on the 4-6-2s and was to be carried out on other classes too.

The D49 4-4-0s were again largely regionally based, the Shires mostly in Scotland and the Hunts in the North East. Very good engines which did a lot of front line work in their respective areas, they were broadly equivalent in power to the LMS (ex-MR) compound 4-4-0s but most objective opinion generally gave the edge to the LMS design. Thompson rebuilt one Hunt with two inside cylinders but this somewhat surprising development was not successful, nor was it repeated.

Turning now to the mixed traffic field, this is another area where (as was the case elsewhere in Britain) the LNER concentrated attention and had achieved a degree of system-wide standardisation by 1947. The Gresley Class V2 type has already been mentioned and these successful 2-6-2s were to be seen everywhere: the LNER called them the engines which won the war, though supporters of the Stanier Class 5 might have had other views. In British mixed traffic terms, the V2 was unique and, some would argue, far too complicated and expensive to build for a common user mixed traffic type. But the rest of the LNER-built fleet had much in common with that seen elsewhere in the country.

The first to appear, chronologically, was the 2-6-0 type where the LNER was to operate a fleet of about the same magnitude as that of the LMS - and had many of them in service well before those of its rival. Their origins go back to the GNR and gave proof that Gresley was not always a 3-cylinder man. Two versions were to be seen, the two-cylinder K2 type (dating from 1914), many of which were actually created in LNER days by rebuilding Gresley's earlier and smaller boilered K1 type of 1912. But a much greater total was represented by the K3 three-cylinder version, the first of which had also appeared in GNR days during 1920 as what many regard as the first of the Gresley 'big' engines. Until the V2 appeared, this was in effect the LNER standard mixed traffic type and very powerful, more so, in fact than the LMS 'Crabs' and Class 5s in tractive effort terms. Both classes did huge amounts of work in late LNER days, Thompson leaving both of them more or less alone save for rebuilding one K3 with two cylinders in 1945 as Class K5. The final LNER 2-6-0 type was the K4, effectively a small wheeled version of the K3, of which six were built (all named) specifically for use on the heavily graded West Highland line where their high power to weight ratio (they were 25 tons lighter than a V2 with 3,000lb more tractive effort) was put to very good use. Again, Thompson rebuilt one of them with two cylinders in 1945 (reclassifying it as K1 in the process) but this time, there was an interesting outcome in that this became the prototype for a new small-wheeled two-cylinder 2-6-0 which Peppercorn developed to the tune of 70 engines. But these all came into service after the LNER had ceased to exist.

Above:
The two principal varieties of Class B17. The upper view shows No.2800 Sandringham *itself (Class B17/1); note the short GER type tender, employed to reduce the overall wheelbase so as to fit existing turntables. The lower view depicts No.2848* Arsenal, *one of the 'Football Club' series (Class B17/4 with larger LNER standard tender) which were regularly used on ex-GCR routes.*
Photos: Both LNER Official

Below:
The LNER had two other useful classes of mixed traffic engine these being the 'Hunts' (named after famous fox-hunting packs such as the Ainsty, Bedale, Zetland and so on; the class D49/2) and the slightly earlier class D49/1 'Shires'. The picture shows No.253 Oxfordshire *(Class D49/1) one of the early Walschaerts motion engines from 1927 and given GCR type tender. It is seen in company with Sentinel steam railcar* Cleveland, *another characteristic LNER sight in the 1930s.*
Photo: Pendragon Collection

Above:

Very few class B1 4-6-0s were actually built during the Thompson period though the design is rightly attributed to him. No.8302 Eland was only the second example to appear and is seen here brand new in works grey condition at Darlington in 1942. It was later numbered 1001.

Photo: LNER Official

Above Right:

Gresley three-cylinder Class K3 2-6-0 No.143 (built 1925) on express passenger duty bound for London at Huntingdon in the late 1930s. The large boilered K3 was the principal LNER mixed traffic type until the advent of the Gresley Class V2 and always played a vital part in LNER main line operations.

Below:

A nice study of Class K2 2-6-0 No.4674 Loch Arkaig on West Highland line duty near Bridge of Orchy in the mid-1930s. Many examples of this former Great Northern design were sent to Scotland in LNER days and given more protective side-window cabs as shown here. The majority were also given suitable names in the best North British Railway tradition, the GNR not having favoured named engines.

Photo: NRM Collection

It will be apparent from the above that Thompson quite regularly rebuilt individual examples from many three-cylinder classes to a two-cylinder form and this seems to have been his preferred method for evaluating the benefits of long term standardisation. However, the LNER did not have the equivalent of the Class 5 4-6-0 which was creating such a fine reputation on the LMS, so in this field, Thompson went for a completely new design, the Class B1 4-6-0. In fact, it used many standard detail components which had emerged in the Gresley period but it is fair to see it as a wholly new type. Ten only were built between 1942 and 1944 so their evaluation was slow, but from 1946, they began to emerge in quantity, 274 being in service when BR took over. The eventual total (including BR-built examples) was 410 and they were scarcely distinguishable from the LMS equivalent in performance terms. For some reason, the LNER preferred to call them 'general utility' rather than mixed traffic.

Moving now to passenger tank engines, where the LNER never introduced a truly standard type, broad generalisation is difficult. Nevertheless, there were a few types which, by virtue of their numbers, took on a more dominant role and need to be singled out. Within them, we encounter for the first time a form of wheel arrangement particularly, though not exclusively, associated with the LNER, largely by virtue of its pre-grouping inheritance: the inside-cylinder 0-6-2T. This was a tank engine derivative of the familiar British 0-6-0 with an extra pair of wheels to support a reasonable sized bunker. Many types came into LNER ownership and three were to assume particular importance.

Largest, numerically, were the Class N7 series whose origins were firmly Great Eastern and which could be seen bustling in and out of Liverpool Street on intensive suburban duty until the end of steam days in BR times. Many of them were built new in the 1920s and others rebuilt from genuine GER originals from 1940 onwards - a typical example of Gresley's alternative approach when a good pre-group design merited such treatment. Thompson followed the same line of policy in 1943 with further rebuilds and all of them (134) went on to see more than ten years service with BR.

A similar situation pertained on the GNR suburban lines from King's Cross where the Class N2 reigned supreme, this time a former GNR type dating from 1920 and, with the addition of new LNER-built examples, totalling 107 units. Of slightly larger driving wheel diameter than the N7, what they may have lacked in acceleration (very important on the intensively operated ex-GER lines) was more than compensated by a higher turn of speed - very useful on the longer distance runs from King's Cross. They were supplemented during LNER days by a further 56 examples of the earlier Ivatt N1 Class from which the N2 was developed.

The Scottish equivalent was the former North British design of 1910 (LNER Class N15) of which 99 existed during the final LNER period (and again well into BR days). Developed from an earlier NBR design of which only six were made (LNER Class N14), these engines were astonishingly similar in both concept and design to the GER and GNR types and did much the same sort of work, although in this case, no new engines were added by the LNER.

The nearest approach to a standard LNER design of passenger tank was the Class V1 2-6-2T, introduced in 1930. Of characteristically good looking Gresley three-cylinder configuration, it was considerably better than the contemporary 2-6-2T from the LMS and was made even more

puissant when ten further examples were built with higher boiler pressure in 1939 (Class V3). In due time, many V1s were upgraded to V3 and eventually, approximately half the total of 92 engines were in V3 configuration. Many of them, not surprisingly, found use in the North East where the 0-6-2T did not dominate and a number of older classes needed either to be replaced or augmented. The LNER did not copy the LMS as far as the larger 2-6-4T arrangement was concerned during the company period, but Thompson was undoubtedly influenced by LMS activities. Indeed he sought to get support from LMS locomotive engineers when arguing that Gresley's ideas were somehow inappropriate to the latter day LNER. "We wouldn't have done it quite that way" is the only known comment to have been offered by Stanier's men on this particular theme; but they never said what they would have done! Gresley and Stanier (exact contemporaries by age as it happened) were close personal friends (bigoted railway enthusiasts please note!) and the LMS team decided to be diplomatic. Whatever, the 2-6-4T made sense and in 1945 Thompson introduced the type in the form of the L1 Class and as with many of his ideas, built but a single prototype for evaluation. Like the K1 2-6-0 rebuild it was the only one to enter service before 1948, it being left to Peppercorn to multiply the class to a final total of 100 in BR days. As with the main post-war production batches of B1 4-6-0s, Peppercorn chose to make no changes to Thompson's design.

Both intermediate and heavy freight categories were again areas where the LNER had no single solution and here, its response was not unlike that of the LMS and probably for much the same reason. It too had a vast army of pre-group 0-6-0s to which, like the LMS, it added substantially in the form of the near-identical Gresley Class J38 (4ft 8in wheels) and J39 (5ft 2in wheels), both of which, like the D49s, had quite a bit of Darlington (ex-NER) thinking to them. The J38 variant totalled but 35 out of the over 300 examples to be built. They were slightly more powerful (and somewhat better) than the comparable LMS Class 4F and did much the same sort of work, supplemented by hundreds of pre-group examples which, like those of the LMS, continued to be seen at work to the end.

The 0-8-0 story was also similar. All LNER examples were pre-group in origin and the best of them were undoubtedly those of the old NER which had made something of a speciality of the 0-8-0 type for its considerable mineral traffic. These remained in front line service right to the end of steam and included 15 of what were undoubtedly Britain's most sophisticated 0-8-0 type: the three-cylinder Class Q7 dating from 1919. But the LNER, unlike the LMS, did not see fit to build additional 0-8-0s (save for Q7s already ordered in 1923) because, and this time unlike the LMS, it already had examples of what has been seen already to be the better heavy freight type: the 'modern' 2-8-0.

Within this wheel arrangement the LNER was fortunate in having available from the first day of the grouping, two of the best ever examples of the genre in the form of Robinson's two-cylinder Great Central design of 1911 (Class O4) and Gresley's more sophisticated but considerably less numerous three-cylinder GNR type, Class O2, only eleven of which existed in 1923. This was the successor to the original two-cylinder Gresley 2-8-0 of 1913 (Class O1 reclassified O3 in 1944) of which the LNER received 20. The O2 was effectively a standard type but because of the large number of O4s, only 56 new O2s were built. They were very much in the Gresley 'big engine' tradition, the original GNR prototype being the first engine to display derived valve motion for the middle cylinder.

Above, upper:
Typifying many 0-6-2T designs inherited by the LNER from the pre-group era, the Class N7 was of GER origin. This is No.9671 (built for the LNER in 1926) at Hackney Downs heading for Liverpool Street with a typical ten coach rake of two Quint-Art suburban sets c.1947-8.
Photo: Pendragon Collection

Above, lower:
Gresley's handsome Class V1 2-6-2T in the shape of No.451, brand new at Doncaster in 1938. It was upgraded to Class V3 (see text) in 1943.
Photo: LNER Official.

Left:
Working an empty coaching stock train an ex-North British Railway Class N15 0-6-2 tank engine from Eastfield depot is seen on trip working No.6 Renumbered as No.9174 in 1946, this engine was built by the North British Loco. Co. in 1916 and was scrapped by BR in November 1958. Many of these inherited pre-group locomotives had a considerable period of longevity, as British design was such as to expect a life-span of anything between 30 to 50 years service. This was in stark contrast with, say, American practice where locomotives were built with a much shorter life-expectancy. The fact that the locomotive stock was re-cycled much more quickly in such countries, enabled them to commence alternate forms of traction at a much earlier stage than the railways here in Britain. For this reason the advent of the diesel traction occured much sooner in America, whilst British railways were still working with designs that could be sixty or seventy years old by the time the railways were nationalised.

The Robinson 2-8-0 was one of Britain's most significant locomotive types, having been deemed suitable for adoption as a War Department standard during the 1914-8 conflict, much as the Stanier 2-8-0 had been so regarded in 1940. Being such a large class, they were progressively improved by Gresley and by the end of his time, several sub-classes existed, some of which now carried Gresley (O2 type) boilers. But perhaps the most surprising tribute to these already venerable engines came when Thompson completely rebuilt one of them in 1944 with a new B1 type boiler and cab, new cylinders and Walschaerts valve gear to produce the prototype of the second LNER O1 Class (the elderly Gresley O1s were reclassified O3 in consequence). Only the tenders revealed their GCR origins and this rebuild was, in effect, Thompson's new standard heavy freight type, 58 of them ultimately being converted.

Meantime, the more elegant O2s continued to perform some fine work but were never increased in quantity, although Thompson did rebuild a handful with the B1 type boiler, this time retaining the three cylinder propulsion. Finally, it should be recorded that towards the end of its existence, the LNER also made use of both the Stanier 2-8-0 type (many of which were built in LNER workshops and regarded as technically 'on loan' to the LNER) and the later WD 'Austerity' 2-8-0, classifying them O6 and O7 respectively.

As far as shunting locomotives were concerned, the LNER mostly made use of its pre-group stock of 0-6-0Ts and 0-4-0Ts (of which they had plenty) and the only approach to standardisation was the continued (but limited) building of the attractive (ex-GNR) Class J50 0-6-0T. But even at the end, there were only just over 100 of these compared with the 400 or more LMS Class 3F tanks. Nor did the LNER adopt diesel shunters, apart from the odd experiment. But it had decided to introduce main line diesels on the East Coast (none were built) and was also significantly involved in the first moves to main line electrification, intended to be initiated on the heavily graded ex-GCR Woodhead route between Sheffield and Manchester. For this purpose, Gresley had, in association with Metropolitan-Vickers - and almost his last work for the LNER - introduced a prototype Bo-Bo 1500V DC electric locomotive in 1941. Wartime prevented the immediate implementation of the scheme and the design was not multiplied until BR days when it eventually totalled 58 units (BR Class EM1), but the first of them did carry LNER colours and was destined to become Britain's first active main line electric locomotive. After the war, it was used in the Netherlands (where it was named *Tommy*, which tribute to the British soldier was retained after its return), but, like its LMS diesel pioneer of contemporary vintage, it was never preserved, more's the pity.

Above:
After the first world war, many ex-ROD (Railway Operating Division) engines were made available to the main line companies at what amounted to a knock-down price. Both the GWR and LMS obtained batches (the LMS mostly for their tenders, apparently!) while the LNER naturally went for them in a big way, they being standard with the inherited ex-GCR machines. In consequence, there were over 400 ex-GCR and ex-ROD 2-8-0s in the LNER list and although not seen as 'standard' in the normally accepted sense, their sheer numbers ensured that they were, in effect, the principal LNER heavy freight type, a role they were to fulfil throughout the LNER period. The picture shows ex-ROD No.1868 running as LNER 6268 c. 1930, very much as built and much as it remained throughout the LNER period. It was built in 1918 and came into LNER stock in 1924, running as No.3774 after 1946.
Photo: C.A.Davies Collection

Right:
Class J50 0-6-0T No.594, built by the LNER in 1926 with but few changes made to the original GNR design and then only in detail. Known to many as 'Ardsley' tanks from their work in that area, their distinctive side tanks were meant to improve forward vision when operating trip freight on the main line.
Photo: Pendragon Collection

Passenger Stock

In the field of passenger stock, much the same sort of analysis as has already been offered for the LMS applied to the LNER so need not be repeated, but there were a few significant differences to be observed by the later 1930s and it is this side of the story which will receive emphasis here.

Firstly, although LNER standard carriages were never built in quite the same huge quantities as were to emerge from Wolverton and Derby (in this as in other areas, they reflected the relative sizes and strategic policies of the two companies), they were generally more technically sophisticated in the main line context. This was because, once again almost certainly in consequence of Nigel Gresley's key position, there was a greater degree of continuity. It is often forgotten that Gresley started his East Coast career as the Carriage and Wagon supremo of the GNR where he was the first to introduce the modern automatic 'buckeye' coupling and associated gangway to the British scene, the gangway, by the way, usually being referred to in Britain as the 'Pullman' type, having been originally adopted by that company in North America.

Likewise, Gresley later designed (for the LNER) the most sophisticated form of carriage bogie to be seen in Britain until well into BR days. It employed a compound bolster which, alongside the more modern couplings and gangways that had long been a feature of East Coast expresses, was to be a dominant influence in this part of the story of carriage evolution in Britain. Furthermore, since the East Coast Joint Stock (held in common between the GNR, NER and NBR) and the far less well known GNR/NER joint stock (for services between the North East and London) was dominantly to GNR styling as well, the resultant LNER standard main line carriage was bound to be something of a foregone conclusion.

Some modest experimentation was made with steel construction and/or flush steel panelling (accompanied by elaborate painted simulation of varnished teak livery) and some tourist stock even employed plywood panelling (painted green and cream in this case), but in general the traditional teak body finish (which went back well into the 19th Century) reigned supreme until Gresley died. This fact alone may well explain why the LNER (for its streamline trains) chose to adopt a completely new type of carriage styling whereas the LMS was able to modify existing Stanier types for its contribution; but we anticipate.

Conceptually, there was very little difference between the LNER and LMS approach to main line expresses and the LNER could offer much the same sort of carriage types as have already been considered in regard to its somewhat larger rival, though generally fewer in absolute carriage numbers both in the ordinary sense and in the more specialised field of, say, dining, sleeping and Post Office vehicles. Main line carriage renewal was also a little slower on the LNER which, in consequence, had proportionately rather more residual survivors from the pre-group era, not that there was much wrong with most of them. There was also a somewhat slower move towards the suppression of individual outside compartment doors on gangwayed stock than on the LMS and the LNER did not favour 12-wheel types, nor adopt the 'open third' to quite the same extent; but in general, the differences were minimal save in cosmetic terms, and it was only in two readily identifiable areas of long distance travel that the LNER pursued a markedly different philosophy by the later 1930s.

Above:
This undated but mid-1930s view in the Vale of York shows a typical LNER southbound express taking water from Wiske Moor troughs and headed by Class A1 4-6-2 No.2561 Minoru *(converted to Class A3 in 1944). The thirteen coach train is entirely composed of bow-ended dome roof stock, some of it undoubtedly of pre-1923 origin, a consistency of outline which was very much a feature of the best LNER trains. Somewhat unusually for the time, there are no examples of the later post-1930 carriages with angle-trussed underframe . The precise working is not identified.*
Photo: Pendragon Collection

Below:
The superbly finished first class interior of one of the coaches in the famous 'Silver Jubilee' streamliner of 1935. The later 1937 'Coronation' sets were developed from this style and were even more palatial with rather paler shades of interior finish than the conventional wood panelling seen in this view. Photo: LNER Official

Above:
Throughout the 1930s, the LNER retained traditional varnished teak finish for most of its stock but the underframe was upgraded to the angle trussed form shown here on Buffet Car No.648. The large windows usually to be found in catering vehicles and open carriages were gradually incorporated into the better side corridor stock as years progressed, but never to quite the extent as on the LMS.

Below:
Sentinel steam railcars were very much a feature of secondary LNER lines from the late 1920s. They were often named after stage coaches which were associated with their running areas and given an attractive two-tone livery (red and cream at first, later green and cream), either of which made them stand out well. In this view, one of the earlier articulated cars (No.29 Rockingham*) is given the full paintshop treatment in York carriage works - note the fine lining round the panel edges.*

Photos: Both LNER Official

Chronologically, the first of these to appear was in the catering field where the LNER adopted the buffet car concept to a much greater degree than did the LMS. This was probably due to the greater number of intermediate range express workings that the LNER offered, largely by virtue of geography, compared with the LMS where, as we have already seen, the greater number of really long distance trains (in the British context) was to justify the presence of a more elaborate catering facility. As a consequence, the LNER developed the buffet car to a high degree of sophistication and it is not unreasonable to postulate that this had important spin-off effects on the BR period which followed.

Similarly in the field of high speed trains, the LNER displayed a somewhat different approach. In this respect, and maybe driven by economic factors, it is undeniable that the LNER pursued the development (and the concomitant publicity value) of 'high speed' to a point which was never rivalled by its competitors. No matter that in the mid-1930s, this rather cash-strapped company also offered a good deal more four and six wheel carriages for public delectation than the rest of the British system put together (sic!), 'high speed' ruled and the LNER milked the publicity value of this side of the story for all it was worth: it made sound commercial sense. The interesting consequence was that alongside some of the most outdated stock to be found in Britain at the time for the more ordinary passenger, the LNER simultaneously offered some of the most sublime examples of passenger carriages to be seen anywhere in the world in the form of its streamlined trains, wherein nothing was spared.

There was thus a considerable dichotomy in LNER passenger operations and the company cannot be fully understood unless this fact is both appreciated and accepted. In the purely suburban field, its offerings were mostly dire indeed, regularly taking the form of cramped non-corridor stock (commonly articulated in four or five coach sets to save both cost and weight) which shuttled in and out of Liverpool Street, King's Cross and elsewhere for many a long year with little by way of consolation to the weary commuter. Gresley's articulated carriages were very well regarded and technically significant, but most examples were to be confined (in the interest of economy) to the suburban field and their value on the main line was, in consequence, rather less important overall than some of their many apologists might aver - a harsh judgement, you may well say, but not without historical justification. At the same time, and outwith the purely suburban arena, the LNER was rather good by contrast with the rest of the Big Four. It really did seem to care about intermediate distance passengers and its carriages rather reflected this fact. A particularly neat and satisfactory solution was offered by way of a semi-corridor type which, though not gangwayed to adjacent carriages, contained internal 'half' corridors that allowed all compartments access to the centrally located lavatories. And, of course, there were many pre-group survivors not to mention some degree of cascading of older corridor stock, much as on the LMS.

Another characteristic LNER approach of this period was to be seen in the widespread use of steam railcars (mostly from Sentinel but a few from Clayton). Though not confined to the LNER, this type of self-propelled solution for the less patronised services was pursued with some vigour during the 1930s. They were painted in an attractive green and cream colour scheme, carried individual names (often repeating those of old stage coaches) and were often associated with an improved service frequency on the routes to which they were assigned.

After the war, the LNER moved swiftly away from teak bodied stock for all new construction and finally adopted a similar form of flush steel panelling as could be seen on all the other lines. It was, of course, painted in imitation 'teak' finish until BR days and once again, the instigator was Edward Thompson. All carriages retained Gresley bogies, while main line gangwayed stock continued to make use of buckeye couplers and Pullman gangways. A new innovation was the incorporation of intermediate cross-vestibules in side corridor stock to speed loading and unloading, the actual compartments themselves having large windows and no individual outside doors. Most of the so-called Thompson stock was not to appear until after he had left and was built during Peppercorn's time and well into the BR period, a further example of where Thompson's successor (as in the locomotive field) chose not to revert to Gresley ideas but retained those of his immediate predecessor.

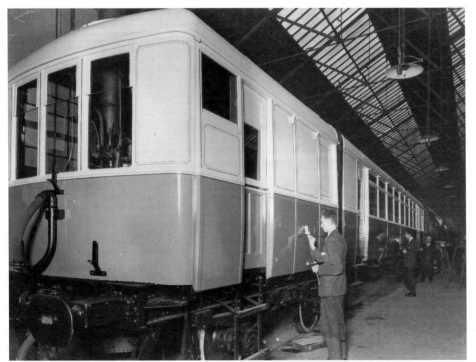

Freight stock

We have seen in Chapter Thirteen that the total LNER wagon stock was only 7% less than that of the LMS and this was largely because the LNER had many more mineral wagons and a slight numerical superiority in the 'other wagon' category (see summary table, page 164). This simultaneously reflected and gave rise to a few differences between the LNER and the other railways in operational terms, though this should not be exaggerated; goods train working was much the same wherever you went in Britain at that time. Many types of commodity were needed on a nationwide basis and only where the local economy was markedly different were significant differences to be seen.

As far as the LNER was concerned, perhaps the most important difference was the intense concentration of mineral traffic in the North East (a legacy from the old NER) wherein the dominant mineral wagon type was not the private owner vehicle as in many (most?) other areas, but the company-owned equivalent. The NER was absolutely dominant on the LNER in terms of wagon fleet size, owning some 43.5% of the total at grouping which was well over twice as many as the next largest goods vehicle contribution, that of the NBR. In fact, the NER was the biggest wagon owning company in the whole of the country in 1922 and while comparative numbers do not tell the whole story - the private owner wagon must also be considered - it can be no surprise that in terms of post-group wagon building, NER influences were to dominate, right down to wagon livery where large identifying letters NE continued to be preferred to LNER in full. Just about the only post-group change in this respect was the adoption of the former GNR wagon colours to identify some specific types of vehicles: fully brake fitted (brown red oxide) and refrigerated vans (white).

Mineral traffic continued to dominate all through the company period and the LNER was fortunate in that its NER predecessor had identified the need for much larger capacity wagons than used in most of the country and had also made provision for their handling. This was usually in the coal, coke and iron ore field and inevitably led to a size difference between such vehicles and the typical private owner wagon to be found in most places - hence the fact that the company itself tended to build its own wagons wherever greater size was needed in the NE region. The LNER continued this practice with its own high capacity mineral wagons, often of patently NER design and/or inspiration as, indeed was also the case for many other types of goods vehicle. In fact, wagon replacement by the LNER was generally good right across the board, the average age of its fleet being just over 16 years throughout its existence, some 80% of the pre-group fleet having been replaced by 1947.

Like that of the LMS, LNER revenue was also dominated by receipts from its freight traffic which was hedged round with much the same sort of constraints as already considered. In consequence, its wagons did not display any marked technological differences from those of its rivals and were much the same in size, shape and design utilisation; excepting the high capacity mineral wagons already considered, the dominant types were open wagons and covered vans, most being for merchandise traffic. There were also, of course, numerous designs of vehicle for specific types of traffic (cattle &c) which were built in smaller quantities and the odd 'one-offs' for highly specialised cargo. The LNER retained dominantly wooden construction for wagon underframes for many a long year (in some cases right to the end), it generally being the most economical solution in terms of previous workshop investment: inertia if you prefer, though the LNER was no worse than the rest.

Almost inevitably, the bulk of wagons continued to be hand braked only and tended to follow the design criteria (if such it may be described) laid down by the Railway Clearing House (RCH). This long established body originally came into being to apportion traffic receipts between the companies when trains traversed more than one system, but soon realised that lack of technical standardisation (even at the primitive levels then ruling) could cause some problems of through running of stock. Accordingly, the RCH tried to set out standard specifications to which goods wagons should ideally conform and, to their credit, most wagon building firms (and the railway companies themselves) went along with this. The pity is that the RCH would have been an ideal body to encourage the increasing use and manufacture of more sophisticated goods stock and specify the standards accordingly, but there is little evidence that this was ever pursued with vigour.

Meantime, the railways muddled on; but at least the LNER managed to run a few reasonably high speed goods trains such as the 'Green Arrow' service already mentioned. It was helped in this respect by having a slightly higher proportion of goods vehicles which would permit such speeds (ie with automatic brakes). But it also had to operate far too many of its more important long distance goods services with only a few fully braked wagons at the front, in effect, rather like the Maltese freights of the LMS. And the LNER also mirrored its rivals by increasing the emphasis on container traffic, a form of operation which was just nicely getting into its stride during the mid-1930s.

Above:
Like the LMS, the LNER adopted the container idea to a quite considerable extent. This 1935 view shows a furniture container being loaded prior to its transit by mechanical horse to be transferred to a rail wagon. Whilst these innovations showed that progress was being made towards modern freight transportation techniques, there were some areas where time seemed to stand still. In retaining things like wooden underframes, it may be argued that, once again like the LMS, the LNER kept the old fashioned wagon building technology going for far too long.
Photo: LNER Official

Below:
Symptomatic of the value to the railways of handling pedigree and prize livestock (high value cargo which thus commanded high movement cost) is this 1946 scene at Leyburn station on the Wensleydale branch, showing the removal of the horses from Armstrong's racing stable to their new home at Newmarket. Note the LNER-owned road van which had probably assisted in bringing these valuable animals to the railhead. Photo: LNER Official

The first truly 'standard' Southern express type was a developed version of the LSWR Class N15, later more popularly known as 'King Arthurs'. This is one of the post-Grouping examples No.782 Sir Brian, one of thirty examples built (from 1925 on) by the North British Loco Company (the so-called 'Scotch Arthurs) seen on an unspecified working on ex-SE&CR metals
Photo: Ransome, Wallis Collection NRM

Below:
One of the progenitors of the successful Class N15 was Urie's 6ft driving wheel LSWR Class H15 of 1914, Britain's first 4-6-0 to embody the two cylinder/outside Walschaerts gear combination which later became so typical across the land. The picture below shows No.485 passing Woking with a Bournemouth train in July 1938.
Photo: Box Collection, NRM

Chapter Seventeen
SR Locomotives & Rolling Stock

Not only was the Southern, by some considerable margin, the smallest of the Big Four, its steam locomotive policy was governed by quite different criteria, in direct consequence of a policy of suburban electrification which it had adopted from the outset. This policy was well advanced by the later 1930s and the steam fleet reflected the fact. Therefore, just as with the other companies, the final years of the Southern can only be understood in the context of earlier events.

At the grouping, the SR inherited a fleet of some 2,275 locomotives which was less in total than any one of the three biggest pre-group systems (GWR, London & North Western and Midland) and only slightly less than that of the North Eastern. By the time of nationalisation, the figure had dropped well below 2,000 units or, put another way, to much about the same as the combined total of Stanier Class 5s, 5XPs and 8Fs built from 1934 onwards.

The Southern received its locomotives from three principal constituents and was like the LNER in the sense that none of them were numerically dominant. However, two of them, the London & South Western and South Eastern & Chatham, had taken locomotive development to a rather more modern position than had the London Brighton & South Coast. The new Southern CME, Richard Maunsell, was an ex-SE&CR man and his general approach until his retirement in 1937 was to blend the best of SE&CR and LSWR practice to form a recognisably Southern approach. Maunsell was succeeded by Oliver Bulleid (Gresley's former assistant on the LNER) who was to prove the dominant influence during the last ten years, much as Stanier had been on the LMS, but with very different consequences.

Another point of similarity between the SR and LNER was the longevity of many pre-group classes after 1922, though the Southern rationale was different. In its case, electrification meant that the need for new steam power was less and there was every incentive to keep older types running during the interim. This strategy was very much set by Southern top management wherein, and this time more like the LMS, the SR was also led by a strong personality, Sir Herbert Walker KCB (curiously enough an ex-LNWR man), who was very much in the Lord Stamp mould but with a somewhat different set of problems to tackle. Walker managed to organise his railway in a remarkably original and successful way against severe financial constraints and in a very real sense, steam locomotive policy had to be subordinated to the needs of electrification.

The latter, of course, was largely a passenger orientated business during Southern days, this being a consequence of the very nature of its constituents; the SR was the only one of the Big Four where passenger revenue exceeded that of freight. This meant, of course, that not only was freight less important, but also that it was passenger locomotives which were most likely to be replaced by new electric trains. In consequence, the Southern never had the need to build standard classes in the all-embracing GWR or LMS sense, either in numerical terms or for the whole range of possible duties. It was not even as uniform as the less standardised LNER in this respect and these circumstances were to give the Southern fleet immense interest, albeit making generalisation difficult.

In effect, steam development on the Southern was concentrated on those areas where electrification was unlikely to occur in the near future and in Maunsell, Sir Herbert had the right man for the job. Not only was he aware of modern developments elsewhere, having started to implement them on the SE&CR system, but he was also something of a diplomat and very soon managed to get these ideas accepted elsewhere on the Southern system, principally, but not exclusively in terms of improving the ex-LSWR fleet. The latter was perhaps made easier by the fact that some LSWR designs were already of great potential and Maunsell was able to develop them in parallel with his ex-SE&CR types.

A natural consequence of the initial concentration of electrification on the London suburban routes meant that one area of activity which would remain steam powered for the foreseeable future (indeed it remained so for the whole SR period) was that of the long and intermediate distance passenger train. One of Maunsell's first tasks was to tackle this problem, for the Southern came into existence with very few really big express types at all. He did not cast his eye round for too long before lighting on the one possible contender which might fit the bill - the Class N15 4-6-0 of the old LSWR, designed by R.W.Urie in 1918 and of which 20 had been built with 6ft 7in driving wheels. These were robust locomotives in the 'modern' idiom with two outside cylinders and Walschaerts valve gear and were part of a family of three related designs which had started with a 6ft driving wheel version (Class H15) in 1914 and were to see a 5ft 7in version (Class S15) added in 1920. The only real problem with the N15 was that by comparison with some of Maunsells SE&CR designs it was not as thermodynamically efficient.

In 1925, Maunsell caused a further ten N15s to be built with his improvements and, prompted by Sir Herbert Walker, was persuaded to give them names as part of Walker's publicity drive. Maunsell is reputed to have informed Sir Herbert that this would not make them work any better (sic!), but names were applied and the choice of theme was truly inspired, The first new Maunsell N15 was called *King Arthur* which was followed by *Queen Guinevere* and eight assorted Knights of the Round Table, *Sir Launcelot* heading the list. These resonant names carried appropriate links with the area wherein they would work and the class thereafter became known as 'King Arthurs'. In very short order, 30 more were built with modified cabs (to suit the ex-SE&CR section) and new bogie tenders, a final batch of fifteen (with the same modified cabs) being given shorter six-wheel tenders for use on ex-LB&SCR routes. Finally, the bulk of the original LSWR engines were then modified to Maunsell standard and also given Camelot-inspired names. Thus, by the late 1920s, the Southern had a truly standard express type totalling 75 broadly identical locomotives, albeit displaying cosmetic variations reflecting their origins, and the Arthurs were to remain in front line service for most of the Southern period. Their value in unifying the system was of considerable importance.

At much the same time, Maunsell also gave attention to the need for a far bigger locomotive than a King Arthur for the very heaviest trains - including the extensive boat train services to Southampton and elsewhere. His solution was a brand new four-cylinder 4-6-0 design, again with 6ft 7in wheels but only 5% heavier for some 40% extra tractive power. This was *Lord Nelson*, the first of an eventual modest-sized class of 16 engines which, over the years, were to be subject to several experiments and changes. As previously stated, the first named was claimed as Britain's most powerful express type when it appeared but the GWR soon put a stop to that! Meantime, the LMS had also showed interest and borrowed the LN drawings. When it first appeared, the LMS Royal Scot type looked rather like a 'Nelson' but in reality they were rather different in concept. Even so, this design was another interesting example of the 'coming together' (albeit reluctantly in some cases) which was beginning to be seen in Britain.

The Lord Nelsons, again all inspiringly named - this time after famous Naval Admirals, the Portsmouth connection being important to the Southern - might well have led to a 4-6-2 (Maunsell certainly had one sketched out for study) but the adoption of this wheel arrangement by the SR was left to Oliver Bulleid to implement. However, before considering these final Southern express designs, we first need to consider the one problem in this area which remained for Maunsell to solve: how to improve express services on those routes where structure clearances were very limited; the Southern had rather a number.

The solution was to be Maunsell's masterpiece, the 'Schools' Class of 1930: not only Britain's largest ever 4-4-0 in dimensional terms but conceivably the best 4-4-0 ever designed anywhere. In simple terms, the Schools Class combined a King Arthur type boiler with three sets of Lord Nelson cylinders and all modern refinements then available. Its cross-profile was carefully designed to the maximum size as would still 'fit' the restricted clearances of, for example, the Hastings route; while the adoption of only four driving wheels gave it greater flexibility on the more curving sections of line. The 40 engines built were as powerful as the Arthurs and some folk even referred to them as 'eight wheeled 4-6-0s', which compliment was well justified.

Maunsell Masterpieces
The two brand new Maunsell express passenger designs for the Southern were quite closely related to each other and to the preceding Arthurs. The upper view shows the first to appear in the form of the four-cylinder Lord Nelson Class 4-6-0 of 1926. The example shown is one of the later examples to appear: No.862 Lord Collingwood. *Four years later, the Schools (or 'V' Class) 4-4-0 appeared combining features from both the LNs and the Arthurs - see text. The lower view shows No.927* Clifton *passing Petersfield in mid-1937 with the 3.50pm from Waterloo.*
Photo: Ransome-Wallis and Box Collections, NRM

Above:

At first glance, the two Bulleid pacific designs were hard to tell apart, save for their names and numbers, the near identical outer casings on the lightweight version serving to hide both the smaller boiler and other weight-saving tricks of the trade which were mostly out of sight anyway; this view of No.21C119 therefore serves for all of them. The engine first came into service, unnamed, in 1945 as one of the first twenty 'light' pacifics and is shown here in that form at the head of the recently re-instated 'Golden Arrow' service, probably c.1946. It was later named Bideford *in the 'West Country' series once that thematic idea had been established. The unique Bulleid numbering system (confined purely to his engines and never applied to those of his predecessors) was similar to continental practice in that the coding before the actual fleet number indicated the number of axles, not wheels. Arabic numerals denoted non-driven axles and letters denoted the driven equivalent. Typically, however, Bulleid did not put them in order, or else 2C1 would have been the code for a 4-6-2; but after BR was formed, the new order put a stop to all this nonsense and the Bulleid 4-6-2s were given conventional plain numbers - 34019 in the case of the example featured.*

Photo: Ransome-Wallis Collection, NRM

All three Maunsell express classes were outstanding in their way and in full charge of most principal expresses when Bulleid took over. At first, he confined attention to detail changes to the Nelsons and Schools, mostly the former, it having been sometimes noted that the engines were not always quite as good as might have been expected. Modified cylinders together with Lemaitre multiple jet blastpipes and consequential larger chimneys cured such problems as did exist on what was, perhaps, the least effective of the three Maunsell types, but when Bulleid fitted the same multiple exhaust to the otherwise unmodified Schools, no real improvement was to be seen nor, in retrospect, was it likely to have been, given the quality of the original design. Just over half the class were so fitted, the rest being left unchanged.

Bulleid, having worked closely alongside Gresley, was no doubt convinced of the value of the 4-6-2 type and events were to see such engines emerge in due course. But even at this range in time with much more evidence coming available down the years, it is still by no means clear how he was able to convince high authority that a new 4-6-2, moreover a streamlined one at that, was justified during the difficult war years, much less that so many hitherto untried features should be incorporated and that the quantities eventually built in the immediate post-war years should be so large. But thus it was and two new types emerged: the physically larger 'Merchant Navy' Class in 1941 and the 'West Country/Battle of Britain' Class (a scaled-down, lighter weight version) in 1945. The three class designations derived from their thematic name series, but the WC/BB types were otherwise identical.

It is, of course, true that the Southern was increasingly burdened by the need to run so many services with elderly pre-group types and wartime traffic was probably more intense than anywhere else given its strategic geographical location, so some degree of additional power was wanted. Very early in the war, the government agreed to new steam locomotive construction resuming, but the great need was for freight engines which could, in *extremis*, haul passenger trains and the SR was building such types (see later), including quite a number of LMS Class 8F 2-8-0s. Against this background, the fact that the first purely Bulleid design took the form of a revolutionary new 4-6-2, was remarkable. The Bulleid pacifics, have become immortalised down the years and to be fair to him, the first proposals were made in 1938; but their introduction at the darkest time of war was probably as much a triumph of Bulleid's will power over common sense. There is some evidence that he gave them 6ft 2in wheels to get them into the 'mixed traffic' category but there is also evidence that he farmed out preparation work between his three main workshops so as not to reveal just how innovative the new engines were intended to be.

Even so, the fact that he managed to get away with streamlining (he called it air-smoothing and argued it would improve economy) and the complexities of chain drive totally encased in an oil bath (he argued ease of maintenance), is still astonishing in retrospect. Ten Merchant Navies appeared during 1941-2 and another ten in 1944-5, while BR added the final ten, ordered by the Southern prior to 1948. Whatever the exact circumstances of their building, the MNs quickly showed themselves to be good and powerful engines and their later reliability problems and maintenance difficulties were not apparent at first. In power terms they were somewhere between a Gresley A4 and an LMS Duchess and carried what was probably the finest boiler design ever fitted to a comparable British type, so Bulleid no doubt had ample cause for satisfaction; and he certainly had not finished....

Because of their size and 21 ton axle weight, the MNs were somewhat route restricted (probably more of a problem on the SR than any other British system), so this remarkable man set about designing a lightweight version with no more than 18 ton axle load. By now, the elderly nature of many SR types was beginning to become irksome so there can be little doubt as to the logic behind the fact of their introduction in 1945; this made sense and since many of the restricted routes lay beyond Exeter, their West Country names were a happy choice. But it is much harder to justify their sheer quantity. By the end of 1947, the Southern had no fewer than 70 in service with 40 more planned (duly delivered during the BR period between 1948-51). As early as 1946, with 48 already in use, the name theme changed to the Battle of Britain - prominent aircraft, personalities and squadrons associated with that conflict - another well-received idea - but the West Country theme returned on most of the last 20, BR-built examples.

All told, 110 Bulleid light pacifics emerged to become, amazingly, the most numerous 4-6-2 design ever to be seen in Britain. In the context of the purely Southern requirement this was patently too many; even in pre-BR days they could often be seen heading but two or three coaches which was manifestly absurd, the wonder being that it should have happened at all. Objectively, of course, they were, like their MN predecessors, very fine engines in strict performance terms, blessed with equally fine boilers and a nominal power output in line with the LMS 5XP category - ie: a bit more than a King Arthur. Not until later in BR days did their fundamental deficiencies become apparent; but that is another story.

Meantime, what of secondary Southern passenger power? Here, the need was less pressing and, for the most part, the Southern made do with inherited pre-group types. No one design was totally dominant but we may perhaps single out a few types which, to the end, were giving valiant service and wholly typical of the latter day SR, not least because Maunsell had deemed them worthy of fine-tuning after 1922. None of them were particularly numerous by comparison with those considered so far for the other three companies; but relative to the size of the Southern they played a significant role and, like many LNER designs, also went some way to maintain the pre-group character of the system, depending, of course, on where you might be at the time.

Numerically dominant as a class, though not in pre-group company terms, were the 66 examples of the former LSWR T9 Class 4-4-0s, designed and built by the formidable Dugald Drummond during 1899-1901. Nicknamed 'Greyhounds' (the Southern and its predecessors were rather fond of such soubriquets) and very much in the traditional 'Scottish' school of locomotive design, these celebrated engines had been given a new lease of life in 1922 when Urie began to fit them with superheaters to vastly beneficial effect. Maunsell simply continued the process, no doubt to the great delight of his ex-LSWR staff and excellent 'PR' consequences all round. They remained at work on ex-LSWR lines for many a long year, alongside others of the Drummond breed, well over half of them still being in active use on BR ten years after nationalisation.

A similar, but more complex story applied to some of the many 4-4-0 types which had come from Maunsell's own pre-group company the SE&CR. Here, the new Southern CME had already begun to build on the foundations of his eminent SE&CR predecessor, Harry Wainwright, by way of taking the latter's D and E Class (the E being a developed version of the D) into a more modernised form with belpaire boilers where relevant (the Es had them already), long travel piston valves and other refinements as D1 and E1 respectively. Collectively, they totalled 77 (51 D/D1; 26 E/E1) and the D and E Class evolution culminated in 22 examples of the L Class of 1914 with detailed (pre-1923) alterations by Maunsell. Here, however, the modified Maunsell L1 version (of which 15 were built with the usual 'modern' trimmings) did not appear until 1926 and was thus, in theory, to SR design. All told, these related but not fully identical 4-4-0s totalled 114 excellent units and the Southern got very good use out of them to the very end.

Actually an interesting feature of the Wainwright -Maunsell continuum on the SE&CR was seen in the outward appearance of the later Maunsell variants, many of which displayed visual lines which were very reminiscent of the Deeley/Fowler period of the old Midland Railway. This was entirely attributable to Maunsell's chief draughtsman, James Clayton, who had come from Derby, bringing many ideas with him. In consequence, many Maunsell designs both for the SE&CR and, later, the Southern, displayed distinct Derby lineaments of pre-1923 type (especially round the cab and tender). Thus, the fact that the Royal Scots looked a bit like Lord Nelsons around the cab and tender was as much a case of 'Derby' coming back home as anything else!

Above:
Of the many noteworthy pre-group 4-4-0 designs which were inherited by the Southern, perhaps the most outstanding were the Drummond Class T9 of the old LSWR ('Greyhounds'). Just prior to the grouping, the LSWR embarked on a process of superheating what were already middle aged engines and this was to transform their performance. After the Southern was formed, Maunsell continued the process and for the best part of another thirty years or so (right through Southern days) this fine group of engines was to give valuable service. This is No.703 on a down train at Exeter Central in April 1939.
Below:
Of the tank engines inherited by the Southern one of the long-lived types was the Wainwright Class J 0-6-4Ts of 1913, designed for Hastings and Tonbridge expresses. With the coming of the L Class 4-4-0s, the 0-6-4Ts then moved to the London-Redhill services as one of the few big passenger tanks to work the Southern prior to BR. No.1595 lasted until 1951.

On the ex-Brighton lines, Maunsell did not find quite the same seed corn available - in any case, the ex-LB&SCR routes, being generally more suburban and short distance were usually amongst the first to be wholly electrified - but no account of the Southern, even in its final days, would be complete without brief mention of the continued survival of ex-LB&SCR Atlantics on the Newhaven boat trains well into BR days (the writer has happy memories of travelling behind one in 1948), not to mention the modest handful of elegant SR-built 4-6-0s (the N15X Class), rebuilt in 1934 from ex-LB&SCR 4-6-4Ts dating from 1914. Neither were of major long-term significance but both were typical of the 'Southern' approach, both in its final years and in earlier times.

Coming now to the mixed traffic field, where the SR did not have anything like the same quantitative need for such engines as did the rest of the British system, its solution was very much in the mainstream of conceptual development nationwide. The eventual form once again represented a typical Maunsell mix of LSWR and SE&CR ideas, the difference in pre-group company origin being manifest on this occasion in terms of wheel arrangement; but the gestation of both types was both complex and interesting.

The Southern 2-6-0 was very much a child of the SE&CR where Maunsell, in 1917, not too long after Churchward and Gresley had come to much the same sort of conclusions on the GWR and GNR, had introduced a fine two-cylinder 2-6-0 in the shape of the N Class, a powerful modern two-cylinder design with outside Walschaerts gear.* Of distinctly Swindon proportions and concept as far as its boiler and firebox design were concerned, but displaying the external lineaments of James Clayton, (Maunsell's Chief Draughtsman who came from Derby) fifteen were built by the SE&CR plus one experimental three-cylinder example with Holcroft's conjugated valve gear in 1922 (Class N1).

After the war, the Southern later added another 65 two-cylinder engines, 50 during 1924-5 (assembled at Ashford using parts made at Woolwich Arsenal and boilers from the North British Loco. Co., the so-called 'Woolworth' engines) and another fifteen during 1932-4. Additionally, these fine engines were supplemented in 1930 by five more N1 Class three-cylinder versions developed from the 1922 experimental example but this time with three orthodox sets of valve gear - a sort of consequence of the Gresley/Holcroft debate about who, exactly invented the conjugated gear.

Southern locomotive class designation letters were confusing and often reflected their pre-group origins, most of which were kept (and in some cases added to) after 1922. Thus, the SE&CR 'N' had no relation to the N15 of the LSWR, neither had any new post-1923 letter prefixes (eg Class V 'Schools') any connection with any of them.

After the N/N1 series, the 2-6-0 group was augmented by a rather similar version with 6ft driving wheels as opposed to the 5ft 6in size of the earlier Class N type. This time, the origin was a 1928 rebuild of the somewhat unhappy SE&CR 'River' Class K 2-6-4Ts of 1917, virtual contemporaries of the original N Class, which had shown both stability problems and minor derailments at speed, before the catastrophe near Sevenoaks in 1927. These twenty engines, along with a further 30 planned but so far unbuilt 2-6-4Ts thus became Class U tender engines (rebuilt ex-2-6-4T or built new as 2-6-0 tender) during 1928-31.

Like the earlier Class N, the original Class K two-cylinder 2-6-4T had been augmented by an experimental three-cylinder version with conjugated valve gear and this too was rebuilt as a 2-6-0 in 1928, retaining its original valve gear (Class U1). This version was also repeated with three independent sets of valve gear in 1931 to the tune of 20 additional Class U1 engines. This raised the U/U1 class total to 71 which, together with the 86 Class N/N1 gave to the Southern a fine modern fleet of 2-6-0s, fully comparable in quality and relative-to-company totals with anything found on the other three systems in this wheel arrangement - yet another 'coming together' of concept.

By contrast with the 2-6-0, the mixed traffic 4-6-0 was not really a major feature on the Southern Railway. Yet it could claim to have the father of the whole breed in the shape of the ex-LSWR Class H15. This type, dating from 1914, not only predated the GWR Halls by nearly half a generation but was also the very first British 4-6-0 to display what eventually became the standard mixed traffic configuration - ie with c.6ft driving wheels, two outside cylinders and Walschaerts valve gear as typified by Stanier and Thompson types a generation later. The Southern inherited eleven of them, built another fifteen in 1924 and from them stemmed the King Arthurs, already described see also page 199.

Rather more numerous than the H15s were the 45 Class S15 engines, Urie's third LSWR 4-6-0 design and effectively a 5ft 7in wheel version of the H15 and N15 (King Arthur) types. Twenty were handed over to the SR and Maunsell built a further 15 in 1927-8 and a final ten in 1936, both series embodying his own 'King Arthur' type variations and again representing a considerable improvement over the LSWR type - and very good engines to boot. It will thus be seen that by the late 1930s, the Southern could call upon well over 200 very modern mixed traffic 2-6-0s and 4-6-0s, a by no means an inconsiderable total! and in proportion to the company size, in every way comparable with the LMS position at much the same time, as indeed was its main line express passenger fleet - an interesting but not often appreciated fact.

Of course, Maunsell introduced a few more new types, notably the Class Z 0-8-0T for heavy shunting in 1929 and, surprisingly, the Class W 2-6-4T for transfer freight duties in the London area in 1932, but neither were in great quantities. After the unhappy experience with the K Class 2-6-4Ts, the company never tackled the big passenger tank, though post-war events showed that it could surely have used one. Yet with its 5ft 6in wheels the Class W was not too far away from the 5ft 8in LMS 2-6-4Ts and might well have justified multiplication; but memories of the K Class presumably lingered long. Nor did the SR ever find need for a truly heavy-duty eight-coupled main line freight engine.

As for the rest, and with but one interesting exception in the purely freight field, the Southern steam fleet of the late 1930s was almost entirely dominated by pre-group types. Thus it was that in the lesser fields of steam motive power, the pre-1923 situation continued with little by way of change, be it freight, local passenger or bucolic branch line. On ex-LSWR lines, Drummond's M7 0-4-4Ts, 0-6-0 'Black Motors' (and others of that ilk) held sway, the SE&CR section was still very much the home of Wainwright Class C 0-6-0 goods and class H 0-4-4Ts (amongst others), while even the increasingly electrified central section (ex-LB&SCR) could always offer a more than reasonable quota of elegant survivals from the Stroudley (and later) periods right to the very end. The enthusiasts loved it!

Passenger stock

The Southern Railway was a carriage enthusiasts' delight throughout its whole existence and this was due to a number of facts of which we can single out the more significant. Firstly, relative to its size, it probably had the largest variety of passenger stock anywhere in the Kingdom in 1923; secondly, it never built any new non-corridor locomotive-hauled stock at all and thirdly, it could never standardise even main line stock on one set of dimensions because of its many routes with restricted clearances. If one adds to this the ramifications of electrification and the fact that Pullman regularly provided catering services rather than the company itself, it will readily be appreciated that variety was at all times a principal characteristic of Southern trains. Yet this apparently diverse state of affairs tended to disguise a fairly simple underlying policy which does lend itself to a fair degree of generalisation.

In the main line field, the Southern inherited a situation in which, apart from a few LSWR examples, and even fewer from the SE&CR, both of which were to be of minimal long term significance, the gangwayed long distance carriage was virtually unknown. Maunsell was thus able to start more or less from scratch when company policy decreed that the SR should

Above:
Maunsell's mighty shunting engine: Class Z 0-8-0T No.950 of 1929. Eight were built for use on the Eastern and Central sections of the SR and all of them lasted well into BR days.
SR Official

Below:
In the old-fashioned 0-6-0 goods field, the Southern was not as well supplied as were most British companies. It had no need for anything much bigger so Maunsell took the logical step of designing some modern new 0-6-0s (Class Q), introduced in 1938 just after he had retired and at a time where other railways were by now favouring 2-8-0s. Only 20 were built, but even the innovative Bulleid could not fault their logic and added twice as many of his own version (Class Q1) in 1942. Their brutally controversial appearance quite obscured the fact that they were in reality very modern and powerful engines and probably the best 0-6-0s ever built in Britain. What is more they had a far wider route availability because of the overall reduction in weight, and were thus able to work many of the rural branch lines on the Southern system that began to see the massive increases in military traffic mentioned elsewhere in this book. In the appended view, an unidentified class Q1 is compared in an official Ministry of War Transport photograph with an older SR freight type.

Classic Maunsell carriage stock.
Both these views typify the problems which Maunsell faced and overcame in building new coaches for his railway after 1923. the upper view shows 'Nondescript' saloon brake No.4448 of 1933. These were built for boat train use which, because the old three-class travel had not vanished on the continent, had to make provision for second class as well as the customary British first and third. These saloons were therefore often used for second class, though built to first class standards and sometimes even used for third class travel! They also had to be built to the more restricted 8ft 6in width, hence the near slab-sided styling. The lower picture shows, at first sight, a conventional 9ft wide corridor third No.10083 of the mid to late 1930s. In fact it has an extra half compartment (at the far end) and was one of many carriages built for use in four-car sets for the Portsmouth and Bognor electrifications of 1937 and later; these new EMUs were fully in the mainstream Southern main line tradition as far as carriage design was concerned.
Photos: Both SR Official

immediately start to catch up with the rest in the longer distance field. meantime,while the new standard main line carriages were being designed, the Southern built a few more corridor examples to both LSWR and SE&CR design to tide things over, so to speak. These were to be the only non-standard main line coaches ever operated by the company and although not without technical interest, they could in no way be considered 'typical' at the end of the 1930s. By that time, Maunsell had given his company a full range of corridor and open gangwayed stock which, albeit very traditional (some would say bordering on the old-fashioned), was fully comparable with most of what its rivals (save, perhaps the LMS) could offer on the majority of their trains. Given that a whole new main line fleet had been put in place in little more than ten years, this was a noteworthy achievement by Maunsell's team.

Maunsell had to design carriages to meet a number of route restrictions, so the standard SR main line carriage, as it existed in the 1930s, was never as wholly consistent in outline as, say, Gresley LNER or Stanier LMS stock; but it was very consistent in quality. Built to three principal widths (9ft, 8ft 6in and 8ft), it was nearly always 59ft long and the full range of generic types was offered, much as anywhere else. The main difference in carriages built to the narrower restrictions was usually confined to a rather more slab-sided outward appearance often combined with a reduction in seat capacity within the coach to allow for the narrowing (eg three per side third class compartments rather than the four per side in full width stock). Like the GWR, the Southern never offered armrests in its third class corridors so the four per side capability of 9ft stock did make a difference at busy times: an 8ft wide third class corridor could carry only 75% of its 9ft equivalent. First class was somewhat similar, two per side (rather than three) being common on narrower stock. And all the corridor stock of this period had a full set of outside compartment doors.

'Special stock' was, of course, different and the Southern had nothing to rival the GWR centenary stock or the LNER streamlined trains, nor did it have (or need) sleeping cars. But it did have some fine dining cars and its open stock with central gangways was probably better than anywhere else, especially in terms of spacious entrance lobbies and passenger luggage racks, often placed transversely above the seat backs rather than longitudinally along the walls as in rival stock. It also operated a number of very well furnished 'nondescript' carriages which, since they could be used for any class of passenger (according to the specific needs of the service), tended to be first class in quality. All Maunsell standard stock had outer steel panelling and exteriors were usually of smooth if not fully flush sided appearance.

Two interesting styling points also distinguished most Maunsell stock from the rest at this time. Firstly, and applicable to all stock after the very first standard batches, fixed windows on the corridor side were taken virtually to the full height of the side and secondly, the brake ends of 9ft wide carriages were recessed to about 8ft 7in width alongside the guard/luggage section, to allow a projecting lookout to be fitted without exceeding the overall width; this idea was probably of LSWR inspiration. A thoughtful touch, exclusive to the Southern and nearly always present, was to mark seat numbers on the carriage exterior so as to enable passengers to find reserved seats more easily, many SR expresses at busy times being fully reserved, especially holiday trains.

Maunsell had been so successful in re-equipping his railway with main line stock that when Bulleid came on the scene, there was no need for any immediate additions, nor any new stock at all for the restricted width lines. This meant that when it did finally appear in 1945, the new Bulleid stock displayed much more consistency of outline, not to mention embodying both new constructional techniques and a completely revised outer form which, in the event, was to prove the main inspiration behind the BR MkI standard stock of the 1950s.

Bulleid's carriages were smooth of outline, fully flush-clad in the manner of all other companies by now, but differed by having a continuously curved side profile from floor to gutter and a smooth transition to the roof above the side. Windows had markedly rounded corners and most elements of his main line stock had been accurately predicted in his earlier electric stock. The first of the main line series copied Maunsell layouts (including outside doors) but it was not long before large picture windows began to appear, along with far less widespread use of outer doors and an increase in the proportion of open carriages relative to side corridor. The thinking here, as on the LMS and LNER, was that to have 2 + 2 seating either side of a centre aisle was less cramped than four per side in a compartment. In this context and alone of the Big Four, Bulleid made widespread use of a semi-open design (ie mixed side corridor and centre aisle within one carriage), ostensibly to give passengers more choice.

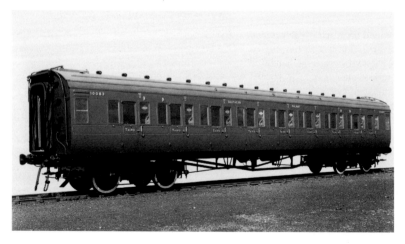

Bulleid's carriages were undeniably handsome and, like the later designs of the other three main companies, continued in production well into BR days, with slight detail variations appearing as time went by. The fact that at first they also coincided with the widespread introduction of a new malachite green livery (introduced in 1938 but not common until after the war) drew added attention - at least until all the older stock had been similarly painted.

Whether they be formed from Maunsell or Bulleid stock (or both), a number of operational aspects were to differentiate Southern expresses from those of the other lines and we can, perhaps single out three as being of particular interest. Firstly, the majority of services made use of fixed formation sets, carriages being regularly built with the deliberate intention of forming them into sets from new and quite regularly, these sets remained as formed until they were withdrawn. These permanent sets could be anything from two to ten coaches long, the general principle being to combine appropriate sets together to form bigger trains if need be. Thus, for example, a typical solution for a busier West of England service might be to take two identical five coach sets and place a dining car between them. Only if this principle did not suffice would the Southern depart from the idea and add extra individual carriages as strengtheners. For this purpose it maintained a separate fleet of what it called 'loose' vehicles and from these it could also form up the many extra trains it would need, for example, at busy holiday weekends.

This idea came very much into its own in the context of working a complex service, of which the Southern had many; indeed the whole idea probably stemmed from that fact. Thus, if a train served a number of destinations, each of which would normally justify a set of vehicles (which could be reduced to but one brake composite for a smaller terminal point or at quieter times), the whole cavalcade set off as one large train (sometimes more than one) which gradually shed itself of the various sets as the journey proceeded. Compared with the alternative of running more (but individually shorter) trains, this both improved the line occupation and reduced the number of locomotives, while still enabling passengers to reach their destination without change of carriage. Those who travel the modern railway may well look back wistfully.......

A second distinctive element was the heavy involvement of the Pullman Car Company in Southern services - a historical inheritance from all three Southern constituents but mostly the LB&SCR and SE&CR. This was intimately tied up with the heavy boat train traffic which all three handled and which the Southern had to face in 1923. Typically, it took the form of either all-Pullman trains (who needs reminding of the various 'Belles' of the time, not to mention the famous 'Golden Arrow' service?) or of Pullman providing the catering facility in an otherwise company-owned train. The latter was especially true on the former Brighton and SE&CR routes and, in due course, was extended to the insertion of Pullman dining cars in the main line electric trains of the mid-1930s and later.

It was Pullman too, via its associated Wagons-Lits partner in Continental Europe, that was responsible for the only sleeping car service operated on SR metals: the celebrated 'Night Ferry' between London and Paris (later including Brussels) wherein the sleeping cars crossed the English Channel on purpose-built ferry vessels. This service was started in 1936 but suppressed during the war; but since the carriages themselves owed everything to continental practice, one can hardly call this a Southern idea at all.

The practical effect of all this was that the Southern never built any sleeping cars at all (save for a maverick one-off Bulleid car which was only ever used by railway officers!) and that its many fine dining cars were mostly confined to the ex-LSWR routes where Pullman had not achieved such dominance. This latter pre-group distinction continued into the electric trains which were eventually built for some of the longer-distance ex-LSWR routes; and it was, of course, the gradual extension of electrification onto the Southern main line services which marked the third differentiating factor mentioned above. But before coming to this, we must first consider the whole matter of the Southern approach to electrification.

The celebrated and on the whole remarkably successful electrification of the inner suburban routes of the Southern Railway was very much down to the determination of Sir Herbert Walker. All three constituents had either started or were about to start such a policy by 1923, so the likelihood of widespread further electrification was strong anyway; but what is perhaps most remarkable is the fact of its post-group achievement against severe financial constraints. These were first manifest in the form of electrification adopted: the familiar and relatively low voltage third rail system. This was the LSWR solution and although in many ways less sophisticated than the existing LB&SC high voltage overhead alternative or the proposed, but not yet started SE&CR scheme, it had the advantage of lower cost - and this was the key factor.

Important too was the likely cost of new rolling stock but this was mostly circumvented by taking advantage of the huge amount of fairly new locomotive-hauled rolling stock from all three companies which would, of course, otherwise be rendered surplus after electrification. Thus, apart from a modest amount of genuinely new stock, the vast majority of the 'new' electric trains were in fact composed of carriages rebuilt from 'steam stock' as it was most usually called - plus conversion of the ex-LB&SCR 'Overhead Electrics stock and the retention of the original LSWR electric's more or less unchanged. Thus, although all trains embodied the new standard electrical equipment, the bulk of the first generation suburban units all to clearly revealed their pre-1923 origins. What is more, they were sufficiently well founded to serve for a generation or more and it was only (for the most part) after the war that a major replacement programme was instituted, mostly in the form of Bulleid's new four-car sets (the familiar 4-SUB units) which themselves also lasted long. Accordingly many of the old pre-group warriors also lasted well into BR days.

But that was not all. When electrification began to extend beyond inner suburban routes and a more cross-country type of unit was needed, the Southern again began to raid its still substantial pre-group fleet alongside building some new trains specifically for this purpose. The result was a very eclectic mix of train styles throughout the system, all utilising common electrical gear. In 1938, such post-1923 stock as did exist was typically Maunsell and it was only when Bulleid began to build new sets for the same cross-country lines (and give them his new styling) that the short/medium distance services began to assume standard (as opposed to pre-group) visual lineaments.

Only when the Southern began to tackle main line electrification did some genuinely new ideas begin to emerge and by the later 1930s, these had taken two principal forms. The earliest was the complete electrification of the Brighton line from 1933, for which two new sorts of train emerged, six-car corridor units for the faster trains and four-car non-corridor sets with lavatories and inside passageways for semi-fast workings. Inevitably Pullman had a shout, so the six car sets had a Pullman diner and the famous all-Pullman 'Southern Belle' became the unique all-electric 'Brighton Belle'. The company stock was typically to the Maunsell style now becoming familiar in the long distance field (above) and the SR did manage to get some six car sets into use with their own catering cars.

In 1937, the Portsmouth line was electrified and this time (being ex-LSWR) there was no inherited Pullman input and the new trains were wholly in the now familiar Maunsell idiom. As with main line steam services, they were delivered in sets (four coaches in this case), some, but not all of which had dining car facilities. Thus, in accordance with best SR practice, trains could be four, eight or twelve cars long depending on need. When these trains were extended to the Bognor line after Bulleid's arrival, new sets were needed. In some of these were included a fairly *avant garde* buffet car which Bulleid had designed to replace the more orthodox restaurant cars of the Portsmouth sets. These cars (but not the rest of the sets) were painted in a shrieking malachite green shade - one of the first hints that a new man was in charge! Thereafter until well into BR days, Southern electrics remained remarkably consistent and, apart from a gradual dilution of the pre-group styled suburban units as Bulleid's new trains came into service during the later 1940s, there was little significant difference to be observed between the Southern of 1937 and its final state as nationalisation dawned.

Meantime, what of the rest of the passenger scene? Here, the Southern, like most of the rest of Britain, tended to rely on its inherited pre-group fleet, the one difference being that no new carriages were ever built for the short and medium distance services which justified neither electrification nor new main line corridor stock. In consequence, one had the interesting situation of a railway whose main line trains (be they electric or steam) were almost wholly post-group in styling, whose electrified suburban services were (carriage styles excepted) equally post-group in philosophy and technology yet whose residual services mostly remained a living museum of the pre-group age. But whilever the Brighton 'Terriers' trundled across the causeway to Hayling Island and Beattie's LSWR tank engines continued to serve the West Country branches, not to mention many other similar examples of that ilk throughout the system, you were never really in any doubt as to where you were. Neither carriages nor locomotives moved appreciably away from their pre-1923 haunts; only the livery changed and no wonder the enthusiasts loved it - and there we must leave it.

Above:

The early Southern suburban electrification was carried out against very severe economic constraints. The third rail low voltage traction system was that of the old LSWR (the least sophisticated and cheapest to install of the three ideas then in play, both the LB&SCR and SE&CR having had rather more grandiose notions), while there was insufficient funding for a total stock re-equipment. Some new carriages were built but most suburban trains were achieved by re-building pre-group non-corridor steam stock, mounting it on new underframes and giving it standard new traction equipment.This assemblage is typical. The first three carriages are of ex-LSWR origin and the last three ex-LB&SCR; both were known as 3-SUB in Southern EMU parlance and could operate independently or in multiple regardless of cosmetic outline. Between the two 3-SUBs are two non-powered ex-LB&SCR 'trailers', added at busy times. After the war, the more logical step was taken to form up permanent four car units (4-SUB) and this was the basis for the huge stock replacement initiated by Bulleid which continued into BR days and was to last a further 40 years or so! When the Brighton line and associated routes were electrified from 1933 onwards, it was found possible to contemplate a complete fleet of new stock and the expresses were put in the hands of very well thought out six-car gangwayed units, coded 6-PUL or 6-PAN, depending on whether Pullman (PUL) or the company (PANtry) did the catering.

Photo: Pendragon Collection

206

Freight stock

If this review of the Southern has, thus far, been dominated by the passenger scene (be it locomotives or carriages), this is no more than the essence of the Southern and the reason for its difference from the rest. The Southern was not a freight carrying railway in the sense of the others and neither had been any of its constituents. In fact, it is surprising to note that it even managed to gain 25% of its revenue from freight traffic. But even this small percentage in company terms must be viewed against its much smaller overall size anyway. It drops to even more minor proportions when viewed against the national picture whether it be in terms of revenue or vehicles owned. As the summary table (page 164) reveals, the SR had no mineral wagons to speak of and its total wagon fleet comprised a meagre 5% of the British total. It can therefore be no surprise, set against the generally backward state of British 'wagonry' overall, that the Southern made no significant contribution to the state of the freight vehicle art; indeed, its own modest complement of merchandise wagons (a category more relevant to the Southern area than in many parts of the country, simply by virtue of its particular hinterland) was actually dominated by the more primitive open version to a far greater degree than other companies; and the latter were bad enough in all conscience!

Such vehicles as it did build were entirely orthodox and mostly confined, as ever, to hand braked common or garden types. There was no specifically new company style, save for a propensity to build covered vans with distinctively semi-elliptical shaped roofs rather than the arc roof form favoured elsewhere in Britain; this may have been ex-SE&CR in origin though ex-LSWR influence usually predominated. Neither was there any one type of wagon which may have been said to be peculiarly Southern in terms of utilisation, though it did build some well-equipped and unique bogie brake vans which, no doubt, pleased the guards. There was also more than a bit of SE&CR influence in that grey area between freight and passenger wherein lay the so-called 'General Utility Van'. This was basically a cargo-carrying vehicle with automatic brakes which was used for higher value traffic and often conveyed by passenger train. All railways had them but the SE&CR design was to become a particularly resilient type and was built throughout the Southern period: well into BR days too. One suspects that its inexpensive first cost (it was basically a wooden goods van after all) had much to do with its continued popularity!

That said, however, the importance of the Southern in freight terms was less a function of the wagons which it built than of the geographical position which it occupied in the total railway network. Visit a typical Southern goods yard and chances are that the company-owned wagons would be dominated by those of 'foreign' companies rather than the home-built product - and we should not be surprised at this. The SR had no great primary traffic flows such as the coal and mineral trade which characterised those railways serving our major industrial regions.

Above: Perhaps the most distinctive feature of Southern Railway freight and non-passenger coaching stock was the roof shape adopted on both its covered goods vans and passenger rated luggage vans etc. This is one of the latter, No.1915 when new. Its styling derived from SE&CR practice and even at the end of the 20th Century, this distinctive vehicle outline is still to be seen in occasional use on our newly privatised railway! It is worth mentioning that because the South London suburbs (and much of the area occupied by the LB&SCR and SE&CR) were probably the largest single domestic market for what we would now call consumer goods and since most of these were carried by rail in the period under study, their distribution within the region was very much the Southern's concern. In consequence, marshalling yards and transfer facilities (whereby could be handled the great volumes of traffic which originated elsewhere in the country, usually in someone else's wagons - sic!) assumed far greater importance than great rafts of brand new vehicles. This was the distinguishing feature of the Southern freight scene and continued thus throughout the company's existence.
Photo: SR Official

CHAPTER EIGHTEEN
A Final Reckoning ?

On the eve of nationalisation, a group of LMS locomotives await the dawning of a new era at Polmadie depot (Glasgow) at the end of 1947. LMS official picture.

Having looked at the pre-war situation, the troubled war years, and the locomotive and rolling stock situation on the Big Four, the reader could rightly expect a conclusion at this point. Yet it is really inappropriate to try and draw a line across history just because we have reached midnight on Tuesday 31st December 1947. Indeed history continued and the Big Four did not just die away at the Birth of British Railways. Therefore we should really continue the story, rather than merely conclude it at this point. As my fellow author has already pointed out in his section on Locomotives & Rolling Stock, the ideas, designs and aspirations of officers in the Big Four continued well on into nationalisation, and when coupled with the hardware and infrastructure that was acquired by BR in 1948, this was to set the trend for regional (in effect the Big Four's) development for at least a further 10 years. This continuance of 'business as usual' in many areas of operation means that the end of the Big Four can not be really signalled until we come to the time when the BR Board had both thought through and actually started the Modernisation Programme - if then! This means that this book naturally lends itself as but the first part of a series charting the social history of Britain's railways and, as this work has been prepared, research has been simultaneously taking place into the next part of the story. Thus it is my pleasure to announce that, a book of similar specifications to this will be released to recount 'The Birth of British Railways'. To set the scene for that book, we will inevitably turn back to the years following the war, which in many ways is both the conclusion to this book and the introduction to the next.

However, suffice it to say, the Big Four were but a period in railway history, and a comparatively short one at that. Yet they were amongst the most significant years ever experienced in our transport history. Change from private to state ownership did not happen easily either, and although the railways were virtually destitute (the LNER was almost on the verge of bankruptcy) at the annual meetings of the four main line companies the various chairmen put forward a concerted and unified objection to the Government plans, stating that nationalisation was unwarranted both on the ground of performance and proposed restoration and efficiency they were programming. Yet the Transport Bill gained Royal Assent on 6th August 1947, establishing the British Transport Commission for the purpose of setting up a publicly-owned national transport system, although air transport services were not included. Its announced intention was to take over, on 1st January 1948, the railway and canal undertakings of the Big Four railway companies, and a number of other minor railways, joint lines and transport systems which had come under the care of the Railway Executive in the period from the summer of 1939. All privately owned wagons which had been taken in to the Government's wartime wagon pool were also to be absorbed, though by this time many were fit only for scrapping. The Commission would also acquire those road-haulage companies that were primarily engaged in long distance haulage for hire.

It is with some regret that we must now leave the story of The Last Years of the Big Four, for it is a story with an abrupt end. Yet it is an account which does not really end, and merely continues in another guise, but this is not necessarily a cause for regret. As William Whitelaw had indicated in 1937, the eventuality of a fully nationalised railway system was clearly evident to the directors of the railway companies themselves, and in the post-war reconstruction period there was little chance of delaying the inevitable. We could spend many hours recounting the superlative achievements of the Big Four, or put forward long and convincing arguments about their various merits, but we too must bow to the inevitable conclusion. The Last Years of the Big Four were, indeed, but a passing phase. They were the inevitable outcome of the First World War, and a publicly acceptable face for what perhaps ought to have been a nationalised railway system at the start of the 1920s. They were indeed a convenient stop-gap measure for a nation beleaguered by a crippling and futile war, and a sensible interim step to restructuring and rebuilding an over-used and badly abused railway system. The creation of the Big Four companies was an answer, but it was not a complete or fully workable solution by any means. At the end of another period of world conflict, history was moving on and so were the railways; but would the Birth of British Railways be as glorious or distinguished as the Last Years of The Big Four! As one railway author wrote at the time; "What may be the railways' future of these days in the melting pot, no-one, I suppose, can tell, but I find it hard to believe that under any other regime it can be conducted with greater keenness and success or with a finer or more loyal tradition. I will only add *Floreat, Florebit!*"